John the Baptizer, *The Voice*, *The Messenger* and *Elijah*, and, "All Israel Shall Be Saved"

An Unexplored Proposal for the Problem of Romans 11:25-27

Vol. III
Torah To Telos: The Passing of the Law of Moses At the Cross or AD 70?

© 2016 JaDon Management

All rights reserved. No part of this book may be reproduced or transmitted in any form or by any means, electronic or mechanical, including photocopying, recording, or by any information storage and retrieval system, except for brief quotations for the purpose of review or comment, without the expressed written permission of the author or publisher, except where permitted by law.

ISBN -978-1530650019   1530650011

Logo Design: Joseph Vincent

Cover Design by:
Jeffrey T. McCormack
The Pendragon: Web and Graphic Design
www.the pendragon.net

Foreword

Romans 11:25-27 continues to interest, perplex and challenge Bible students. When Paul spoke of the salvation of "all Israel" what exactly did he mean?

Did he mean to communicate that all Jews alive at the coming of Jesus at the proposed "end of human history" would be saved, as Jesus comes out of heaven and they at last recognize him as their promised Messiah? Did he mean that all the faithful Jews, those who had been faithful through the centuries, would then receive their reward? Was Paul actually embracing universalism under the guise of the salvation of Israel?

What coming of the Lord "out of Zion" did Paul have in mind? Was he actually referring to the Incarnation of Jesus and the ensuing conversion of Jews since that time? Was he speaking of a yet future coming of Christ at the end of the current age, when masses of Jews instantly turn to Jesus in faith?

Amillennialists, Postmillennialists and Dispensationalists alike, all suggest, with different nuances in the respective camps, that Paul anticipated the conversion of the mass of ethnic Jews at the end of human history. He did not necessarily envision the salvation of every single Jew, but nonetheless, he did predict the conversion of the mass body of Israel.

On the other hand, a significant number of notable scholars insist that Paul simply meant that all Israel, or any of Israel, will be saved throughout the Christian age, when individual Jews turn to Christ in faith.

These are but a few of the important questions to be pondered and investigated in any serious study of Paul's discussion of Israel's condition when he wrote, and his prediction about their fate. These questions demand answers, but, to read the literature, the answers are not easy to come by.

As a young man in seminary, I well remember how my professors, Amillennialists, admitted to the difficulty of Romans 11:25f. When I would attend lectureships, the men I admired as my heroes in the faith, that I considered to be excellent Bible students, would all but throw up their hands in frustration when questions were posed about this text. They would agree that the text is difficult, but, one thing they knew for sure was that, "The Dispensationalists are wrong on it!" This was hardly satisfactory to me then, and even less so now.

In 1982, I was challenged to my first formal public debate. I spent the next year in preparation. My opponent often wrote in the local newspaper about Romans 11:25f, and how it is definitive proof of Dispensationalism and the future salvation of the Jews. To be honest, at the time, I had no solid, substantive answer for his arguments. I needed help.

I met one day with a friend of mine, a prominent Bible scholar. When I asked him about Romans 11, he sat and looked at me for a moment and then said, "Don, you just have to hope and pray that your opponent does not go to Romans 11:25 and camp out. I do not know how to deal with that text. I don't have any answers for you." To say I was disappointed is a huge understatement.

For some reason, in the debate, my opponent only referred to Romans 11 almost in passing. I offered a sort of rebuttal, and he never returned to the text - much to my relief! But after that debate, I determined that I was going to find some answers to my questions on Romans 11:25f.

In the ensuing years, I began to focus more and more on the prophetic background and source of Paul's expectation of the salvation of "all Israel." I read commentary after commentary. I got journal article after journal article.

What astounded me then, and now, is that while most commentators readily state that Paul quotes directly from Isaiah 27, Isaiah 59 and Jeremiah 31:29f, I have yet to find, as I finalize this book, even one commentator that actually examines the content and context of those prophecies that serve as Paul's source! Not one! Why is this important?

It is important because in both Isaiah 27 & 59 the very ground of the promise of the coming of the Lord is His coming in judgment of Israel for shedding the blood of the martyrs! This is explicit in both prophecies (not to mention Daniel 9 which is loudly echoed in Romans).

The question is, since Isaiah 27 & 59 conflate the time of Israel's salvation with the time of the judgment of Israel for shedding innocent blood, what is the hermeneutic for ignoring that relationship in Romans? This is particularly relevant since, as I will show in this work, the motif of martyrdom is very strong in Romans.

So, the salvation of Israel promised in Isaiah is tied directly to the vindication of the martyrs at the Day of the Lord. In Matthew 23, Jesus is unambiguous and emphatic about when all the blood, of all the righteous, all the way back to Creation, would be judged and vindicated - it would be in the judgment of

Jerusalem that took place in AD 70. When I discovered this connection, I was, and am, convinced that it is critical for a proper understanding of Romans 11. And yet, to reiterate, I have not found a single scholar that develops this. Some "dance around it" but never connect the dots. But, my research then went a bit further.

I have long been fascinated with John the Baptizer. Through the years, I have collected a number of books that have explored John's role and his importance. What began to dawn on me was that virtually all of the critical works took note of the ancient Hebraic view of the eschatological role of Elijah when he would come and how John was the promised Elijah. Many of the commentators speak of the critical role of John as a last days prophet to usher in the resurrection and the kingdom. But, something was wrong, or at least it seemed so.

While the commentators acknowledge John's role as the herald of the Great and Terrible Day of the Lord, and as the Voice in the Wilderness to prepare for the salvation of Israel, there was absolutely no discussion of John in the epistles, and particularly in Paul's writings when Paul spoke of the coming salvation of Israel! What happened to John and his message? Why did (do) none of the commentators draw the lines of connection between John, Paul, Peter and Revelation? After all, if John was all about the restoration of Israel, and Paul discussed the salvation of Israel, should we not find some testimony of John that might – just possibly - help us understand Paul? And since 1 Peter is about the salvation of the Diaspora, and he cites Isaiah 40 - *a prophecy of John's ministry* - shouldn't we be able to correlate John with 1 Peter? Since Peter also echoes Malachi 3 - that foretold John's ministry as *The Messenger* - should we not be able to glean some help from an examination of the Baptizer and Peter? Since Revelation is patently about the restoration of Israel, why do virtually no commentators even hint at John and his ministry as important evidence to understand the Apocalypse. (I will take note below of one commentator that made some connections between John and Revelation, but, that commentator makes no mention of the connection with Romans 11!)

This book seeks to establish that the ministry of John the Baptizer as *The Voice* of Isaiah 40, *The Messenger* of Malachi 3 and *Elijah* of Malachi 4 is in fact paradigmatic and determinative for a proper understanding of Paul's doctrine of the salvation of Israel. I am convinced that when we take John's message into proper consideration, that all futurist applications of Romans 11:25f fall to the wayside. Romans 11 was fulfilled at the end of the Old Covenant age of Israel that took place in AD 70. That is when the blood of the martyrs was vindicated, in fulfillment of Isaiah 27 & 59. That is when the Lord came to take away the

Old Covenant of sin and death. That is when Old Covenant Israel, the exclusivistic nation, gave way to the inclusive body of Christ.

It is my hope and desire that this book will be accepted in the spirit of inquiry and desire for the truth that it is intended, and that God and His Truth will be glorified.

(My special thanks to Sam Dawson for generating the Indices for this book. His efforts are greatly appreciated).

TABLE OF CONTENTS

Introductory remarks on the significance of Elijah

Page 3 – Salvation and Judgment: Siamese Twins. A Critical Element of Eschatology.

Page 7 – John as End Time Prophet, full of the Spirit. A Demonstration of the eschatological significance of John - and his role in the salvation of Israel foretold in Romans 11.

Page 13 – John as *The Voice* of Isaiah 40, proclaiming the salvation of Israel, the taking away of Israel's sin at the Day of the Lord. This is precisely what Paul anticipated in Romans 11. Yet, this connection is all but ignored in the commentaries.

Page 23 – John as *The Messenger* to prepare for the coming of the Lord to the Messianic Kingdom Temple - the time of Israel's salvation. As the Messenger, we discover the nature of the Day of the Lord - a time of national judgment on Israel. Yet, this connection is all but ignored in the commentaries.

Page 38 – Elijah Has Already Come! John as *Elijah*, would "restore all things" i.e. the time of the resurrection. Paul's anticipation of the salvation of Israel at the parousia was John's message as Elijah of the Great Day of the Lord. Yet, this connection is all but ignored in the commentaries.

Page 44 – John as *Elijah*, Paul and the Ministry of Reconciliation. Nothing spoke more eloquently of the time of Israel's salvation than the concept of "reconciliation." Paul continued that ministry, proving that John's message had not failed or been postponed. This connection is not found in the commentaries.

Page 56 – The Nature of the Day of the Lord Proclaimed by John as *The Voice, The Messenger* and *Elijah*

Page 71 – Did Paul Anticipate a Different Day of the Lord From That Preached by John?

Page 84 – Romans 11 and Martyr Vindication. Few scholars make the connection between the salvation of Israel at the coming of the Lord in

Romans 11 with the theme of *Martyr Vindication*. Yet, theme permeates Romans.

Page – 140 - John, *the Voice*, *the Messenger* and *Elijah*: Revelation and the Salvation of "All Israel."

Page 150 - What Kind of Coming of the Day of the Lord Did John, Jesus and Paul Envision / Expect / Predict? Were They Truly the Same?

Page 157 – Paul, Jesus as *The Deliverer* and John's Message of, "The Wrath To Come."

Page 163 – Paul and the Little Apocalypse Of Isaiah 24-27. A Critical But Often Ignored Connection.

Page 166 – What About: "Blessed Is he Who Comes in the Name of the Lord'"? Is this not a prediction of the conversion of "all Israel" at the coming of Christ - like Romans 11?

Page 177 – What About: "Jerusalem Shall Be Trodden down of the Gentiles, until the Times of the Gentiles Are Fulfilled" (Luke 21:24)? Does this not show that Jerusalem and Israel will be finally delivered - like Romans 11?

Page 183 – Some Unexplored But Corroborative Issues

Page 186 – The Implications of Our Proposal for Futurist Eschatologies.

JOHN THE BAPTIST AND THE SALVATION OF ISRAEL: AN OVERLOOKED *CRUX INTERPRETUM* FOR ROMANS 11:25-27

Romans 11:25-27 continues to be a source of tremendous interest and speculation. It is believed by many to be some of the most difficult of all of Paul's writings. Did Paul posit - as held by Dispensationalists and classic Postmillennialists[1] – a future conversion of the great majority of ethnic Israel? Or, does Paul in Romans 11 have in mind the total number of Israelites that will be eventually be converted through individually turning to the Lord in faith until that number is finalized at the coming of Christ, as suggested by many Amillennialists? Or is "Israel" to be saved inclusive of Jew and Gentile alike who will be saved until the consummation, as scholars such as N. T. Wright suggest?[2]

Are the events of 1948 a key to understanding Romans 11? Was the "restoration of Israel" in 1948[3] a key indicator that the fulfillment of Romans 11 and the coming of the Lord is near? Was 1948 the, "Super Sign of the End" as posited by Tim Lahaye and Thomas Ice?[4] For the Dispensational / Zionist world, Romans 11:25f is a critical, foundational and necessary part of their

---

[1] Cf. Kenneth Gentry, *He Shall Have Dominion*, (Draper, Va. 2009).

[2] N. T. Wright, *The Letter to the Romans, New Interpreters Bible*, (Abingdon, Nashville, 2002).

[3] The majority of "Israel" in 1948, by Dispensational admission, was comprised of "atheists, agnostics and unbelievers." Yet, we are to believe that God blessed that unbelieving, Christ denying, nation by restoring them in that state of rebellion and unbelief? In my book, *Israel 1948: Countdown to No Where*, I demonstrate that 1948 had nothing to do with the fulfillment of prophecy. That book is available on Amazon, Kindle, my websites and other retailers.

[4] Thomas *Ice and Tim LaHaye, Charting the End Times*, (Eugene, Ore. Harvest House, 2001)84, 119). 1948 is called, "God's Super Sign of the End Times," and they say, "Israel's re-gathering and the turmoil are specific signs that God's end-time program is on the verge of springing into full gear. In addition, the fact that all three streams of prophecy (the nations, Israel, and the church) are all converging for the first time in history constitutes a sign in itself."

eschatological narrative. Romans 11:25f is likewise critical to the classic Postmillennial eschatology.

I am convinced, as I survey the literature, that there are some issues being almost totally ignored or at the least overlooked. One of those elements is the connection between the ministry and message of John the Baptizer and Paul's concern with the salvation of Israel at the coming of Christ. This connection is of critical, I would go so far as to say determinative, importance. And yet, I have not found a single commentator that has made the connection that I will present in this book. What the commentators do at times is to comment on related texts and themes. They even speak of John's eschatological role. But, they do not then "connect the dots" with Romans 11. That is what I do.

I want to propose a "solution" to the conundrum that is Romans 11. What I will propose should, I am convinced, at least be considered in the discussions of this great text. I propose here that John the Baptizer, in his role as *The Voice* (Isaiah 40), *The Messenger* (Malachi 3) and *Elijah* (Malachi 4:5-6) to herald the "restoration of Israel" provides us the historical and theological context for the proper understanding of Romans 11:25f.

Before proceeding to that main point, I think it is important to establish what some may see, on first blush, as an insignificant or even superfluous point. However, as we proceed, I think it will become evident that that issue is vital for understanding John's role and its impact on Romans 11.

SALVATION AND JUDGMENT - SIAMESE TWINS

Wanamaker, commenting on 1 Thessalonians 2:14f says that Paul's strident "anti-Judaism" language, "Has led many to deny that Paul could have written these verses[5] because of his supposedly positive stance toward the people of Israel in Romans 9-11."[6] The failure of commentators to see that in scripture, salvation and judgment occur synchronously, has, I am convinced, caused some to divorce Romans 11 from its OT prophetic moorings,[7] and perhaps, just perhaps, to divorce it from the message of John the Baptizer as well. However, the Tanakh indisputably links salvation and judgment. I will offer only a few examples from Isaiah. Other prophetic books make the same connection.

In Isaiah 1:27-28 YHVH spoke of the impending judgment of Israel. In that judgment, both deliverance (for the remnant) and the judgment of the nation are conjoined: "Zion shall be redeemed with justice, And her penitents with righteousness. The destruction of transgressors and of sinners shall be together, And those who forsake the Lord shall be consumed." Redemption and judgment go hand in hand.

Wagner comments on two Isaianic prophecies of Israel's last days fate and Paul's use of them: "These two Isaianic prophecies of remnant (Isaiah 10:22-23)

---

[5] There is no MSS support for this rejection. The exclusion of the text by some commentators is based on the failure to acknowledge that in scripture, Israel's salvation would come through, and at the time of, her judgment.

[6] Charles Wanamaker, *New International Greek Testament Commentary, Commentary on 1 & 2 Thessalonians*, (Grand Rapids, Eerdmans, Paternoster, 1990)114.

[7] In 2015, I had a two hour YouTube debate with noted Christian apologist Dr. Michael Brown (Premillennialist). Our topic was the salvation of Israel in Romans 11. I noted that the prophetic source of Romans 11, Isaiah 27 & 59, emphatically posit Israel's salvation at the time of her judgment for shedding innocent blood. Dr. Brown strongly objected, stating that in Romans, Paul is discussing the salvation of Israel, not judgment. When I noted that Isaiah joins salvation and judgment, Dr. Brown had to admit that this was true. Dr. Brown's attempt to divorce Israel's salvation from the time of her judgment is far too common.

and seed (Isaiah 1:9) function *together* in Romans 9:27-29 not only to evoke the severe judgment of God on wayward Israel, but also to foreshadow God's ultimate restoration of his people."[8] Salvation and judgment are conjoined.

In Isaiah 27:9f, one of the prophetic springs from which Romans 11:26f flows, Israel's salvation is posited as accomplished through her judgment, and like in chapter 1, her judgment would be at the time of the vindication of the martyrs, at the Day of the Lord (Isaiah 26:21). In that Day of Salvation, the fortified city would become a desolation, and YHVH would "forget" the people He had created (Isaiah 27:11f).[9] Isaiah conflates Israel's salvation with the time of her judgment (when her sin would be removed. cf. Daniel 9:24 which also conflates salvation and judgment).

Likewise, in Isaiah 59, YHVH accused Israel of being guilty of shedding innocent blood three times, (v. 3-12). As a result of those sins, He promised to come in judgment and vengeance, but, also salvation (v. 16, 20) in fulfillment of His covenant promises. Thus, once again, judgment and salvation are siamese twins and cannot be severed from one another. It is important to realize this in any discussion of Romans 11, but as noted, many commentators fail to see that while Romans 11 is focused on salvation, lying behind that promise was the prophetic reality that Israel's salvation would come at the time of her judgment for shedding innocent blood. The commentators fail to see that Paul joins judgment and salvation right there in Romans 11 - "Behold therefore, the goodness and the severity of God" (v. 22).

N. T. Wright, though he fails to draw the connection between John and Romans 11, calls our attention to the fact that prophetically, salvation and judgment go hand in hand:

---

[8] J. Ross Wagner, *Heralds of the Good News*, (Boston, Brill Academic Press, 2003)116. See also Motyer who makes the same connection between judgment and salvation: Alec Motyer, *The Prophecy of Isaiah*, (Downer's Grove, IVP Academic, 1993)301+.

[9] I concur with Hays' comments on *metalepsis*, i.e. that when a NT writer cites part of an OT text, that he is drawing the reader's attention to the entire prophetic context. (Richard Hays, *Conversion of the Imagination*, (Grand Rapids, Eerdmans, 2005)18.

> "There was, in other words, a belief hammered out, not in abstract debate, but in and through poverty, exile torture and martyrdom, that Israel's sufferings might be, not merely a state *from* which she would, in YHWH's good time, be saved and redeemed, but paradoxically, under certain circumstances and in certain sense, part of the means *by* which that redemption would be effected."[10]

This is what Isaiah 27:9 explicitly says: "Therefore *by this* the iniquity of Jacob will be covered; And this is all the fruit of taking away his sin: *When* he makes all the stones of the altar like chalk stones that are beaten to dust."[11] (My emphasis).

Wright also says, speaking of Israel's expectation of the Day of the Lord,

> "The promise of that return is stated most fully at the end of Ezekiel, balancing the dramatic story, near the beginning of the book, in which the divine presence takes its leave. But the aching sense of absence, coupled with further promises– and warnings!– that this absence will not last forever, continue to echo through the post-exilic period, summed up vividly by Malachi. The priests, ministering in the renewed temple, are bored and careless. But, Israel's God is not finished. There will come a final messenger of warning, and then 'the Lord whom you seek will come suddenly to his temple.' But, as with Amos several centuries earlier, so now, 'who can endure the day of his

---

[10] N. T. Wright, *Jesus and the Victory of God*, (Minneapolis, Fortress, 1996)591.

[11] I suggest that what is at work here and in Isaiah 1, 26-27 and 59, and a host of other eschatological texts, is the principle of Blood Atonement. I cannot develop that here, but this is a critical principle lying behind many OT prophecies of the Day of the Lord. The Law of Blood Atonement demanded the death of "murderers",(Numbers 35). There is a slight allusion to this concept in Keener,(Craig Keener, *Acts: An Exegetical Commentary, Vol. 2*, (Grand Rapids, Baker Academic, 2013)1117, n. 760. This law led, perhaps, to the concept of "atonement through suffering."

coming, and who can stand when he appears?'"[12] Finally, McKnight says: "Thematically, Jesus' vision of AD 70 concerned both redemption and judgment."[13]

It should be evident that judgment and salvation are posited as synchronous events and some scholars even realize that Jesus posited both salvation and judgment for AD 70.

This brief survey of critical messianic prophecies, and the commentators, is sufficient to establish the concept that Israel's salvation at the coming of the Lord is inextricably linked with the judgment on Israel.

Let's turn now to an examination of my main point, and that is the eschatological role of John the Baptizer and its relationship with Romans 11.

---

[12] N. T. Wright, *Paul and the Faithfulness of God*, Vol II, parts III & IV, (Minneapolis, Fortress, Vol. II, 2013)1051.

[13] Scott McKnight, *A New Vision For Israel*, (Grand Rapids, Eerdmans, 1999)12.

JOHN: END TIME PROPHET

We begin our examination of John's eschatological role with Luke 1, where his father, Zecharias, full of the Holy Spirit, is given insight into his son's role. That role is nothing less than the salvation of Israel:

> "Now his father Zacharias was filled with the Holy Spirit, and prophesied, saying: "Blessed is the Lord God of Israel, For He has visited and redeemed His people, And has raised up a horn of salvation for us In the house of His servant David, As He spoke by the mouth of His holy prophets, Who have been since the world began, That we should be saved from our enemies And from the hand of all who hate us, To perform the mercy promised to our fathers And to remember His holy covenant, The oath which He swore to our father Abraham: To grant us that we, Being delivered from the hand of our enemies, Might serve Him without fear, In holiness and righteousness before Him all the days of our life. "And you, child, will be called the prophet of the Highest; For you will go before the face of the Lord to prepare His ways, to give knowledge of salvation to His people By the remission of their sins, Through the tender mercy of our God, With which the Dayspring from on high has visited us; To give light to those who sit in darkness and the shadow of death, To guide our feet into the way of peace." So the child grew and became strong in spirit, and was in the deserts till the day of his manifestation to Israel." (Luke 1:67-80).

Volumes could be written on this, but, it is manifestly clear that John was the fulfillment of prophecy. He *was a prophet* - indeed, per Jesus - he was, "more than a prophet" (Matthew 11:9). As Edwards says: "This child will be the true eschatological harbinger, a 'prophet of the Most High God.'"[14] As we are about to see, this fact alone signaled that the eschaton had arrived.

Murphy reminds us: "All the Synoptics associate John's appearance with the fulfillment of prophecy (Isaiah 40:3 / Malachi 3:24). They suggest that John is inaugurating the new age promised in Jewish Scripture, an age that would be a time of healing, cleansing and purification (See Luke 1:51-55, 68-79; 3:14-

---

[14] James Edwards, *The Pillar New Testament Commentary*, *Luke,* (Nottingham, England, Apollos, Eerdman, 2015)63.

30).""[15] France rightly says John's role was that of,

> "Leading to a new order, the kingdom of heaven of which John was only the herald, and which is the fulfillment of all that went before."[16] Hagner adds: "A correct assessment of the significance of John the Baptist can only be made in relation to Jesus and the kingdom he brings. If Jesus brings the era of the fulfillment of the OT promises, then John is by definition the turning point of the aeons, the last and greatest of the old, announcing and preparing the way for the new kingdom of the messianic king..... "John cannot be Elijah if Jesus is not the Messiah."[17]

As Turner says, John stood, "at the apex of the old order of promise"[18] – the time of fulfillment had arrived! Jesus said that no human ever born was the equal to John, (Matthew 11:12f). Wright says, "John announced imminent judgment on the nation of Israel and urged her to repent, warning that her status as YHWH's covenant people would not be enough, by itself, to deliver her from the coming disaster." Then, commenting on the importance of John's command that the people be baptized, Wright says:

> "Anybody inviting those who wished to do so to pass through an initiatory rite of this kind was symbolically saying: here is the true Israel that is to be vindicated by YHWH. By implication, those who did not join in had forfeited the right to be regarded as the covenant people. ...what John was doing must be seen, and can only be seen, as a prophetic renewal

---

[15] Catherine M. Murphy, *John the Baptist, Prophet of Purity for a New Age*, (Barbara Green, editor), Collegeville, Minn, Liturgical Press, 2003)130.

[16] R. T. France, *Matthew, Tyndale New Testament Commentaries,* (Grand Rapids, Eerdmans, IVP, 1985)194.

[17] Donald Hagner, *Word Biblical Commentary on Matthew* 11:14, Vol. 33, (Dallas, Word Publishers, 1995)308.

[18] David Turner, *Israel's Last Prophet*,(Minneapolis, Fortress, 2015)131.

movement within Judaism - a renewal, however, that aimed not at renewing the existing structures, but at replacing them."[19]

The significance of Wright's comments will, hopefully, be more fully appreciated as we proceed. John was not a prophet heralding the end of time, or judgment on the planet. He was, however, a prophet declaring that Israel's long awaited salvation – the kingdom - was near. But, that would demand a cataclysmic age changing event - the judgment of the Old Covenant world. Thus, when we see Paul's discussion of the salvation of Israel, we are wise to reflect back on John's mission. And this challenges all prevailing views of Romans 11. So far as I have determined, Wright does not, however, make the connection between John's ministry and Romans 11.

Finally, of many similar citations that could be given, McKnight says John's mission was a movement that was a, "prophetic and restorationist movement, a movement anchored in the vision of renewing Israel."[20] He adds: "To have watched, and heard. And participated in John's prophetic movement would have awakened the hopes of the nation for the end of its exile and the dawn of its restoration. John surely stirred the eschatological fires of the expectant among Israel" (1999, 4).

We could multiple these kind of quotes many times over. Many, perhaps even most scholars, at least *verbalize* the significance - the eschatological significance - of John the Baptizer. However, as noted above, *they then ignore John in their discussions of the salvation of Israel in Romans 11*. But, if John's mission was related to the salvation of Israel and if Paul was anticipating the salvation of Israel, *how do we divorce John's message from Paul's?* A look at John's role as described in scripture clearly shows that John can serve as the *crux interpretum* for understanding Paul's enigmatic statement.

According to Zecharias, the time for Israel's end time deliverance was now near with the birth of his son. John would be instrumental in the salvation of Israel (cf. Romans 11:25). His role was in fulfillment of God's covenant with Israel to bring salvation (cf. Romans 11:26). That salvation would come through the

---

[19] N. T. Wright, *Jesus and the Victory of God*, (Minneapolis, Fortress, 1996)160.

[20] Scott McKnight, *A New Vision for Israel*, (Grand Rapids, Eerdmans, 1999)3.

forgiveness of sin (cf. Romans 11:27). YHVH had "visited" His people through the presence of John.

In light of this announcement, it is a huge under-statement to say that John should be seen as a penultimate eschatological figure.[21] In light of Zecharias' description of John, it is perplexing that I have not found one commentator who makes the connection between John and Romans 11:25f.[22]

John's end time role, *as an eschatological prophet* must be noted, even if briefly. Notice how Zecharias says that through John's ministry:

✔ In John, the Lord was proclaiming and initiating the salvation of Israel: "Blessed is the Lord God of Israel, For He has visited and redeemed His people, And has raised up a horn of salvation for us In the house of His servant David."

✔ Through the fulfillment of John's ministry and message, *God's covenant with Abraham* would be fulfilled. Zecharias said the Lord had raised up John: "To perform the mercy promised to our fathers And to remember His holy covenant, The oath which He swore to our father Abraham: To grant us that we, Being delivered from the hand of our enemies, Might serve Him without fear."

✔ The Davidic Kingdom promises would be fulfilled. In John, the herald of that salvation, God had, "raised up a horn of salvation for us In the house of His servant David, As He spoke by the mouth of His holy prophets."

✔ That salvation, the fulfillment of those Covenant promises to Abraham, David and Israel, was nothing but resurrection, the deliverance of Israel: "the Dayspring from on high has visited us; To give light to those who sit in darkness and the shadow of death." These descriptives of sitting in darkness and the "shadow of death" are Hebraisms for *death*. (See Job particularly, where

---

[21] I am convinced that other than Jesus and Paul, John is the most significant -yet commonly overlooked - eschatological figure in the NT. McKnight is surely correct to say: "No significant prophet-like figure in Jewish history has been more neglected than John" (1999, 3).

[22] Even Webb, who produced a major study (almost 400 pages) of the Baptist and his mission does not so much as mention John and Romans 11:25f. Robert Webb, *John the Baptizer and Prophet*, (Eugene, Or. Wipf and Stock, 1991).

"shadow of death" is a euphemism for death itself). Thus, fulfillment of the Abrahamic, Davidic Covenants, the salvation of Israel, was nothing but resurrection! See Isaiah 25:6-9).

The significance of this is that from the perspective of Zecharias, through inspiration, *there was no distinction between the covenant promises of Abraham, David and Israel*. There was *one hope*.[23] That one hope may have been, and was, expressed in different terminology with different nuances, at different times, but, there was no substantive difference. The fulfillment of the David Covenant was viewed as the fulfillment of the Abrahamic Covenant, which was seen as the salvation of Israel.

This unity of hope is highly important. There are, amazingly, some who seek to dichotomize between those "hopes." In July 2012, I had a formal two day debate with Joel McDurmon, now president of American Vision, of Powder Springs, Georgia. In that debate, McDurmon claimed that eschatological resurrection hope of Israel was not the resurrection hope of Job or Abraham![24]

Likewise, in preparation for a 2016 formal public debate with Dr. David Hester, of Faulkner University in Montgomery, Alabama, I asked if his eschatological hope was taken from and based on God's Old Covenant promises, made to Old Covenant Israel. His answer was: "No - My hopes are firmly rooted in the past promises made by God to Abraham, being fulfilled in Christ and witnessed and recorded in the New Testament." Thus, like McDurmon, Hester is affirming that the Abrahamic promises are different from the promises to Israel because God's last judgment on Israel was in AD 70, and we are waiting on the final consummation of the Abrahamic Covenant.

---

[23] See Hebrews 11, where the writer speaks of the one hope, the one eschatological, resurrection hope, that was continuous from Abel through Abraham, to Moses. But, the writer affirms clearly that his audience stood on the cusp of fulfillment, since they had arrived at Zion, the eschatological locus of that salvation (Isaiah 25:6-8; Hebrews 12:21f).

[24] A book of that debate is available from Amazon, my websites and other retailers: *End Times Dilemma: Future or Fulfilled?*

These views are, to say the least, unfortunate and specious, totally falsified in Zecharias' song. Through the Spirit, he affirmed that the Abrahamic Covenant, the Davidic Covenant and Israel's covenant hope was "One." Now, for a brief look at John as an eschatological prophet.

From the NT record, the Holy Spirit was on John and he was a "prophet of God" (Luke 1:17). This is significant, for in Jewish thought the prophetic office had ceased long before John. Edwards notes that in Jewish thought, it was believed that, "at the death of the last prophets, Haggai, Zechariah, and Malachi, the Spirit of prophecy disappeared from Israel and communicated henceforth only occasionally through the inferior *bat-quol*."[25]

Wright likewise notes that the Jews believed that the Spirit had departed from Israel, but, He would be poured out in the last days as a sign of the Day of the Lord.[26] He adds that in Rabbinic and scholarly literature it is accepted that the second temple did not have the Spirit, the Shechinah. He shows that during the entire second temple period, there were no writers that affirmed that the Spirit had returned. No prophet or priest ever said that YHVH had come to the second temple! They always pointed to the last days and the Messianic temple. (Ibid).

Thus, for Jesus (Matthew 11:9F) and the gospel writers to speak of John *as the prophet of God, full of the Spirit from his mother's womb*, this was, for the first century Jew, a powerful declaration that the last days had arrived. YHVH was once again among His people and He was about to bring about their salvation. And He chose John the Baptizer to be the herald of that coming salvation. We now turn to an examination of John's role in bringing about the salvation of Israel.

---

[25] James Edwards, *The Pillar New Testament Commentary, Luke,* (Nottingham, England, Apollos, Eerdman, 2015)117, n. 56. Edwards does mention that some of the rabbis of the first century denied this, affirming the presence of the Spirit. He says, however, that their reason for claiming this was to support their authority over the temple.

[26] N. T. Wright, *Paul and the Faithfulness of God,* Vol. I, (Minneapolis, Fortress, 2014)105.

JOHN AS *THE VOICE* TO PREPARE FOR THE COMING OF THE LORD - AND ISRAEL'S SALVATION

There is no doubt that as far as the Gospel writers - and John himself (John 1:23f) - were concerned he was "the Voice" foretold by Isaiah the prophet.

Mark 1:1-3:

> "The beginning of the gospel of Jesus Christ, the Son of God. 2 As it is written in the Prophets: "Behold, I send My messenger before Your face, Who will prepare Your way before You." "The voice of one crying in the wilderness: 'Prepare the way of the Lord; Make His paths straight.'"

An examination of the prophecy of the coming of *The Voice*, will confirm the eschatological role of John.

Isaiah 40:1-11:

> "Comfort, yes, comfort My people!" Says your God. "Speak comfort to Jerusalem, and cry out to her, That her warfare is ended, That her iniquity is pardoned; For she has received from the Lord's hand Double for all her sins." The voice of one crying in the wilderness: "Prepare the way of the Lord; Make straight in the desert A highway for our God. Every valley shall be exalted And every mountain and hill brought low; The crooked places shall be made straight And the rough places smooth; The glory of the Lord shall be revealed, And all flesh shall see it together; For the mouth of the Lord has spoken." The voice said, "Cry out!" And he said, "What shall I cry?" "All flesh is grass, And all its loveliness is like the flower of the field. The grass withers, the flower fades, Because the breath of the Lord blows upon it; Surely the people are grass. The grass withers, the flower fades, But the word of our God stands forever." O Zion, You who bring good tidings, Get up into the high mountain; O Jerusalem, You who bring good tidings, Lift up your voice with strength, Lift it up, be not afraid; Say to the cities of Judah, "Behold your God!" Behold, the Lord God shall come with a strong hand, And His arm shall rule for Him; Behold, His reward is with Him, And His work before Him. He will feed His flock like a shepherd; He will gather the lambs

with His arm, And carry them in His bosom, And gently lead those who are with young."

Isaiah was predicting the end time coming of YHVH for the "restoration of Israel," "the Redemption of Zion," the, "Second Exodus."[27] Hays, commenting on Mark 1:1-3 and the citation of Isaiah there, says,

> "Mark weaves together citations from Malachi 3:1, Exodus 23;20, and Isaiah 40:3 to portray John the Baptizer as the messenger sent by God as a harbinger of the new exodus and the restoration of Israel." He continues: "Isaiah's announcement of a new exodus is predicated on the bold claim that the all

---

[27] Our focus in this work is on the relationship between John the Baptizer, as *The Voice* of Isaiah 40 and the salvation of Israel in Romans 11. However, John's role as *The Voice,* likewise has tremendous influence on our understanding of the eschatology of 1 Peter. Dubis, for instance, shows that Peter is focused on the return from exile, the second exodus, accomplished in Christ. His discussion of Isaiah 40 and the "Word" of God, i.e. the word of God's promised deliverance, being the gospel that was preached to those to whom Peter writes, is important, and reinforces the points we are making in this work. He says: "Peter equated the good news of what has happened in Christ with Isaiah 40's glorious hope of Israel's restoration. For Peter, the long anticipated restoration has found (and at the *parousia,* yet will fully find) its realization in the readers of 1 Peter themselves" (p. 53). Mark Dubis, *Messianic Woes in First Peter, Suffering and Eschatology in 1 Peter 4:12-19*– Studies in Biblical Literature, Vol. 33, (New York, Peter Lang, 2002)48f. As Dubis cogently notes, according to Hosea and the other prophets, "it is only when God re-gathers Israel and Judah to the promised land that they are once again called 'Sons of the Living God....Thus, when 1 Peter 2:10 takes up the language of Hosea 1:6, 9, 2:25 (LXX), and says that those who were formerly called, 'Not a people' (*ou laos*) are now called 'People of God' (*laos theou*), and that 'Not pitied (*ouk eleemenoi*) has now received pity (*nun...eleethentes*), this is tantamount to saying that Israel's restoration from exile has taken place." (P. 59). Thus, Peter, like Paul in Romans 11, was focused on the "salvation of Israel." Sadly, enough, however, Dubis, like the commentators on Romans, does not even mention John's role in the fulfillment of Isaiah 40 and the restoration of Israel.

powerful God is coming to save his people."[28]

So, *The Voice* - John - was to prepare the way of the Lord who was coming to save His people. Is this not the salvation of Romans 11? That salvation would arrive at the Day of the Lord. It would be at the Lord's coming to reward His saints. It is when, "all flesh shall see the salvation of the Lord" (Isaiah 40:5). That might have suggested to Paul's readers that the salvation of the Gentiles was to have been expected and accepted, as well as conveying to the Gentiles in his audience that they were not being saved "independently" of Israel, but as part of God's faithfulness to Israel (Cf. Romans 1:16-17 / 15:16-27). Either way, Paul's citation of Isaiah 40 in Romans 11 should cue us into the fact that the coming of the Lord that he was anticipating was not the Incarnation.

Dunn adds to this by noting that in Romans 11:25f, Paul's reference to Christ coming "out of Zion" is counter intuitive to the suggestion that Paul is looking back at Jesus' Incarnation. He says the coming of the Lord in Romans 11 refers to Israel's final conversion. Paul's, "out of Zion,"

> "Would give the text a, "particular Messianic interpretation to this passage." Paul would not have been thinking of Jesus' origin as a Jew, and so of his incarnation... but of his eschatological appearance in (and so, 'from') Jerusalem (2 Thessalonians 2:4, 8) or of his coming from heavenly Jerusalem (Galatians 4:26; Hebrews 12:22; Revelation 3:12; 21:2)... that is, of Jesus' parousia."[29]

There is something important here.

In Romans 11, Paul reassures his Jewish audience that God's promises to Israel had not, and would not fail. He does this by citing Isaiah 40:28:[30]

---

[28] Richard Hays, *Reading Backwards*, (Waco, Baylor University Press, 2014)20, 24.

[29] James Dunn, *Romans 9-16, Vol. 33b*, (Dallas, Word Publishers Word 1988)680.

[30] Beale and other scholars acknowledge Paul's citation of Isaiah 40 here. Greg Beale, *Commentary on the New Testament Use of the Old Testament*, (Grand Rapids, Baker Academic, 2007)678.

"Have you not known? Have you not heard? The everlasting God, the Lord, The Creator of the ends of the earth, Neither faints nor is weary. His understanding is unsearchable."

What was Isaiah saying? He was assuring Israel, in bondage and alienated from YHVH, that the time was coming - the Day of the Lord - when Israel's sin would be taken away. God would save His people. Isaiah 40:28 is an affirmation of God's faithfulness to Israel to accomplish her salvation. This is precisely how Paul is using that citation. To those in his audience who were pondering, "Has God cast off His people?" (Romans 11:1f), Paul cites Isaiah 40, and other OT texts, as reassurance that it was not true. He assures his audience that the gifts and calling of God are "irrevocable" (11:28) and that YHVH had not cast them off. He would accomplish the promised salvation! That salvation would come, just as Isaiah 40 foretold, at the coming of the Lord.[31] This ties Romans 11 directly to the ministry and message of John, *The Voice*. But Romans 11 is not Paul's only citation of Isaiah 40 in his discussion of the future of Israel.

In Romans 10:18, the apostle cites Isaiah 40:21 in his discussion of Israel's recalcitrance and rejection of the gospel he was preaching.[32] His point in Romans is that Israel stood without excuse.[33] They should have known that in their own prophecies, YHVH had foretold their stubbornness and disobedience. They were, as it were, "following the script" but, that knowledge should have prompted them to obedience! As Wagner says, Paul found in the OT scriptures, including Isaiah 40, "an analogue to the resistance his message now faces from

---

[31] Wagner notes that Romans 11:34f is a direct citation of Isaiah 40, but makes no connection between John as *The Voice* and Romans 11 (2002, 303 & 304).

[32] Paul likewise quoted from Isaiah 65 in his discussion of Israel's unbelief and as part of the justification for the calling of the nations (Romans 10:20-21). This ties Isaiah 40 and 65-66 together, and therefore, ties the ministry of John to the coming of the New Creation!

[33] There is a strong threat lying behind Paul's statement that Israel was without excuse for rejecting his message. That threat is found in the OT prophecies that Paul quotes from, including Isaiah 40 and Isaiah 65. God was offering them salvation through Jesus, their promised Messiah. That message had gone to them throughout the world. Israel *knew* of the offered salvation. Thus, God would be just to judge them for that rejection (Romans 3:3; see Acts 3:23f also).

his contemporaries, as they question how Paul's gospel could be the announcement of their long-awaited deliverance" (2003, 304).

In other words, *The Voice* of Isaiah would predict the coming of the Lord for the salvation of Israel, and yet, *The Voice* - or the One sending *The Voice* - knew and foretold Israel's rejection of *The Voice* and the salvation he would herald. That rejection carried with it severe consequences in the Day that the Lord would come to reward. If Israel had heeded their own prophecies, and *The Voice*, they could avoid that judgment. Instead, they would reject him. They would reject God's message and they would be "without excuse" (cf. Romans 2:1f; 3:1f). That is what Paul was saying in Romans 10.

This brings John's ministry into sharp focus. John's mission as *The Voice* was to prepare for this coming of the Lord and the salvation of Israel. This shows that Isaiah 40 - and thus, Romans 11 - is not the coming of the Christ in his Incarnate ministry of humility as suggested by many commentators, like Riddlebarger for instance.[34] Hendrikson agrees, claiming that, "Paul is not thinking of what Jesus will do at his second coming, when he will come not 'out of Zion' but 'from heaven' (1 Thess. 4:16). And when forgiveness of sin will no longer be possible."[35]

In preparation for my aforementioned debate with professor David Hester, I asked him to which coming of the Lord did Paul refer in Romans 11, when he anticipated the salvation of "all Israel" at the coming of the Lord out of Zion. Hester's response is not only remarkable, but illustrative of the confusion that exists in the Amillennial world in regard to Romans 11. Hester said, "To say that there is a specific 'coming of the Lord' that Paul refers to is to miss the point of his argument." This is specious and untenable.

---

[34] Kim Riddlebarger, *A Case For Amillennialism*, (Grand Rapids, Baker, 2003)194. Commenting on Romans 11:25-27: "Paul, therefore, probably understands the future tenses of the Isaiah prophecy as fulfilled in the first coming of Christ, which set in motion the apostolic mission of the church." As we shall see, this view completely ignores the context of the prophecies that Paul cites, as well as the message of John as *The Voice*.

[35] William Hendrickson, *New Testament Commentary, Romans*, (Grand Rapids, Baker, 2002)383.

Paul anticipated the coming of the Lord out of Zion in fulfillment of Isaiah 27 & 59. Both Isaiah 27 and Isaiah 59 foretold *a very specific coming of the Lord for the salvation of Israel. That coming was to be at the judgment of Israel for shedding innocent blood.* Thus, the idea that Paul did not have a specific coming in mind is facile and in fact misses his entire point!

Of course, to appreciate why Hester would argue as he did, one has to realize that he is on record that NT eschatology is not taken from, or based on God's Old Covenant promises made to Old Covenant Israel as noted above. Thus, for him, or Riddlebarger, or Boettner, et. al., to admit, for one moment, that Paul was anticipating the coming of the Lord in fulfillment of God's OT promises is to surrender his entire eschatology.

Riddlebarger and Hendrikson say that the coming of the Lord out of Zion was the Incarnation. But, they then posit a future salvation of Israel[36] at the end of the age, i.e. at the coming of the Lord out of Zion:

> "Is there a future for ethnic Israel? Paul's answer was yes. And the presence of a believing remnant was proof. But the future salvation of Israel is not connected to a future millennial kingdom. It is connected to the end of the age. When all Israel is saved, the resurrection is near." (2003,194).

This is self-contradictory and confusing. Paul posits the salvation of Israel at the coming of the Lord. Riddlebarger says the coming of the Lord was Jesus' Incarnation, and yet, he says the coming of the Lord – when Israel is saved! - is yet future!

Paul is clear that the salvation of Israel that he had in mind would occur at the coming of the Lord "out of Zion" in fulfillment of Isaiah 27 and 59. If the coming of the Lord he had in mind was the Incarnation, then surely it can be argued that Israel's salvation was past. However, while Riddlebarger says that the parousia that Paul speaks of was the Incarnation, he then posits that the salvation of Israel will not take place until the end of the current age, i.e. *at the parousia of Christ out of Zion!* That essentially means that Paul had two

---

[36] Hendrikson says the salvation of "all Israel" is the salvation of the predestinated righteous remnant of the Jews who are saved throughout the entirety of the Christian age. (P. 381-382). This is not substantively different from Riddlebarger.

comings of the Lord "out of Zion" in mind and two salvations of Israel in mind. This turns the text on its head and is hardly tenable.

The coming of the Lord foretold in Isaiah, and thus, the coming that was to be the focus of *The Voice* was the coming of the *Kurios* in *judgment*, as well as salvation.[37] Not only does Isaiah's reference to the Lord's coming to reward and save indicate this, but, the language he utilizes suggests this.

The mission of *The Voice* would be: "Every valley shall be exalted And every mountain and hill brought low; The crooked places shall be made straight And the rough places smooth." Given the fact that John was *The Voice*, and yet, he undertook no literal landscaping work, it is important to understand that his language was taken directly from *the language of warfare.*[38] Thus, the imagery is that of the Day of the Lord, the time of the "holy war" – YHVH's end time coming.

---

[37] Jesus echoes Isaiah 40:10, as well as Isaiah 62:11, ("his reward is with him") to speak of his coming in judgment (Matthew 16:27 / Revelation 22:12). Matthew 16:27-28 is an extension of John's message of the coming kingdom and judgment. Jesus, like John, said those things would occur in the lifetime of the first century audiences.

[38] Josephus described Vespasian's invasion of Galilee and his approach to besiege Jotapata. Vespasian designated soldiers to, "measure out the camp withal; and after them, such as were to make the road even and straight, and it were anywhere rough and hard pressed to be passed over, to plane it, and to cut down the woods that hindered their march, that the army might not be in distress, or tired with their march." (Wars, Bk. 3:6:2). See also, David Pao, *Acts and the Isaianic New Exodus*, (Grand Rapids, Baker Academic, 2000)42f, where he shows that the language was used of Pompey's conquests, in Psalms of Solomon 8:17. Motyer says the language here combines the ancient picture of the Lord coming to his people's aid (Dt. 33:2) with the practice of constructing processional ways for visiting dignitaries or for use by the gods as they were carried in procession." (J. Alec Motyer, *The Prophecy of Isaiah*, (Downer's Grove, ILL, IVP Academic, 1993)300). But, the coming of YHVH in the context of Isaiah 40 is more than a mere "processional." It is His coming to reward / recompense.

So, twice in Paul's discussion of Israel's future he draws directly from Isaiah 40,[39] the ground of John's ministry as *The Voice*. Paul's message was John's message. The Lord was coming. He was coming for the salvation of Israel. There was danger in rejecting that message - and no excuse for doing so. In spite of any rejection on the part of the nation however, God was faithful and would bring to pass His promises when the Redeemer / Deliverer came out of Zion.

There is another element of John's mission as *The Voice* to note. As Mark 1:4 says, John came preaching the baptism of repentance "for the remission of sin." Wright calls our attention to the fact that:

> "Centuries of Christian usage have accustomed readers of the New Testament to think of 'forgiveness' as primarily a gift to the individual person, which can be made at any time. It is, in that sense, abstract and ahistorical, however much it may burst upon one's consciousness with fresh delight in particular historical situations. On this basis, analysis of Jesus' offer of forgiveness have tended to focus on the piety (the sense of forgiveness) or the abstract theology (the fact of forgiveness, or the belief in it) of Jesus' hearers and / or the earth church. ... What is regularly missing from analyses of forgiveness is that which, arguably, stands front and center in precisely those biblical and post-biblical Jewish texts upon which Jesus and the early church drew most heavily. *Forgiveness of sins is another way of saying 'return from exile'*" (1996, 268).

While Wright was speaking of Jesus' message, there was no distinction between John and Jesus in this regard. This connection between "end of exile" and forgiveness is undeniable in Isaiah 40, and thus, in John's message.[40] When we read Mark 1:1-4 where we are told of John's identity and his message, it seems

---

[39] Paul's citation of Isaiah 40 in Romans 10 and then in chapter 11 makes one wonder if he intended an *inclusio*. If so, that would emphasize his reliance on the message and ministry of *The Voice*.

[40] See Wright's additional comments on this 1996, 434+. However, even in his 2013 productions, *Paul and the Faithfulness of God*, in his expansive discussion of Romans 11:25f, he makes no mention or connection to John and his mission.

to me that we should see an arrow pointing directly to Romans 11:26f since there, Paul, just like John and Jesus, was anticipating the forgiveness of Israel's sin. This is particularly true since, as noted just above, Paul cites Isaiah 40 twice in Romans 10-11. Very clearly, Paul had in mind the same thing that John did. *What John had begun to declare and promise Paul was promising that it would be brought to pass at the parousia.*

As we shall see, this demands that the coming of the Lord of Romans 11:26f - the climax of Israel's covenant history - was to take place at the catastrophic fall of Jerusalem in AD 70. As Wright suggested just above, John was warning Israel to accept the offer of forgiveness or face "imminent judgment" on the nation. That imminent coming must be seen as not only the time of judgment, but, the time of Israel's salvation as well, since, as we have seen that salvation and judgment go hand in hand. The coming of the Lord *in judgment and salvation* are explicit in Isaiah 40 – the very text that John fulfilled and that Paul cited.

So, when John called on his audience to repent and be baptized for the forgiveness of sin, he was not functioning like a modern evangelist calling on individuals to become "Christians."[41] He was calling on Israel to repent and turn back to YHVH so that her long exile – her separation from her God - would come to an end. We should of course, see Paul's expectation of the coming forgiveness of Israel's sin in Romans 11 as a continuation of that same eschatological narrative. The work of forgiveness / restoration of Israel – calling them to believe in the coming "Second Moses," initiated the Second Exodus, and the parousia of Christ would lead them to their promised land of salvation.

Needless to say, both John and Jesus "subverted" the expectation of Israel in regard to the return from exile / forgiveness / restoration. As Wright noted, for John to offer forgiveness of sin by being baptized by him, and not at the temple, by the priests, was nothing short of revolutionary! And, when Jesus offered to forgive sins through his word, e.g. Mark 2:5f, this contravened the accepted views. As Wright says, "In first century Jewish reality, the way YHWH forgave sins was ultimately through the established and authorized channels of temple and priesthood. Jesus was claiming to be in that sense 'speaking for god', claiming by strong implication that he carried in himself the authority normally

---

[41] This is not to disparage or deny, in any way, the Gospel call for men to become Christians today. It is simply to better understand the specific, eschatological role of John as *The Voice*, preparing for, and calling Israel to her destined covenant climax.

vested elsewhere." (1996, 435). Subversive indeed!

Not only did John and Jesus' message of forgiveness subvert the accepted methods of forgiveness, the rest of their message demonstrated that the normal expectation about *the nature of Israel's restoration* was likewise wrong. National restoration, ethnic superiority, possession of land, even the praxis of Israel, (e.g. Sabbath, foods, circumcision, etc.) that set her off from the nations were all rejected by John and Jesus. Neither John or Jesus and thus, not Paul in Romans 11, anticipated or predicted a nationalistic restoration of Israel to land, city or temple. Those things were temporary, *always destined to pass*, at the true restoration.

John did offer what Isaiah 40 said YHVH would give. The nation might have rejected his offer, but, just as Paul would write later, the remnant did respond to that invitation and entered into "that for which Israel sought" (Romans 11:7). Furthermore, Paul affirms that God was not only faithful, but, Israel's unbelief would not, and could not, affect God's plan: "What if some did not believe? Shall their unbelief make the faith of God without effect? God forbid! Yea, let God be true and every man a liar" (Romans 3:3f).

In light of these things, when we view John's role in offering Israel forgiveness, it forces us to reject the Dispensational claim that Jewish unbelief postponed God's purposes. Dispensationalists / Zionists have the same misguided expectation of Israel's restoration that the early Jews did, but, which was rejected by John, Jesus and Paul.

JOHN *AS THE MESSENGER* TO PREPARE FOR THE COMING OF THE LORD

> "Behold, I send My messenger, And he will prepare the way before Me. And the Lord, whom you seek, Will suddenly come to His temple, Even the Messenger of the covenant, In whom you delight. Behold, He is coming," Says the Lord of hosts. "But who can endure the day of His coming? And who can stand when He appears? For He is like a refiner's fire And like launderers' soap. He will sit as a refiner and a purifier of silver; He will purify the sons of Levi, And purge them as gold and silver, That they may offer to the Lord An offering in righteousness. "Then the offering of Judah and Jerusalem Will be pleasant to the Lord, As in the days of old, As in former years. And I will come near you for judgment; I will be a swift witness Against sorcerers, Against adulterers, Against perjurers, Against those who exploit wage earners and widows and orphans, And against those who turn away an alien— Because they do not fear Me," Says the Lord of hosts" (Malachi 3:1-5).

"This is he of whom it was written: 'I send my messenger before my face'" (Matthew 11:10).

> "The beginning of the gospel of Jesus Christ, the Son of God. As it is written in the Prophets: "Behold, I send My messenger before Your face, Who will prepare Your way before You." "The voice of one crying in the wilderness: 'Prepare the way of the Lord; Make His paths straight.'" (Mark 1:1-2).

As we have noted, Jesus was emphatic in declaring that John was both *The Voice* and *The Messenger*. There was no, "If you accept it" conditionality.

In Isaiah, the salvation of Israel is at the forefront and judgment is in the background. In Malachi, the opposite is true: judgment is in the focus, while salvation and deliverance are more implicit. This reinforces the point that we made earlier: salvation and judgment are synchronous events in scripture.

Space forbids a full analysis of the impact of Malachi on New Testament eschatology. A look at a few instances of this influence however, is worthwhile and revealing - not to mention having tremendous implications

☛ Acts 17:30-31 - When Paul spoke of the "about to be" judgment, he said that it was a day that had been "appointed." In Malachi 4, the Great Day of the Lord, as in Daniel, i.e. the "appointed time", was in view.[42]

☛ 1 Thessalonians 1:10- The wrath to come of Thessalonians is the wrath that John, as *The Messenger* and *Elijah* foretold (Matthew 3:7).[43]

☛ 1 Peter 1– The Refining of the new priesthood to offer acceptable sacrifices is clearly echoed in 1 Peter 1-2. What is so significant is that Peter patently "re-interprets" the entire concept of the priesthood, "universalizing" the Levites, interpreting them as all believers. In similar fashion, he sees the body of Christ as the spiritual temple, wherein spiritual sacrifices are offered by this new, radically different priesthood.

Note that in 1 Peter 2:9, Peter tells his audience that they were "His own special people." He cites Exodus 19:6, where YHVH said Old Covenant Israel was supposed to be a distinctive people for His possession. Unfortunately, Israel had failed to live up to that high calling. But, in Malachi, the Lord was promising that in the Day of His coming, the righteous remnant would be His "jewels."

---

[42] In Daniel, "the appointed time" plays a prominent role. The end time narrative is focused on the climactic "appointed time" which included the end of the age and the resurrection. Since Paul draws from Daniel a good bit, when we read his discourse at Athens and his focus on the "appointed day" we should hear the echo of Daniel. The significance of this is that in Daniel, the "appointed time of the end" cannot be extrapolated beyond the days of Rome.

[43] Like other connections between John and the NT eschatological texts that are mostly overlooked, as of the writing of this work, I have found only one commentator, Adam Clarke, (*Clarke's Commentary,* Vol. 6, p. 540) who connected Paul's reference to the coming wrath to AD 70. One could conjecture that he connected this with John's ministry, but, he does not explicitly make that connection.

Hill notes that the word used here is *segulla* and,

> "The word is unique to Malachi among the prophetic books of the OT/HB (Hebrew Bible, DKP). The term is used in the Pentateuch (Exodus 19:5; Deuteronomy 7:6; 14:2; 26:18) and the Psalms to describe the privileged status of the people of Israel (Psalms 135:4) In two instances, *segulla* refers to unusual or special treasure acquired by royalty (Ecclesiastes 2:8; 1 Chronicles 29:3)."[44]

The connection between Exodus, Malachi and 1 Peter is tantalizing, intriguing and significant. In Malachi, YHVH was pointing to the eschatological consummation as the time when Israel would reach her destiny– in Messiah. This is Romans 11 and Revelation 20.

☞ 2 Peter 3 - Peter foretold the Day of the Lord, the Day of Fire. As most commentators agree, he was drawing from Isaiah 66:15f. What is commonly overlooked however, is that Malachi is drawing on Isaiah as well. Malachi's Day of Fire is the Great Day of the Lord and the judgment of the wicked, just as Peter's Day of the Lord is the time of the judgment of the wicked. This means that John's message as *The Messenger* and *Elijah* is paradigmatic for understanding 2 Peter 3.

☞ Revelation 6:9-17 - The Great and Terrible Day of the Lord, for the vindication of the martyrs in Revelation is the fulfillment of the Great Day of the Lord of Malachi, the Day in which no man could stand.

☞ Revelation 20 - John anticipated the Great White Throne Judgment when the books would be opened, and those written in the Book of Life would enter the New Creation. In Malachi, YHVH promised that in the Day of His coming, His book of remembrance would be opened and those written there would make up His "jewels."

This is only a small sampling of NT citations or echoes of Malachi. John was *The Messenger* to proclaim the message of Malachi. Clearly, Malachi - and thus, John - had a profound influence on the NT writers.

---

[44] Andrew Hill, *Anchor Bible, Malachi*, (Yale University Press, 1998)342.

I want now to look closely at Malachi 3 and the prediction of *The Messenger*. Our purpose is to determine the nature of the Day of the Lord that *The Messenger* would herald. What we will find is that John, as *The Messenger* of the coming salvation of Israel at the parousia, was not a messenger of an end of time, cosmos destroying event. He was in fact to be a "covenant messenger" warning Israel that if she did not repent and accept Jesus as their promised messiah, the full brunt of Mosaic Covenant wrath would fall on them. To say the least, the implications of this for our understanding of Romans 11:25f are powerful!

Let me say this: If the coming of the Lord of Romans 11 is the coming of the Lord foretold by John as *The Messenger*, this means that the events of 1948 have nothing to do with the fulfillment of prophecy. It means that modern Zionism is built on a faulty foundation and should be rejected. It likewise means that *any* futurist application of Romans 11 is false. It means that "all Israel" has been saved - no matter what our personal concept of that might be.

Malachi, *The Messenger* prophet,[45] foretold a future coming of another Messenger, one who would prepare for the coming of the Lord to His temple:

> "Behold, I send My messenger, And he will prepare the way before Me. And the Lord, whom you seek, Will suddenly come to His temple, Even the Messenger of the covenant, In whom you delight. Behold, He is coming," Says the LORD of hosts. But who can endure the day of His coming? And who can stand when He appears? For He is like a refiner's fire And like launderers' soap. He will sit as a refiner and a purifier of silver; He will purify the sons of Levi, And purge them as gold and silver, That they may offer to the LORD An offering in righteousness" (Malachi 3.1-3).[46]

---

[45] In Hebrew, "Malachi" means messenger.

[46] Taking the size of Malachi into consideration, in comparison with the other OT books Malachi is cited more often than any other book, according to the Logos Bible Software Blog: http://www.crossway.org/blog/2006/03/nt-citations-of-ot/.

The eschatological nature of this coming of the Lord is clear and undeniable. The Lord would come "suddenly to His temple"[47] and no one could stand before Him at that coming.[48] The word translated as *come*, (*bow, Strong's #0935*) is a word commonly used in the OT to speak of the coming YHVH in judgment.[49]

The eschatological nature of this coming of the Lord is reinforced in Malachi, in verse 5:

> "And I will come near you for judgment; I will be a swift witness Against sorcerers, Against adulterers, Against perjurers, Against those who exploit wage earners and widows and orphans, And against those who turn away an alien— Because they do not fear Me."

So, there is no doubt that the coming of the Lord in view is his coming in judgment. Now, take particular note again of the things that God said He was going to judge:

> "And I will come near you for judgment; I will be a swift witness:
> Against *sorcerers*.
> Against *adulterers*.
> Against *perjurers*.
> Against those who exploit wage earners and widows and orphans.
> And against those *who turn away an alien*."

---

[47] Baldwin says the reference to the Lord coming "suddenly" was "ominous", "for suddenness was usually associated with a calamitous event (e.g. Isaiah 47:11; 48:3; Jeremiah 4:20)." Joyce Baldwin, *Tyndale Old Testament Commentaries, Haggai, Zechariah, Malachi*, (Downers Grove, Ill., Intervarsity Press, 1972)243.

[48] The concept of "standing" before the Lord in connection with his "coming" is invariably related to the judgment parousia of Christ in the NT.

[49] There is a beautiful thematic connection between the coming of the Lord to his temple in Malachi and Psalms 24, but we cannot develop it here.

Keep in mind that God was saying that this judgment would be at His coming in judgment, when the kingdom arrived. The entrance of the "Messenger of the Covenant" into his temple is an undeniable eschatological doctrine. The language is the language of enthronement. It is the language of the Messianic temple. It is the language of the kingdom.

So, the kingdom would come when Messiah's Kingdom temple was perfected and he entered that temple to rule and reign. Of course, this implies that the old temple would become passe when the new temple was fully established. Needless to say, John's message was, "the kingdom of heaven has drawn near" (Matthew 3:2). He was proclaiming the imminent fulfillment of the coming of the Lord into His Messianic temple.

As a side bar, there is another possible connection here that bears examination. If Malachi 3 is referent to the Lord's coming into the perfected Messianic temple,[50] do we have here an echo of Daniel 9:24? In Daniel's prophecy of the seventy weeks, he was told, "Seventy weeks are determined...to anoint the Most Holy." The identity of "the Most Holy" is disputed with many commentators taking the view that it is referent to the anointing of Jesus at his baptism. On the other hand, many commentators believe the term is referent to the dedication of the completed Messianic temple. I personally favor the later view. If that is accurate, here is what we would have.

John, as *The Messenger*, would tell Israel that the time for the Kingdom and the Messianic temple at the coming of the Lord was near.

John's message as The Messenger was that the Day of the Lord was to be a national judgment on Israel and the old temple. Thus, the Messianic temple would be dedicated at the time of the national judgment on Israel.

This agrees perfectly well with Daniel 9, where the full end of the seventy weeks is the destruction of the city and the temple – the dissolution of the old temple

---

[50] See my discussion of Matthew 24:29f as the dedication of the Messianic kingdom by Christ's coming in the Shechinah Glory Cloud in my book *Like Father Like Son, On Clouds of Glory*. Jesus was discussing the passing of the Old Covenant temple (24:2f) and the building of his Temple. My book is available on Amazon, Kindle, my websites and other retailers.

to make way for the Messiah's temple.

So, John's message as *The Messenger* was one of impending national judgment, warning of the impending destruction of the old temple,[51] but the full arrival of the Messianic temple would be at the end of the seventy weeks. The salvation of Israel - of Romans 11 - is inextricably bound up with the concept of the end times temple (cf. Isaiah 2:2f / Ezekiel 37 / Zechariah 6:13, etc.). Daniel 9 delimits the dedication of that temple to the seventy weeks. Since John's mission as *The Messenger* posits that temple at the imminent Day of the Lord in national judgment of Israel, this powerfully suggests that Romans 11 must be interpreted within that framework, consummating in AD 70.

Remember that in Mark 1:1-3, John is unequivocally identified not only as *The Messenger* of Malachi, but, *The Voice* of one crying in the wilderness of Isaiah 40. *The Voice*, just like *The Messenger*, was to prepare the people for the coming of the Lord in his kingdom and in judgment (Isaiah 40:1-11). Is this not the coming of the Lord of Romans 11? If not, what is the difference?

It cannot be emphasized enough that the task of *The Messenger / The Voice* was to proclaim impending *judgment*. There is nothing in Isaiah 40 or Malachi to indicate that the mission was to prepare for the Incarnation of Messiah. The coming of the Lord to his temple – when no one could stand before him - is a coming in judgment of the wicked (Malachi 3:5). The coming of *The Voice* was to be the coming of the Lord "with his reward" when he would rule over the kingdom. This is not the Incarnation. It is the parousia of Messiah in judgment. But, as established above, that coming in judgment was also the time of the kingdom, the time of salvation.

So:

John the Baptizer was *The Messenger* foretold by Malachi 3.

But, *The Messenger* foretold by Malachi was to prepare the way for the

---

[51] As we will see below, scholars recognize that John's baptism was itself a harbinger of the end of the temple system in Jerusalem. In fact, John's entire ministry was one of "good news / bad news" for it heralded the imminent fulfillment of Israel's eschatological hope, while warning that the coming New Creation demanded the passing of the Old.

coming of the Lord in judgment, at the time of the kingdom.

Therefore, John, as *The Messenger* foretold by Malachi 3, was preparing for the coming of the Lord in judgment at the time of the kingdom.

The question is, what was the nature of the Day of the Lord that *The Messenger*, John heralded and foretold?

The answer to this question has a direct bearing on our understanding of Romans 11 and we will address further below. As we have seen, the coming of the Lord that John foretold was the Day of the Lord for the salvation of Israel - the salvation of Israel foretold by Paul in Romans 11. If John, as *The Messenger*, was not predicting an end of time coming, then Paul was not predicting one either.

To help answer the question, note the further connections between John's message in Matthew 3 (remembering that he was *The Messenger* of Malachi 3) and what Malachi said of the Day of the Lord:

> "For behold, the day is coming, Burning like an oven, And all the proud, yes, all who do wickedly will be stubble. And the day which is coming shall burn them up," Says the LORD of hosts, That will leave them neither root nor branch. 2 But to you who fear My name The Sun of Righteousness shall arise With healing in His wings; And you shall go out And grow fat like stall-fed calves. You shall trample the wicked, For they shall be ashes under the soles of your feet On the day that I do this," Says the LORD of hosts" (Malachi 4:1-3).

So, *The Messenger* was to prepare the people for the Day of the Lord when the wicked would be burned as stubble - this is Matthew 3:7, 10-12. This would be the time of his coming to his temple when he would judge the sorcerers, the adulterers, the liars, those who mis-treated the widows and the orphans, and those who turned away the alien. There is something very critical to note about this judgment. *It was to be an outpouring of Covenantal Wrath - national judgment - on Israel for violating Torah.*

Look again at Malachi 3:5. God said in the judgment to come Messiah would come to his temple and:

"I will come near you for judgment; I will be a swift witness:[52]
Against *sorcerers*.
Against *adulterers*.
Against *perjurers*.
Against those who exploit wage earners and widows and orphans.
And against those *who turn away an alien*."[53]

What cannot be missed or dismissed is that this is a direct allusion to Deuteronomy 27:19: "Cursed is the one who perverts the justice due the stranger, the fatherless, and widow." This connection is undeniable and the implications are profound.

Deuteronomy also foretold curses on Israel for the time when she would commit the sins listed in 27:19 (and of course, other sins as well). Chapters 28-30, called the Law of Blessings and Cursings, described the curses that would come. Those curses involved *national judgment, invasion, captivity*. It did not involve the end of the Christian age. It did not involve the events of 1948. This is therefore, incredibly important. Nothing could more unambiguously establish the fact of *Torah To Telos* than John's role as *The Messenger* who would proclaim the application of Mosaic Covenant sanctions at the Day of the Lord.

If it is true that the judgment to come in fulfillment of the ministry of *The Messenger* / John the Baptizer was to be in application of the Law of Blessings and Cursings in Deuteronomy 28-30, and if that judgment is the time of the

---

[52] The word *witness* used here is itself proof that this is a covenantal judgment. Taylor and Clarendon say: "The term 'witness' calls to mind the covenant between God and Israel, which Israel swore to uphold. The book of the Law was a witness against them (Deuteronomy 31:26), as was Israel's God, who had pledged to enforce the covenant (Deuteronomy 28:15-68)." Richard Taylor and E. Ray Clendenen, *The American Commentary, Haggai-Malachi*, (Nashville, Broadman, 2004)392.

[53] I will not develop this here, but, in 1 Thessalonians 2:14-16, Paul condemned the Jews of his day because they refused to allow the Gospel to be preached to the Gentiles so that they might be saved! This is an echo of Malachi. God had always provided that foreigners could participate in Israel's blessings, thus, to turn away the alien from those blessings was a heinous crime. How much more so when the Jews sought to turn away the Gentiles from entering Christ and the kingdom?

salvation of Israel in Romans 11, then it is undeniably true that the coming of the Lord in Romans 11 was in application of the Law of Blessings and Cursings. Since the coming of the Lord of Romans 11, as we shall establish, was still future to Paul, and since that coming would be in fulfillment of John's message of the coming of the Lord in fulfillment of the Law of Blessings and Cursings, then, once again, this fully establishes the truth of *Torah To Telos*. The law of Moses and its sanctions would remain in effect until the coming of the Lord of Romans 11:25f.

That Day of the Lord of Malachi 3 was to be national judgment *when YHVH would bring the sword against the nation* of Israel. This is explicitly stated in Exodus 22:18-24, where the same list of sins found in Malachi and Deuteronomy are listed. YHVH said violation of those laws would result in: "My wrath will become hot, and I will kill you with the sword: your wives will be widows, and your children fatherless."

So, John as *The Messenger*, was to warn Israel that their sins would lead to *national judgment for violating the Law of Moses*. That judgment would be at the Great and Terrible Day of the Lord.[54] But again, to re-emphasize, if that Day proclaimed by *The Messenger* was the Day of Israel's salvation, as well as her judgment, this demands that Romans 11, being the time of Israel's salvation, was at the time of Israel's national judgment in AD 70.

So, what does it mean that Malachi identifies the Day of the Lord that he was predicting as the application of Mosaic Covenant Wrath?

Malachi was predicting the coming of the Lord in judgment – as well as the salvation of the remnant, the jewels of the Lord. That coming would be when He would judge those who had violated *Torah* through neglect of the widows and orphans, and by turning away foreigners. But, provision for the judgment of those sins was delineated in Torah, the Law of Moses.

The Day of the Lord of Malachi 3:5 – the Day to be heralded by John as The

---

[54] Numerous commentators note that the list of sins in Malachi 3:5f were violations of *Torah* and yet, the commentaries consulted made no comment about the nature of the coming Day of the Lord. In fact, some, like Peter Adam, claim that the judgment foretold by *The Messenger* will occur at the so called end of time. Peter Adam, *The Message of Malachi*, (Downers Grove, InterVarsity, 2013)120+.

Voice & The Messenger- would have to be at a time when the Law of Moses and its provisions for Covenant Wrath were still in effect.[55] And since the coming of the Lord of Romans 11, the Day of the Lord for the salvation of Israel, is the Day of the Lord proclaimed by John, then the parousia of Romans 11 would have to occur when the Law of Moses, including the Law of Blessings and Cursings, when the Law of Moses was still in effect.

Keep in mind that all three futurist eschatologies tell us that the Law of Moses has been abrogated. Generally speaking, they tell us that Torah was removed at the Cross. But here is the problem: If the Law of Moses passed away at the Cross, this demands that the Day of the Lord foretold by Malachi 3-4 - the Day proclaimed by John as *The Voice, The Messenger* and *Elijah,* had to have been fulfilled *prior to the Cross and the annulment of Torah. The Law of Moses had to be in effect for the fulfillment of John's prophecy of the impending judgment!*

It is interesting that Dispensationalists, both Progressive and Classic, realize that the Law of Moses had to be in effect at the time of the destruction of Jerusalem in AD 70 in order for the covenant sanctions to be applied. However, in a bit of self-contradictions, they deny the current validity of Torah in their predictions of the supposedly future Great Tribulation.[56]

Blaising and Bock, commenting on the threatened judgment against Jerusalem in Isaiah 1 say:

---

[55] This point is completely missed by Hester, who insisted that the Law of Moses was nailed to the cross, but that the decree / promise / prophecy of the end of the Mosaic Commonwealth did not take place until AD 70. But, this means that the provisions for Mosaic Covenant wrath were applied 40 years after the Mosaic Covenant was annulled! Such is the illogic of the view that the Law was removed at the Cross.

[56] See my extensive discussion of this in my book: *The Resurrection of Daniel 12:2: Future or Fulfilled*? The bottom line is that the Abomination of Desolation and the ensuring Great Tribulation must be seen as covenant sanctions / punishments on Israel for violation of Torah. Yet, at the time of this writing, I have not found even one Millennialists who acknowledges this fact. This undeniable truth is devastating to Premillennialism. My book is available on Amazon, at my websites and other retailers.

"Technically, one could not be prosecuted for violating the covenant if there were no witnesses. In Isaiah 1, we have an example of God 'suing' Israel before the witnesses, heaven and earth, for having broken the Mosaic Covenant. The punishment, of course, is the curses of that covenant."[57]

This comment is surely spot on. But, to say the least, it is troublesome for Blaising and Bock. If the threat of the judgment of Jerusalem in Isaiah 1 was made in the context of the sanctions of the Law of Moses, then the Day of the Lord of Malachi 3-4 must likewise be viewed as the threat of the application of the Law of Moses.

That raises the question once again: If the Day of the Lord foretold in Malachi 3-4, the Day of the Lord proclaimed by John the Baptizer as *The Messenger* and *Elijah*, was to be in the application of Mosaic Covenant sanctions, then at what point, from the time of John's ministry, to the cross (where Torah was supposedly abrogated) did that Day of the Lord come? The undeniable answer is, it did not happen from John to the cross. But there is more.

The Day of the Lord of Malachi 3-4, the Day foretold by John as *The Messenger and Elijah*, had to take place while the Law of Moses was still binding. It would therefore, have to be a time when Israel remained God's covenant people.

The Day of the Lord of Malachi 3-4, the Day proclaimed by John as *The Voice*, is the same Day of the Lord of Romans 11:25f - The Day of Israel's salvation.

But, all futurists say the Law of Moses was abrogated in the first century.[58]

---

[57] Craig Blaising and Darrell Bock, *Progressive Dispensationalism,* A BridgePoint Book, (Wheaton, Ill, 1993)313, n. 19. Significantly, neither Blaising or Bock even mention John in his role as *The Voice*, *The Messenger* and *Elijah* in their book. This is true even though they cite Isaiah 40 as predictive of the future kingdom, and they likewise posit Malachi 3:1-5 as the future Davidic kingdom (1993, 226+). Such a position clearly ignores John's eschatological role.

[58] Amillennialists and Postmillennialists, by and large, also say that Israel is no longer the covenant people of God. But if that is so, then the coming of the Lord of Romans 11 is, of necessity, fulfilled. The salvation of Israel in Romans 11 is patently about the fulfillment of God's covenant with Israel.

Of necessity, then, the Day of the Lord of Malachi 3-4 - the Day of the Lord foretold by John, *the coming of the Lord of Romans 11:25f,* - had to have occurred in the first century while the Law of Moses was still binding and its provisions for Covenant Wrath applicable.[59] The point to be made of course is that if the destruction of Jerusalem in Isaiah was in the application of Mosaic Covenant sanctions, then the destruction of Jerusalem in AD 70 was likewise in application of Mosaic Covenant sanctions. The Law stood valid until it was totally fulfilled, when the full power and the full application of Torah came crashing down on Israel, bringing her covenant history to its close.

Thomas Ice likewise inadvertently posits the continuation of Torah until AD 70, in his comments on Luke 21:22. In his written debate with Kenneth Gentry, on the Great Tribulation, Ice wrote the following:

> "Luke 21:20 must be A.D. 70 because it speaks of the days of vengeance, and this means "Those first century days are called 'days of vengeance' for Jerusalem is under the divine judgment of covenantal sanctions recorded in Leviticus 26 and Deuteronomy 28. Luke records that God's vengeance upon His elect nation is 'in order that all things which are written may be fulfilled.' Jesus is telling the nation that God will fulfill all the curses of the Mosaic covenant because of Israel's disobedience. He will not relent and merely bring to pass a partial fulfillment of His vengeance. Some of the passages that Jesus said would be fulfilled include the following: Lev. 26:27-33; Deut. 28:49f; 32:19-27; 1 Kings 9:1-9; Jeremiah 6:1-8; 26:1-9;Daniel 9:26; Hosea 8:1-10-10:15; Micah 3:12; Zechariah 11:6)."[60]

---

[59] Note that in Hebrews 8:13, Torah, the Covenant, (not the external observances of Torah, but the *Covenant* itself) was, "nigh unto passing." See my *Torah To Telos: The Passing of the Law of Moses*, (Ardmore, Ok. JaDon Management Inc., 2012) for a full discussion of this text. That book is available from Amazon, Kindle, my websites and other retailers.

[60] Thomas Ice, (Kenneth L. Gentry and Thomas Ice, *the Great Tribulation past or Future?*, (Grand Rapids, MI: Kregel Publications, 1999)98.

It should be noted that the passages that Ice adduces to prove his point are in fact prophecies of *the application of the sanctions of Torah*. Thus, to reiterate, if AD 70 was, as Ice affirms, the application of the sanctions of the Law of Moses, then of necessity the Law of Moses stood valid until AD 70.

Both Bock and Ice fail to see the implications of their own comments. And unfortunately, Gentry failed to point out the implications of Ice's comments. But, as a general rule, commentators either fail to see, or they ignore, the fact that John, as Elijah, was predicting the coming of the Lord in application of the covenant sanctions of Torah, and that those penalties were not applied until AD 70 – demanding that Torah remained valid until that time.

This is confirmed further in Malachi 4.

Notice that God foretold the coming of "the Day" that would burn up the wicked like fire consumes the stubble. In contradistinction, Messiah would rise "with healing in his wings" for those who would put their trust in him. But, it is in light of that Day that YHVH then called on Israel: "You shall trample the wicked, For they shall be ashes under the soles of your feet On the day that I do this," Says the LORD of hosts. "Remember the Law of Moses, My servant, Which I commanded him in Horeb for all Israel, With the statutes and judgments" (Malachi 4:3-4). Note the conflation of judgment and salvation.

So, God called on Israel to return to faithful observance of Torah in light of the coming "Great and Terrible Day of the Lord." One would be hard pressed to find a more direct connection between Torah and eschatology. God was calling on Israel to obey Torah to avoid destruction at the Day of the Lord.

If the Great Day of the Lord is an earth burning, time ending event, then one can only conclude that Israel remains God's covenant people, bound to obey Torah until the end of time.

If the Day of the Lord - the parousia of Romans 11 - is still future, then since the Day that John foretold was the same Day anticipated by Paul, then the Law of Moses, with all of its provisions for Covenant Wrath on Israel, will remain valid until that Day comes.

To reiterate, this is problematic for any view that says the Law of Moses passed away at the cross. It is illogical to suggest that the Law of Moses passed, and yet, then posit a future coming of the Lord in fulfillment of texts that predicted that Day *as the time when those Covenant sanctions would be applied.*

Malachi's prophecy is patently problematic for the traditional views of Torah. And, if that Day of the Lord was indeed the same Day of the Lord as in Romans 11, then needless to say, the futurist paradigms that see in Romans a yet future salvation of national Israel are misguided and falsified.

The fact is that there was no covenantal Day of the Lord judgment on Israel, after John's ministry but before the Cross. Has anyone in the history of exegesis ever suggested that it did? So, here is what we have:

Malachi 3-4 predicted the outpouring of Mosaic Covenant Wrath at the Great and Terrible Day of the Lord.

That Day of the Lord was to be heralded by *The Messenger* of Malachi 3:1-2.

John the Baptizer was *The Messenger* foretold by Malachi 3, and he foretold the coming of the Lord in judgment.

John as *The Messenger* said the coming of the Lord in judgment – which was to be the application of Mosaic Covenant Wrath – was near.

Therefore, the coming of the Lord in the application of Mosaic Covenant Wrath – at the Great and Terrible Day of the Lord -- was near when John ministered.

It should be clear that the Day of the Lord of Malachi 3-4, the Lord's coming in judgment, was near in John's ministry. That Day would be a covenantal judgment of Israel for violating Torah. That Day of the Lord was also the coming of the Lord for salvation, the coming of the Lord of Romans 11:25f. That means that the coming of the Lord for the salvation of Israel in Romans had to be imminent when Paul wrote, and, it means that it had to be a covenantal judgment on Israel for violating Torah. As we proceed, it will become abundantly clear that Paul did indeed have this very thing in mind, because that judgment is a foundational element of the prophecies that he cites as he anticipated the coming of the Lord for the salvation of Israel.

It should be more than apparent that John the Baptizer was pre-eminently important as regards to eschatology. Yet, most commentators seem to dismiss him once he was killed by Herod. I believe this is a tragic oversight, and fails to see his influence on the rest of NT eschatology - and particularly Romans 11. I want to turn now to a brief examination of John as *Elijah*.

ELIJAH HAS ALREADY COME!

According to many rabbinic sources, Elijah was to come in the last days to prepare Israel for the Great Tribulation, the coming of the Lord and arrival of the kingdom.

There is nothing in those sources to suggest that Elijah would foreshadow another, more critical, eschatological figure or another consummate eschatology.[61] Elijah was to appear before, and be the herald of the consummate Day of the Lord.

Even in church history, it was believed that Elijah and the resurrection were connected. Tertullian cites Malachi 4:2-3 (and Isaiah 26:19f) as a prediction of the coming resurrection.[62] Keener shows that prior to the establishment of the church the Rabbis linked Elijah with the resurrection at the end of the age.[63] Pitre likewise documents how in Jewish expectation and in Malachi, Elijah was to come in or immediately before, the Tribulation period and the resurrection.[64] John's own father stated that John was to offer resurrection life (Luke 1:79). He would, "give light to those in darkness and the shadow of death."

During his ministry, Jesus unambiguously identified John as Elijah.

> "Assuredly, I say to you, among those born of women there has not risen one greater than John the Baptist; but he who is least

---

[61] Significantly, in the Dominionist / Postmillennial literature, it is almost unanimously agreed that John was Elijah and that he did not foreshadow another "real" Elijah who is to someday appear before the "real" end of the age. This is clearly true, but the Dominionists fail to see the implications of their admission. Elijah was to appear before "the" Day of the Lord. I chronicle the Dominionists' views in a large work on Daniel 12 that, as I write this, is almost ready for the printer.

[62] Tertullian, in *The Church's Bible, Isaiah*, Robert Lewis Wilken, (Grand Rapids, Eerdmans, 2007)229.

[63] Craig Keener, *Commentary on John, Vol. 1*, (Peabody, Mass, Hendrickson, 2003)435, n. 51.

[64] Brant Pitre, *Jesus, The Tribulation and the End of Exile*, (Grand Rapids, Baker Academic, 1975)181f.

in the kingdom of heaven is greater than he. And from the days of John the Baptist until now the kingdom of heaven suffers violence, and the violent take it by force. For all the prophets and the law prophesied until John. And if you are willing to receive it, he is Elijah who is to come. He who has ears to hear, let him hear! (Matthew 11:11-15).

There is no actual conditionality in Jesus' statement, "If you are willing to receive it," as Dispensational writers claim. As Wright says, Jesus' statement, "He who has ears, let him hear" cued the audience into the fact that it took spiritual discernment to realize who John was. Wright says, "To add that to a public utterance implies that what has been said is cryptic, and suggests that a certain secrecy is necessary to the present circumstances."[65] Gentry concurs, adding this:

> "Matthew 17 is unambiguously clear. In Matthew 11, Christ is rebuking spiritual obstinacy (11:16)f of the crowds that come to hear him (11:7). He urges them to hear and understand (11:15). He does not fear that they will derail prophetic fulfillment by their unbelief. When he says 'He who has ears to hear' (11:15) he does not imply that his views of John are invalid; rather he alludes to the spiritual dullness of those who reject his teaching (Matthew 13:9, 43; Mark 4:9; Luke 8:8; 14:35). The reason why John comes in the spirit and power of Elijah (Luke 1:17) and why Israel should receive him as "Elijah who was to come' (Matthew 11:14) is because he fulfills the Elijah prophecy." (Gentry, *Dominion*, 2009, 373).

The unconditional identification of John as Elijah is confirmed when we conflate his identity as *The Voice* and *The Messenger*, with that of Elijah. As we have noted, there is no, "He is *The Voice if* you will accept it", or, "If you will accept it, John is, "The Messenger of Malachi 3." Furthermore, in the book of Malachi there is no distinction between *The Messenger* and *Elijah*. Thus, if John was *The Messenger* (and he patently was) then there can be no dispute: John was *Elijah*. That means that *The Voice* was *The Messenger* who was *Elijah*.

---

[65] N. T. Wright, *Jesus and the Victory of God*, (Minneapolis, Fortress, 1996)229.

Matthew 17:9-13 is unequivocal.

> "Now as they came down from the mountain, Jesus commanded them, saying, "Tell the vision to no one until the Son of Man is risen from the dead." And His disciples asked Him, saying, "Why then do the scribes say that Elijah must come first?" Jesus answered and said to them, "Indeed, Elijah is coming first and will restore all things. But I say to you that Elijah has come already, and they did not know him but did to him whatever they wished. Likewise the Son of Man is also about to suffer at their hands." Then the disciples understood that He spoke to them of John the Baptist."

On the Transfiguration Mount, the disciples had just seen the "real" Elijah appear with Jesus and Moses. Needless to say, even though Moses and Elijah had disappeared, and the *Bat Kol*, the voice from heaven, had identified Jesus as the voice of authority they were to now listen to, the disciples could not keep from thinking of the prophecy of Malachi and the prediction of the coming of Elijah! And now, they had seen Elijah! Why then did Jesus tell them not to tell anyone about what they had seen? After all, did the prophets and the scribes not say that Elijah was to appear before "the end" and the arrival of the kingdom? So why keep silent about what they had just seen?

I suggest that the reason why Jesus told the apostles not to broadcast what they had seen is because the Jewish expectation of the day was that the literal, physical Elijah was to return. However, Jesus had already indicated to the apostles that it would take spiritual understanding to know that Elijah had come - and it was not the literal reappearance of the revered Old Covenant spokesman. Jesus wanted his disciples to realize who John truly was. He wanted them to exercise spiritual discernment.

Jesus' words must have been challenging and perplexing, yet, Jesus left no doubt, John was Elijah foretold by the prophets.

What then did Jesus mean by saying, "Elijah truly must come"? Some commentators insist that Jesus was foretelling a still future coming of Elijah. But that is not supported by the text.

When Jesus told the disciples not to tell others of what they had seen, the disciples asked, "Why then do the scribes say that Elijah must come?" Jesus' response, "Elijah must come" is a confirmation of what the scribes taught, and had taught for four centuries. But, you see, *the scribes simply reiterated what the ancient prophecies foretold!* Jesus was not making a new prophecy of a future coming of Elijah. He was confirming that the scribes were correct to say, based on the ancient prophecies, that Elijah would come. But, we must realize that the scribes did not have the ears to hear, and eyes to see that John was Elijah!

After confirming the scribes' teaching concerning the coming of Elijah, Jesus then said, plainly, unequivocally: "But I say to you that Elijah has come already, and they did not know him but did to him whatever they wished. Likewise the Son of Man is also about to suffer at their hands" (Matthew 17:11-12). Remember that the scribes also said Messiah will come, but, they did not recognize Jesus as Messiah (John 1:11f).

Many commentators ignore these interpretive words from Jesus, waving them aside as if they carried no meaning. But could words be any clearer: "Elijah has already come!"? After clearly stating that Elijah had come, and, "they have done to him (Him *who*? Elijah!- DKP) what they wished," the text declares, "the disciples understood that he spoke to them of John the Baptist." Again, words could not be clearer. John was Elijah, or else Jesus was wrong. John was Elijah, or else the disciples were wrong to make the connection between Jesus' declaration that, "Elijah has already come," and John the Baptizer. But, there is nothing in the text to suggest that the disciples were wrong, or that Jesus was telling them that John was a "type" of the still future "real" Elijah.

The eschatological significance of acknowledging that John was the predicted Elijah are profound. Drury shows that Elijah was expected to come before the Day of the Lord in judgment: "He is clearly an eschatological figure "signaling the beginning of the end", and he was to come "immediately before the coming wrath of God."[66]

So, if John was Elijah - and he was - then the relationship between his ministry and Romans 11:25f cannot fail to influence our understanding of Romans 11. Elijah was to come and, "restore all things" (Matthew 17:11). That most assuredly included Israel, did it not? In Romans 11, wasn't Paul talking about

---

[66] John Drury, "The Elijah who was to come: Matthew's Use of Malachi" (Matthew 11:2-15) (2007) www.drurywriting.com/john/The%20who%20was%20%20to%20%come.htm.

the restoration of Israel? How is it possible for us to divorce John's ministry of restoration – particularly in light of Luke 1 as noted above - from Paul's anticipation of restoration? But again, if John's ministry of restoration and Paul's eschatological hope for Israel in Romans 11 are the same, then we must sharpen our focus on the time frame, the context and nature of that restoration.

With this in mind, let me re-emphasize that the Day of the Lord in Malachi 3-4 would be *the time of judgment on Israel for violating Torah*. We have shown that in v. 5, where the Lord said, "I will come near to you in judgment," that judgment would be for violating Exodus 22:21f and Deuteronomy 27:19f. Those were the mandates against sorcerers, extortioners, abusers of widows, etc.. Those passages make it clear that the judgment for those sins would be *national judgment on Israel* (Exodus 22:24). But do not forget, the time of national judgment is likewise the time of the end of Israel's exile, the time of the salvation of Israel.

The connection between the restoration of Israel, the ministry of John as Elijah, and the destruction of Jerusalem is a relationship that is seldom sufficiently explored or even noticed.

Pitre does discuss, more than any other scholar I have seen thus far, the connection between the fate of Jerusalem and the end of exile, i.e. the salvation of Israel (2005, 185f; 228f; 250+; etc.). In fact, he says, "The implication of this prayer (1 Kings 8:33-34, DKP) should be clear: the *End of the Exile* and *the forgiveness of Israel's* sins are not only inextricably tied to one another - as both the Law and the prophets bear witness - they are also inextricably tied to *the Jerusalem Temple*." (2005, 375 - all emphasis his).

Pitre even has an excellent chapter on the significance of the appearing of John, as Elijah, demonstrating the relationship between John, the Great Tribulation, the fate of the temple and the promised resurrection and the restoration of Israel (pp. 177-198). Remarkably, however, Pitre makes no comment on the mission of John as Elijah, the restoration of Israel, the fate of Jerusalem and any connection with Romans 11:25f. He references Romans 11 but once in his entire work.

If what Pitre suggests is accurate, it reinforces what we propose in this work. John was *Elijah*, the herald and sign that the last days had arrived. His message, "The Kingdom of heaven has drawn near" (Matthew 3:2) was the long awaited, wonderful message of the impending salvation of Israel - which is nothing but the salvation of Israel of Romans 11:25f. But, as *Elijah*, his appearance also meant that the Great Tribulation was about to fall. It meant that Israel's "final judgment" in which the nation would be "slain" (Isaiah 65:13f) but the remnant saved, was at hand. To divorce John's message of the impending kingdom and salvation, from the time of national judgment is misguided. That also means that to divorce Romans 11 from that time of impending national judgment on Jerusalem would totally separate John's ministry from Paul's message. I find this untenable.

If this assessment is correct, and I fail to see how it isn't, the only real question remaining is, did Paul in Romans 11:25f have that same Day of the Lord in mind when he spoke of the Lord coming "out of Zion" for the salvation of Israel? In other words, did Paul anticipate a yet future "end of time, time ending" parousia of Christ for the salvation of national Israel, in sharp contrast to the Day of the Lord foretold by John as *The Voice*, *The Messenger* and *Elijah*? As just suggested, this really creates a disjunctive message about the salvation of Israel, which is not proper. This is demonstrated by the fact that Paul (not to mention the other NT writers) very clearly continued John's message. That is shown by an examination of the role of Elijah as the herald of Israel's "reconciliation" and Paul's "ministry of reconciliation."

JOHN AS ELIJAH, PAUL AND THE MINISTRY OF RECONCILIATION

Normally, commentators focus on the role of John as herald of the impending eschatological Day of the Lord, the time of the kingdom and resurrection, as demonstrated below. However, we should not lose sight of the fact that the ministry of Elijah was likewise to be that of reconciliation. (See our discussion below on John's message of *forgiveness* - which is nothing but reconciliation).

Many Bible students seem ignorant of the fact that in the Tanakh, the soteriological and eschatological narrative follows in this order:

☛ Covenant between YHVH and Israel - the covenant was seen as a marriage covenant.

☛ Covenant obedience was the condition for Israel's possession of the land.

☛ Israel violated Torah, thus, forfeiting the right to the land.

☛ As a direct consequence of that covenant violation, the Lord removed Israel from the land and sent her into exile.

☛ The Lord promised that if Israel would remember Him in their captivity and repent, that He would restore her. He would forgive their sin. He would end their exile. He would "return" to her and raise her from the dead (Hosea 6:1-6).

So, as far as Torah is concerned, sin / captivity / repentance / remission of sin / reconciliation / the end of exile and salvation are all bound up together. What should not be missed is that the "reconciliation" would be on the corporate level. While, naturally, individuals had to repent, the restoration and reconciliation was viewed as a corporate restoration.[67] So, when we think of Elijah as one who would, "turn the hearts of the fathers," we should see this as his role in the eschatological reconciliation. Elijah would help bring about the "return from exile" - the salvation of Israel.

---

[67] Note Jesus' words in Matthew 23:37 - "O, Jerusalem, Jerusalem, how often I wished to gather you..." This speaks eloquently of the "corporate" nature of the Jewish thought.

The role of Elijah as "reconciler" is clearly set forth in Malachi 4:5-6:

> "Behold, I will send you Elijah the prophet Before the coming of the great and dreadful day of the Lord. And he will turn The hearts of the fathers to the children, And the hearts of the children to their fathers, Lest I come and strike the earth with a curse."

Malachi was not positing the role of Elijah in a vacuum isolated from and different from earlier promises of the salvation of Israel. In fact, Daniel 9 had predicted the framework for the accomplishment of the final reconciliation - by the end of the seventy weeks: "Seventy weeks are determined... to make reconciliation" (Daniel 9:24). The fact that Daniel well realized and confessed that Judah was in exile as a direct result of her sin, adds emphasis to his prayer for forgiveness and reconciliation.

Daniel's prophecy, needless to say, was considered programmatic in Israel. There can be little doubt that the Jews of Jesus' day believed that Daniel's countdown had almost reached its terminus. This is one of the reasons for such strong messianism in Jesus' day. It is almost certainly also why Jesus said, "The time is fulfilled, the kingdom of heaven has drawn near" (Matthew 4:17).

As Bruce observed: "These words (Matthew 4:17, DKP) express, among other things, the assurance that an ardently desired new order, long since foretold and awaited. was now on the point of realization."[68] Likewise, Gentry comments on Jesus' words: "Christ asserts 'the time is fulfilled.' What is 'the time' to which he refers? The Greek term here is kairos, which indicates 'the fateful and decisive point' that is ordained by God.' This 'time' surely refers to the prophetically anticipated time, the time of the coming of David's greater Son to establish the kingdom, for he immediately adds: 'the kingdom of *God* is at hand.'"[69]

---

[68] F. F. Bruce, *The Time is Fulfilled*, (Exeter, Paternoster Press, 1978)15.

[69] Kenneth Gentry, *He Shall Have Dominion*, (Draper, VA., Apologetics Group, 2009)218.

Since Daniel 9 is the most "precise" OT prophecy of the time of the kingdom and the promised reconciliation,[70] it is plausible that the Jewish calculations gave rise to their eager expectation of the appearance of Elijah and of Messiah.

Now, if the seventy weeks were to terminate no later than the destruction of Jerusalem in AD 70,[71] this agrees perfectly with what we have seen about John as *The Messenger,* who would warn Israel of impending national judgment. Daniel said that the eschatological reconciliation would be no later than the overthrow of Jerusalem and the temple in "the overwhelming flood." John as *The Messenger* proclaimed the coming of the Lord to His temple in national judgment, i.e. the judgment of Jerusalem. That time of judgment, per Isaiah 27 & 59 would likewise be the time at which the Lord would take away Israel's sin – as Romans 11 anticipated. These texts are synchronous in their application and demand a first century fulfillment of the message of John as *Elijah*, who was to bring in that reconciliation.

Remember that Romans 11 anticipated the "taking away" of Israel's sin. Daniel 9:24 also foretold the taking away of Israel's sin by the end of the seventy weeks. Thus, Daniel 9 should be seen as pivotal in our understanding of Romans 11. Yet, few commentators make the connections.

So, we have Isaiah 27 positing the taking away of Israel's sin at the time of Jerusalem's destruction and judgment for shedding innocent blood.

We have Isaiah 40:1-2 predicting the taking away of Israel's sin at the Day of the Lord as the focus of the ministry of *The Voice*.

---

[70] It appears that it was widely held that Rome was the fourth kingdom of Daniel 2 and the fourth beast of Daniel 7. If that is true, then the fact that the first century was "in the days of these kings" along with the calculations of the seventy weeks, would surely give rise to the sense of the imminent kingdom.

[71] See my book, *Seventy Weeks Are Determined...For the Resurrection*, for an in-depth study of Daniel 9 as a prediction of the resurrection. When exile was equal to "death" in the mind of the ancients, then the promise of return to the land was the same as resurrection. See Ezekiel 37. My book is available on Amazon, Kindle, my websites and at other retailers.

We have Isaiah 59 predicting the taking away of Israel's sin at the Day of the Lord in judgment of Israel for shedding innocent blood.

We have Daniel 9 predicting the eschatological reconciliation and the taking away of Israel's sin - inclusive of her guilt for killing Messiah the Prince (9:26) - no later than the time of the destruction of "the city and the temple."

These are not mere coincidental comparisons. The prophecies are synchronous in their anticipation. When we see John as Elijah, the one to bring in that final reconciliation, we must acknowledge his pivotal role in our understanding of Romans 11.

If, as shown, Elijah was *The Messenger,* then he was *The Voice* of Isaiah 40. Mark 1:1-3 leaves no doubt that John was *The Voice* and *The Messenger*. Thus, he was *Elijah*. This means that the promise of the restoration / reconciliation / salvation of Israel in Isaiah was the message of John / Elijah. This demands that the salvation of Israel foretold in Romans 11, *being the reiteration of Isaiah,* was to occur at the Day of the Lord foretold by John.

To drive this home, I want to examine another key "reconciliation" prophecy in Isaiah and then "connect the dots" between John and Paul in his epistles.

I want to focus on Isaiah 49:6f, since I will discuss it a bit below in my comments on the salvation of Israel in Revelation.

Isaiah 49:6-18:

> "Indeed He says, 'It is too small a thing that You should be My Servant To raise up the tribes of Jacob, And to restore the preserved ones of Israel; I will also give You as a light to the Gentiles, That You should be My salvation to the ends of the earth.'" Thus says the Lord, The Redeemer of Israel, their Holy One, To Him whom man despises, To Him whom the nation abhors, To the Servant of rulers: "Kings shall see and arise, Princes also shall worship, Because of the Lord who is faithful, The Holy One of Israel; And He has chosen You." Thus says the Lord: "In an acceptable time I have heard You, And in the day of salvation I have helped You; I will preserve You and give You As a covenant to the people, To restore the earth, To cause them to inherit the desolate heritages; That You may say to the prisoners, 'Go forth,' To those who are in darkness,

'Show yourselves.' "They shall feed along the roads, And their pastures shall be on all desolate heights. They shall neither hunger nor thirst, Neither heat nor sun shall strike them; For He who has mercy on them will lead them, Even by the springs of water He will guide them. I will make each of My mountains a road, And My highways shall be elevated. Surely these shall come from afar; Look! Those from the north and the west, And these from the land of Sinim." Sing, O heavens! Be joyful, O earth! And break out in singing, O mountains! For the Lord has comforted His people, And will have mercy on His afflicted. God Will Remember Zion But Zion said, "The Lord has forsaken me, And my Lord has forgotten me." "Can a woman forget her nursing child, And not have compassion on the son of her womb? Surely they may forget, Yet I will not forget you. See, I have inscribed you on the palms of My hands; Your walls are continually before Me. See, I have inscribed you on the palms of My hands; Your walls are continually before Me. Your sons shall make haste; Your destroyers and those who laid you waste Shall go away from you. Lift up your eyes, look around and see; All these gather together and come to you. As I live," says the Lord, "You shall surely clothe yourselves with them all as an ornament, And bind them on you as a bride."

Here is the epitome of the promise of "reconciliation!"[72] Here is the "comforting" of Zion foretold in Isaiah 40 – the message of *The Voice*. Isaiah

---

[72] Notice also the imagery of the marriage. An examination of this motif would take us beyond the scope of this book, but, take note that the restoration / salvation of Israel can be summarized under that very image. YHVH had been married to Israel, but due to her adultery He "divorced" her (Hosea 2:1f). Yet, He promised that in the last days, He would make a New Marriage Covenant with all Israel (Hosea 2:18f). The marriage / re-marriage motif, is, needless to say, powerfully present in Jesus' parables. And that motif was proclaimed by John in John 3:29f where he proclaimed Jesus as the Groom and himself as the "friend of the bridegroom" thus indicating that the time of Israel's restoration was near. So, when Paul in his epistles and John in Revelation continued the theme of the impending Wedding, they were continuing to proclaim the message of John, as *The Voice*. This shows in graphic fashion that they had no sense that John's ministry - or his predictions - had in any way failed or been postponed.

said the Messiah would restore the "tribes of Jacob" i.e. reconcile Israel with Judah.[73] Now, since the comforting of Zion of chapter 40 is the comforting of Zion in chapter 49 this means that the promise of the reconciliation of chapter 49 was the message of *The Voice*, and thus of Elijah. According to Jesus, Elijah was to "restore all things" in fulfillment of the OT promises (Matthew 17:10f; cf. Acts 1:6f). But, Isaiah 49 did not just promise the reconciliation and restoration of the "tribes of Jacob." He would do much more than that.

Isaiah said that it would be "too small" a thing if all Messiah did was to restore the tribes of Jacob. He would also, "show light (which means *life*!) to the nations. Here is the grand scale of reconciliation. Here is the idea that through Israel, *through the restoration of Israel*, the nations of the world would be blessed. This is the "wider" story of reconciliation.[74]

So, John, as *Elijah* and *The Voice*, came to declare that the time of reconciliation and restoration had arrived: "The kingdom has drawn near" was that promise. But, we are reminded, John was martyred. His ministry was cut short. He did not "restore all things" - at least according to most commentators. But, did he fail? Did the writers of the NT who followed John (and of course Jesus who clearly continued to proclaim John's message) express any sense of failure, of disappointment, or delay in the fulfillment of John's message? Did they even continue to proclaim the promised restoration / reconciliation? The answer is an unambiguous, Yes! Romans 11:25f is irrefutable proof of this.

We will examine John's message below as it is developed in Revelation. For now, we need to see that Paul clearly did not believe that John's work- as *Elijah* - had ceased, been interrupted, or failed. To the contrary, Paul affirmed that what

---

[73] Ezekiel 37 would later promise (based on Isaiah?) that "both houses of Israel" would be reconciled (resurrected) under Messiah,

[74] Beale points out that there is no Hebrew word for "reconciliation" in the OT. Greg Beale, *A New Testament Biblical Theology*, (Grand Rapids, Baker Academic, 2011)527. However, the idea and the concept permeates Torah in the promises of the kingdom. Beale (op cit+) has an extensive discussion on the idea that the reconciliation motif found in the NT must be seen as the fulfillment of those OT promises. Unfortunately, Beale, as most commentators, envisions that restoration / reconciliation as inextricably tied to the restoration of material creation.

was promised in Isaiah - and thus, what was promised by *The Voice, The Messenger* and *Elijah* was taking place! I offer 2 Corinthians 5-6 as proof.

> "Therefore, if anyone is in Christ, he is a new creation; old things have passed away; behold, all things have become new. Now all things are of God, who has reconciled us to Himself through Jesus Christ, and has given us the ministry of reconciliation, that is, that God was in Christ reconciling the world to Himself, not imputing their trespasses to them, and has committed to us the word of reconciliation. Now then, we are ambassadors for Christ, as though God were pleading through us: we implore you on Christ's behalf, be reconciled to God. For He made Him who knew no sin to be sin for us, that we might become the righteousness of God in Him. We then, as workers together with Him also plead with you not to receive the grace of God in vain. For He says:
>
> "In an acceptable time I have heard you,
> And in the day of salvation I have helped you."
>
> Behold, now is the accepted time; behold, now is the day of salvation. We give no offense in anything, that our ministry may not be blamed. But in all things we commend ourselves as ministers of God: in much patience, in tribulations, in needs, in distresses, in stripes, in imprisonments, in tumults, in labors, ..."

A reading of this text, (2 Corinthians 5:17- 6:1-3) Paul's longest discourse on the subject of "reconciliation," quickly communicates the fact that for Paul, reconciliation and *the New Creation* are inseparably tied to one another. The implications of this are incredible. Beale notes this: "Paul understands both 'new creation' in Christ as well as 'reconciliation' in Christ as the inaugurated fulfillment of Isaiah's and the prophets' promise of the new creation in which Israel would be restored into a peaceful relationship with God" (2011, 529).

Paul was, of course, the apostle to the Gentiles. However, it should be noted that when Paul went to the Gentiles, he went into the areas of the Diaspora, where the ten northern tribes had been scattered. There, he preached to the members of the synagogues first of all. Sometimes, he had to turn from those audiences to the Gentiles (Acts 13) but this does not mitigate the fact that Paul envisioned himself as the minister to bring about the restoration of the tribes of Jacob, in fulfillment of Isaiah 49 and the subsequent and related calling of the Gentiles.[75]

For our purposes, we need to take note that Paul says the Lord had given him the ministry of reconciliation. Thus, when he went to the Diaspora regions - inclusive of Corinth - and reasoned in those synagogues that Jesus is the Messiah (Acts 17:2-3) he was in effect, offering them the restoration of Israel - the salvation promised in Isaiah, that was to be perfected at the parousia.

There can be no doubt that Paul believed that the promised salvation was underway: "Israel has not received that for which he sought, but, the elect has received it, and the rest were blinded" (Romans 11:7). This was not a declaration of failure or postponement. It was Paul's way of saying that what was taking place was the *fulfillment* of the eschatological narrative - the salvation of the remnant. This is no where more powerfully expressed than in 2 Corinthians 6 where Paul cites Isaiah 49 and the promise of the Day of Israel's restoration / reconciliation and salvation, and declares, "Now is the Acceptable Time; Today is the Day of Salvation!" (2 Corinthians 6:1-2).[76] That "Now" was Paul's *Now*, and his "Today" was his generation, not some protracted, delayed time in the distant future.

---

[75] In Paul, there is an interplay and inner connection between the restoration of Israel and the calling of the Gentiles. In Romans 9, it appears that he identifies Gentiles as Israel, at least in some manner. What appears to be at work here is that since Israel was, "swallowed up by the nations" (Hosea 8:8) that God intended to restore Israel by: 1. Calling Israel out of the nations (not geographically, however) to which they had been scattered, and then, 2. Calling the nations themselves. The fact that Paul went to the *Diaspora synagogues* is rooted in his realization that salvation was "to the Jew first" but, he likewise knew that salvation was to flow to the Greeks, the Scythians, the Romans - to the nations.

[76] Later in this same chapter Paul declared that the body of Christ in Corinth was the fulfillment of Ezekiel 37, where the Lord promised to restore Israel and set His tabernacle among them so that the nations would glorify and serve Him. Paul said to the church, "you are the temple of the living God, as it is written" and cites Ezekiel 37:26! Thus, once again, for Paul, there was not thought of a failed or postponed kingdom message.

To say that Paul's citation of those OT prophecies of Israel's restoration and reconciliation were taking place in the first century is fatal to Dispensationalism. Zionism tells us that due to Jewish rejection, John was not Elijah, and Jesus could not establish the kingdom, until some future time, i.e. Romans 11:26f.

But, that was not Paul's message. His repeated claims that Isaiah and Ezekiel were being fulfilled are prima facie proof of this. Likewise, Peter's affirmation that Hosea's prophecies of Israel's restoration were being fulfilled, serve as total falsification of the postponement doctrine of Dispensationalism. There is not a syllable of proof in the NT that the kingdom predictions of John or Jesus had failed or been postponed.

So, when we realize that the message of Isaiah 49 was the message of John, as Elijah who was to "restore all things," and when we realize that Paul affirmed the fulfillment of that message of reconciliation and restoration was taking place in the body of Christ, then certain things become clear:

1. John's mission had not failed and had not been postponed, as we just noted.

2. The nature of the fulfillment is seen to be spiritual, not focused on, or concerned with, the salvation of "all of ethnic Israel" in a restoration to the land, the City and with a physical temple. After all, since Paul said that Isaiah and Ezekiel were being fulfilled in Christ and his body, it should be glaringly obvious that he had no concern for a physical temple, city or land.

Unless we simply want to dismiss Paul as deluded or wrong, then since he tells us repeatedly that he preached nothing but the hope of Israel found in Torah, then since he cites Israel's prophecies of reconciliation and "return from exile" as being fulfilled in the body of Christ, this demands a radical re-evaluation and re-definition of that return and reconciliation from what is posited in the modern Dispensational world. Paul's definition of the return from exile is patently diametrically opposed to Dispensationalism, and the claims that 1948 was the fulfillment of prophecies like Ezekiel 37.

This is why I think Davies is correct in his assessment of why Paul never mentions the land promises:

"Paul ignores completely the territorial aspect of the (Abrahamic, DKP), promise."[77] ... "In Galatians we can be fairly certain that Paul did not merely ignore the territorial aspect of the promise for political purposes; his silence points not merely to the absence of a conscious concern with it, but to his deliberated rejection of it. His interpretation of the promise is a-territorial."...for Paul, Christ had gathered up the promise into the singularity of his own person. In this way, "the territory' promise was transformed into and fulfilled by the life 'in Christ.' All this is not made explicit, because Paul did not directly apply himself to the question to the land, but it is implied. In the Christological logic of Paul, the land, like the Law, particular and provisional, had become irrelevant." (1974, 179).

He then comments on Paul's application of some of the key OT Messianic "land promises":

" Paul applies to the new community passages from the O.T. applied to the tabernacle and to the future temple in the land: first, Leviticus 26:12 and then Ezekiel 37:27; then Isaiah 52:11, which has reference to priests 'who bear the vessels of the Lord,' the whole community being a priesthood; then 2 Samuel 7:14 form the chapter promising that God would make a house for David. The reference to Lev. 26 is particularly telling in 2 Cor. 6:16b." (1974, 186).

Finally, he gives us this: "The church is for Paul the fulfillment of the hopes of Judaism for the Temple: the presence of the Lord has moved from the Temple to the church....It is easy to conclude that there was a deliberate rejection by Paul of the Holy Space in favour of the Holy People–the church." (1974, 188).

I find little, if anything to disagree with here. But, once again, to reiterate our point, if Paul saw the OT prophecies of Israel's restoration and reconciliation to God - in the land - as being fulfilled "in Christ" and the church, this gives us a

---

[77] W. D. Davies, *The Gospel and the Land*, ((Berkley, University of California Press, 1974)178.

powerful indication of the nature of the Day of the Lord that John as Elijah and Paul anticipated. As we have and will show, John's message as *The Messenger* and *Elijah* was that the Day of the Lord, the time of Israel's salvation, was to be *the time of her national judgment.*

So, Elijah was to have a ministry of restoration / reconciliation as well as warning. Furthermore, his mission was focused on Israel, to call her to, "remember the Law of Moses" and to return to faithful Torah observance. His promise of "remission of sins" as we shall see, was the promise of restoration through repentance. And yet, not a word was uttered about national restoration, the physical land, city or temple. In fact, John's actions were a highly symbolic counter-cultural action that indicated that the temple-centric time of Israel was coming to an end.[78]

What is so important is, as we have noted, the message of John was continued by Jesus and by the NT writers, particularly Paul in Romans and Corinthians. The Cilician apostle's citation of the key restoration / reconciliation texts, drawn from the very context that gave John his identity as *The Voice*, effectively communicates, if we are attuned to hearing it, that John's message was being fulfilled. John had not, in spite of his martyrdom, failed. His mission was not delayed or postponed. Jesus continued to preach it. Paul continued to proclaim it. But, what had begun with John was to be consummated and fulfilled at the parousia, as Isaiah 40 foretold, as Isaiah 27, 59 and other prophecies predicted – and as Romans 11:28f said.

With these things in mind, we need to look closer at the nature of the Day of the Lord that Paul speaks of in Romans 11:25f. We can definitively determine the nature of that Day by examining the OT prophecies that he both quotes and "echoes."

What is so amazing is that the commentators, as a general rule almost totally ignore the prophetic background and context of Paul's parousia references in Romans. Now, make no mistake, the commentators almost universally acknowledge that Paul quotes from Isaiah 27 and Isaiah 59. However, as I

---

[78] Jesus likewise continued that counter-cultural teaching in John 4:20f, where he said that the kingdom would be "de-centralized" and that Jerusalem would no hold any covenantal significance. Jesus was drawing from Jeremiah 3:14f a prophecy of the restoration of Israel! This is stunning stuff!

finalize the writing of this work, I have not found a single commentator who comments on the *context* of those prophecies and the nature of the Day of the Lord that they foretold. This is a stunning oversight and failure.

THE NATURE OF THE DAY OF THE LORD PROCLAIMED BY JOHN AS THE VOICE, THE MESSENGER AND ELIJAH

I believe we have sufficiently demonstrated from Isaiah and Malachi particularly that the Day of the Lord that John was to declare was not to be an earth burning, time ending, cosmos destroying event.[79] Rather, it was to be a "covenantal judgment" the application of the Law of Blessings and Cursings found in Torah. It would be Israel put "to the edge of the sword," for violating Exodus 22 and Deuteronomy 27. That is essentially undeniable. The evidence is clean, clear and emphatic.

This has, needless to say, profound implications for our understanding of Romans 11:25f. It is probably safe to say that most commentators today see Paul predicting a yet future literal, bodily, physical coming of Christ at the end of the current Christian age when the corporate body of national Israel is saved. Moo posits such an event stating that Paul, "refers to the second coming of Christ"... and "the spiritual rejuvenation of the nation of Israel."[80] But, if Paul was anticipating the same Day as that foretold by John as *The Voice* and *The Messenger*, then it is patently obvious - although in the literature it is not seen - that Paul did *not* have a still future, literal, bodily coming of Jesus at the end of time in mind. He was expecting the impending national judgment on Jerusalem and Judah.

Scholars such as Beale and Wright see Romans 11 as predictive of a future coming of the Lord. However, Wright views the "salvation of Israel" as an on-going event realized in the conversion of individual Jews throughout the Christian age. Beale says that at some point in the future, "Israel will see and believe in him as the coming Redeemer, as Paul himself did. The final act in the

---

[79] Needless to say, many scholars do believe that the OT prophets, John the Baptizer and certainly Paul, spoke of the end of time and the collapse of the material cosmos. Allison for instance, argues that the Jews did in fact expect the destruction of material creation. He cites the Sibylline Oracles. Allison then applies 2 Peter 3 literally. Dale Allison Jr., *Jesus and the Restoration of Israel*, Chapter "Jesus and the Victory of Apocalyptic" (Downers Grove, Paternoster, 1999)139.

[80] Douglas Moo, *New International Commentary on the New Testament, The Epistle to the Romans,* (Grand Rapids, Eerdmans, 1996)724.

drama of redemption is not the formation of a church that consists largely of Gentiles, but the creation of salvation for the people of Israel."[81] But, once again, if the parousia of Romans 11 is the same coming of the Lord in Malachi 3, that suggestion is falsified.

A significant number of scholars recognize that John was not predicting the end of the time-space continuum. And yet, they fail to make the connection with Romans 11.

McKnight says,

> "Jesus entered Jerusalem at the beginning of the last, fateful week of his life, realized the utter gravity of Israel's situation, and knew that he had to offer himself consciously and intentionally to God as a vicarious sacrifice for Israel in order to avert the national disaster, and he did so as an atoning, substitutionary sacrifice... ... Not only in theological truth but in historic fact, the one bore the sins of the many, confident that in him the whole Jewish nations was being nailed to the cross, only to come to life again in a better resurrection, and that the Day of the Son of Man which would see the end of the Old Israel would see also the vindication of the new." (Citing Caird, *Jesus and the Jewish Nation*, p. 22). (1999, 13).

It is widely conceded that John's message of the kingdom was Jesus' message of the kingdom. There can be no doubt of this. Thus, if Jesus was not envisioning an "end of time" event, then John did not predict such an event, and *vice versa*.

It is interesting that McKnight adds this comment:

> "It might be argued that Jesus made a distinction between the climactic events pertaining to the nation and to Jerusalem, on the one hand, and to the final events of history, on the other; that is, that Jesus distinguished the events of AD 70 from the final events (judgment, kingdom, etc.). This would be very difficult to prove and need not be proved, since Jesus' method

---

[81] Greg Beale, *Commentary on the New Testament Use of he Old Testament*, (Grand Rapids, Baker Academic, 2007)673.

was so typical of Jewish prophecy: the next event, an event that God enabled a prophet to see, would take shape as the last event that would wrap up God's plan for history."[82] (1999, p. 12).

I concur with McKnight here: Jesus (and John) did not see beyond AD 70 and they were not describing the end of time. But, unlike McKnight who seems to be joining Schweitzer in his claim that Jesus' *ultimate* eschatological expectations were wrong, I do not believe it is correct to say that there was another eschatological climax beyond that which Jesus envisioned.

Wright takes note that the Day of the Lord envisioned by the OT prophets (and thus, by John and Jesus, DKP): "Was seen in various ways, but, among the most obvious was that of military action. So-called 'natural' disasters or unexpected events might also figure in the mix." (2013, Vol. III & IV, 1050). This agrees well with what we have seen about the language of making straight in the desert a hiway for God in Isaiah 40.

Webb suggests that this is hinted at in the words of John when he said that the one coming after him was "mightier than" him. Webb shows that John was saying that the one coming after him, "indicates that the figure will have the power and authority necessary to carry out the judgment and restore the repentant to their new situation." (2006, 302). He then demonstrates that the words used by John have an association with other words that were, "used of military might... used to describe a warrior who is a hero in battle. It is used to describe Yahweh as might when He fights on behalf of His people (i.e, acting as a figure of judgment and restoration)" (2006, 303).

In addition to this, Webb investigates the language that John used, the language of the axe at the root, the winnowing fork, the wrath to come, and concluded:

---

[82] McKnight's mistake, like Allison, Nolland and a host of others, is the belief that the Jews believed in the end of the time, the end of the cosmos. If, however, one acknowledges that John, as Elijah, and that Paul and the NT writers did not have any such consummation in mind, the common occurrence of charging Jesus and the NT writers with a failed eschatology disappears. They were expecting the end of the age to be sure, but, *not the end of time.* They were expecting the end of the Old Covenant age, represented by temple and Torah (Matthew 24:2-3).

"We can clarify the expected situation in one other way by observing what this restoration is *not*. It is not the end of the world or universal, cosmic judgment or the destruction of the earth by fire. ... Thus, the righteous experience a reversal within their present environment, but this restoration involves in some sense a continuation of their present, human existence, and is not some type of translation into a new dimension of existence such as ascension to heaven or resurrection" (2006, 304).[83] (His emphasis).

If John was predicting a "historical" Day of the Lord, as we have shown that he was, then if the Day of the Lord of John's message was the same Day of the Lord predicted by Paul in Romans 11:25-27, this means that Paul was not predicting a cosmos destroying, visible, physical, bodily coming of Christ. He was anticipating the imminent national judgment on Old Covenant Israel. This is supported by a closer look at the language of Matthew 3.

In Matthew 3:7, John said to the Pharisees and Sadducees: "Who has warned you to flee from the wrath to come?" (It is literally, "about to come"- from *mello, DKP*). This wrath is none other than the Day of fire of Malachi 4:1-3, the Great Day of the Lord of Malachi 4:5-6. John draws directly from Malachi. As Davies and Allison note: "Who has warned you to flee from the wrath about to come", '*mello* here implies not so much purpose as imminence or futurity.'"[84] Alford's Greek Testament offers this:

---

[83] I would add this caveat to Webb's comment about resurrection. In Hebraic thought, deliverance from oppression, from bondage, from sin was viewed as resurrection. That study lies beyond the scope of this work, but, see N. T. Wright, *Resurrection of the Son of God* (253) - "the metaphorical 'resurrection' in the second temple Judaism" has its 'concrete referent' Israel's 'return from exile.'" (cited in Pitre, 2005, 321, n. 225). Likewise, Pitre says, commenting on Daniel 12: "This prophecy of the resurrection and justification of the 'many' like all 'resurrection' texts in the Old Testament, is also a prophecy of the restoration of Israel." *Jesus, Tribulation and the End of Exile*, (Grand Rapids, Baker Academic, 1975)414.

[84] W. D. Davies and Dale Allison Jr., *International Critical Commentary, Matthew 1-7*, (London, T and T Clark)304.

> "The reference of John's ministry to the prophecy concerning Elias, Malachi 3:1; 4:5 would naturally suggest to men's minds 'the wrath to come' there also foretold. It was the general expectation of the Jews that troublous times would accompany the appearance of Messiah. John is now speaking in the true character of a prophet, foretelling the wrath soon to be poured out on the Jewish nation."[85]

Nolland says that John's message about the coming wrath, "gained pressing urgency in light of an imminently expected act of judgment on the part of God."[86] Hagner says:

> "John's apocalyptic message involves an imminent judgment of the unrighteous in *tes mellouses orges*, the coming wrath.' This eschatological wrath, associated with fulfillment, is further alluded to in v. 10-12. Abundant parallels indicate that this was a fixed component in the Jewish apocalyptic expectation (see esp. Daniel 7:9-11; Isaiah 13:9; Zephaniah 1:15; 2:2-3; Malachi 4:1f). ...What frightened John's listeners was the insistence that the judgment was about to occur (*mellouses*)."[87]

To put this another way, the Great and Terrible Day of the Lord foretold by Malachi, the coming of the Lord in judgment of Israel for violating Torah and the coming of the Lord for the redemption of Israel, was now near. This means that the time for the salvation of "all Israel" - at the Day of the Lord - was not far off. Clearly, Paul was anticipating the fulfillment of what John foretold.

Matthew 3:10, 12:
> "And even now the ax is laid to the root of the trees. Therefore every tree which does not bear good fruit is cut down and

---

[85] *Alford's Greek Testament, Matthew - John, Vol. I*, (Grand Rapids, Baker, 1875 / 1980)22.

[86] John Nolland, *New International Greek Testament Commentary, Matthew*, (Grand Rapids, Eerdmans, Paternoster, 2005)144.

[87] Donald Hagner, *Word Biblical Commentary, Matthew*, 33a, (Dallas, Word, 1993)50.

thrown into the fire. ... His winnowing fan is in His hand, and He will thoroughly clean out His threshing floor, and gather His wheat into the barn; but He will burn up the chaff with unquenchable fire."

John emphasized the imminence of the impending judgment when he said, "even now the axe is laid to the root" (Matthew 3:10). Nolland reminds us that, "The felling of trees is a prophetic image of judgment in a number of OT texts." (2005, 145). Webb comments on John's imagery:

> "The use of the verb *keimai* might indicate that the farmer has 'laid down' the axe at the base of the tree, but it is more probable that the sense is that the axe blade has been placed against the root and the farmer is about to draw the axe back for the first swing. The emphatic position of the adverb *ede* (already) at the beginning of the sentence serves to highlight this sense of imminence."[88]

So, John, in line with previous prophets of Israel who warned earlier generations about impending national judgment that would come on them for violating Torah, used the same imagery, the same language. Did he "re-define" the definition of those terms and language? No. And this is significant for our understanding of how even the rest of the NT writers used that highly wrought language.

Minear, commenting on the Day of the Lord language of 2 Peter 3, and how Peter does not "explain" what he meant by it, says:

> "As one recalls Old Testament passages like these, one is forced to conclude that every constituent essential feature in the New Testament prophecies was an echo of these. No Christian prophet tried to explain the meaning of these references to solar disasters, a fact that suggests that the audience was expected to understand the language. Modern readers, therefore, must compare this idiom not with modern views of the cosmos, but with an ancient outlook within which an intelligible message

---

[88] Robert Webb, *John the Baptizer and Prophet*, (Eugene, Or. Wipf and Stock, 2006)297+

was conveyed without undue difficulty."[89]

In the same vein, R. T. France says,

> "The unwary reader is in danger of assuming a note of finality in the future hope of the Old Testament that is in fact foreign to it. The "eschatology" of the Old Testament prophets was not concerned with the end of the world, but with the decisive act of God which will bring to an end the existing order of things in the world, and inaugurate a new era of blessing, of a totally different order."[90]

Brown, commenting on the language of Christ's coming in Matthew 24:29f, concurs that this language is from the OT, and that there is no justification for taking it literally. It is metaphoric language to describe Jehovah's powerful intervention into history, not to end history.[91]

So, since Paul is incorporating citations of OT prophecies of the Day of the Lord into his eschatological hope in Romans, should we not honor the way that language is utilized by those OT prophets. When it is demonstrable that the OT prophets consistently used hyperbolic, metaphoric language to predict and describe the coming of the Lord, in both salvation and judgment, what is our hermeneutical justification for saying that the NT writers so radically redefined that language?

I propose that this imagery illustrates or lies behind Paul's, "Behold therefore, the goodness and the severity of God" (Romans 11:22). Just as John was warning Israel not to reject his message, Paul likewise warned Israel, who, as we have seen was being offered the kingdom message, not to reject that message (Romans 10). God is gracious, kind and forgiving. He is also just, and those who

---

[89] Paul Minear, *New Testament Apocalyptic,* (Nashville, Abingdon, 1981)52+.

[90] R. T. France, *Jesus and the Old Testament*, (Grand Rapids, Baker, 1982)84.

[91] Colin Brown, *New International Dictionary of New Testament Theology*, vol. 2, (Grand Rapids, Regency Reference Library, Zondervan, 1986)35f.

rejected His message were without excuse. John had warned them, and Paul reiterated that warning.

John's message of the coming day of fire is the message of Malachi 4:1, the Day of the Lord to be heralded by Elijah would be against the wicked and would leave them, "neither root nor branch." So, Malachi said *The Messenger* and *Elijah* would herald the Great Day of the Lord when the wicked would be cut down, leaving neither root or branch. That was to be a day of national judgment. John (Elijah) said the axe was already at the root. We are given no recourse but to see John as Elijah and that he was predicting, not the end of time, but impending national judgment on Israel.

Reiser drives the point home:

> "With the motif of the cutting down of the bad trees, the Baptizer expanded on the original image and thus created a genuine similitude not only pointing to the end time cleansing of Israel by the removal of sinners, but giving vivid expression to the immediate proximity of that event, and thus the urgency of repentance. The axe is already at work!"... "This temporal urgency is underscored still further in the Greek text by the present tenses of all three verbs."[92]

Malachi also said that in that day of fire, an awful day to be sure, there was also hope for the righteous: "But to you who fear my name The Sun of Righteousness shall arise with healing in His wings; and you shall grow fat like stall fed calves (Malachi 4:2). Here again we find judgment and salvation tied together. Thus, Webb reminds us: "John is sometimes considered to be exclusively a prophet of judgment or doom. But this is not an accurate portrayal, because the figure he proclaimed also had the ministry of restoration." (2006, 220).

The "positive side" of John's message is revealed in his promise that the coming One would, "gather his wheat into the barn" (Matthew 3:12). It should not be overlooked that the time of the harvest is the time of the salvation of the whole house of Israel (Revelation 7 & 14) – the salvation of "all Israel" in Romans 11. As Webb notes, after examining the OT language of harvest and the threshing floor,

---

[92] Marius Reiser, *Jesus and Judgment,* Minneapolis, Fortress, English translation, 1997)175.

> "John's use of this imagery was probably associated with expectations of the eschatological future to be experienced by the restored people of God. The gathering of the grain into the granary symbolizes the positive act taken by the expected figure to preserve the prepared repentant from the imminent judgment which will fall upon the wicked." (2006, 300).

John also said, "his winnowing fork is already in his hand." The imagery tells us that the end of the age harvest, when the chaff would be burned up was already approaching! Once again, this is the Day of the Lord of Malachi 4:1-2 - the Great and Terrible Day of the Lord of Malachi 4:5-6– the Day for which Elijah (John) was *The Voice* and *The Messenger*.

Consider here how Malachi 4 and the prediction of the coming of Elijah confirms that the Great and Terrible Day of the Lord was to be a time of national judgment on Israel, not an end of time event.

Malachi 4:4 called on Israel – through the coming Elijah - to "remember the Law of Moses My servant." Nothing could more powerfully set the covenantal tone and context for the ministry and message of Elijah / John. What we find here is the warning to Israel that Elijah would come and remind Israel that her continued obstinance and disobedience would bring to bear the full - and final - force of the Law of Blessings and Cursings of Deuteronomy 28-30.

So, if the Law of Blessings and Cursings was to be the fountain for the message of *The Voice*, *The Messenger* and *Elijah*, as is evident from our discussion of Malachi 3:5, nothing could more powerfully demonstrate that the Great and Terrible Day of the Lord foretold by John was not, in any way, to be a time ending, earth burning event. The message of *The Voice, The Messenger* and *Elijah* was that YHVH was coming in national judgment of Israel for violating the Law of Moses. And the implications for understanding Romans 11 are profound.

Wagner takes note that Paul draws from Deuteronomy 28, 29 and 30 in Romans 10-11 (2003, 254). So, as just seen, the Law of Blessings and Cursings served as the source of the message of John and his mission for the salvation of Israel, which would be at the time of national judgment of Israel. So far as I can tell, Wagner never develops the connection between John and Paul's use of the Law of Blessings and Cursings. But if the Law of Blessings and Cursings was at least part of the source of John's message of the impending Day of the Lord, then since Paul cites that same covenant in his discussion of the fate of Israel in his day, upon what basis do we create a dichotomy between John's coming judgment and that which Paul anticipated?

Notice the common theme of blindness in Deuteronomy 28:28f; 29:4, and Paul's reference to Israel's blindness in his day as he cites the Law of Blessings and Cursings. This theme of blindness plays a prominent role in Jesus ministry, as he castigated his generation for their blindness, in fulfillment of Isaiah 6:9f. That blindness, as foretold in Deuteronomy, would lead to national judgment. Paul, like Jesus, cited Isaiah 6 in Acts 28:25f as he spoke of the kingdom to the Roman Jewish leaders. It is remiss of the exegete to overlook or ignore the latent threat of national judgment that would have been understood by those Jewish leaders.

Wright calls our attention to this, commenting on Israel's blindness in Romans 2 and 11:

> "Much as we might like to hope for a sudden universal unhardening, this is simply not how the notion of 'hardening' itself functions. As we saw, the 'hard and impenitent heart' of 2. 4-5 was what came about when the 'kindness' of God, meant to lead to repentance, was refused, so that the 'hardening' was the prelude, not to a sudden mercy despite the lack of repentance, but to judgment" (2013, 1237).

So, since Paul draws on the Law of Blessings and Cursings in his discussion of Israel and her fate in Romans 9-11, should we not see that his entire discussion must be viewed and interpreted within the matrix, within the framework of covenant fulfillment - and thus - impending judgment? Would his utilization of that covenant not virtually demand that the fulfillment of Romans 11 would be in fulfillment of that Law of Blessings and Cursings? Once again, this would point us, not to a "cosmic," universal Day of the Lord at the end of the current Christian age, but, to the national judgment of Israel in AD 70, when, "These be the days of vengeance when all things written must be fulfilled" (Luke 21:22).

I must offer just an additional thought or two here that "connects the dots" between John and Romans 11:25f.

As we have seen, Paul quotes directly from Isaiah 27:9f in his anticipation of the coming salvation of Israel. Isaiah tells us that Israel's salvation would come at the time of, and by means of her judgment. That salvation would be when the fortified city would be desolated, the temple destroyed. It is the time when the people of "no understanding" - the people that YHVH had created - would receive no mercy. Take note that Isaiah draws directly from Deuteronomy 32:28 - "They are a nation void of counsel, there is no understanding in them."

The concept of "no understanding" is directly related to the motif of blindness, of Deuteronomy 28 and 29 (and, needless to say, Romans 11:10f and 11:25) that we have just noted. We cannot fail to note also that in Romans 11:8, Paul quotes Isaiah 29:10 which is about Israel's blindness. That blindness would lead directly to the Lord working a "marvelous work" – the destruction of the wise, those who drew near to Him with their lips but their hearts were far from him. Of course, Jesus applied this very passage to Israel of his day in Matthew 15, the blind leading the blind *into the ditch*! Israel's refusal to "know," to heed, to see, would lead them into the ditch of destruction.

According to Isaiah and Paul, the people have no understanding because they refuse to hear, because they blinded themselves to the Lord and His word.[93] So, when Paul draws directly from Isaiah 27 & 29, he is appealing to the Law of Blessings and Cursings as well as the Song of Moses. Paul creates a matrix of allusions to Deuteronomy (as well as Isaiah). The Law of Blessings and Cursings warned Israel of the dangers of refusing to hear and to heed, while the Song described Israel in her last days. All of this ties Paul's message directly to John as *The Messenger*.

Remember that John, as *The Messenger*, would warn Israel of the coming Day of the Lord, a time of national judgment, when the Law of Blessings and Cursings would be brought to bear on the nation. Just like John, Paul cites the Law of Blessings and Cursings in Romans 10-11, as he speaks of Israel's blindness. We should never lose sight of the fact that lying latent, but forebodingly present, behind any description of that blindness and recalcitrance was the threat that national judgment was about to fall on the nation. The Law of Blessings and Cursing was about to be fully applied. These connections define the nature of the Day of the Lord that Paul was anticipating. Like John,

---

[93] There is a direct correlation between the blindness motif and the filling of the measure of sin concept that Jesus spoke of in Matthew 23:29f, and that Paul and John likewise address (1 Thessalonians 2:14f / Revelation 17). Israel's blindness to the calling of the gospel led to her persecution of the "Heralds of the Good News," which in turn led directly to the filling up of the measure of her sin. The result was her destruction.

Paul envisioned the impending judgment on Old Covenant Jerusalem.

The Immerser described that Day of the Lord as the time of the salvation of Israel, the time of gathering into the barn of those faithful to God. Keeping in mind the fact that Luke 1 describes John's mission as the salvation of Israel, this should force us, in light of the above, to see the Day of the Lord, for both the judgment and salvation of Israel as a first century, fulfilled reality. The connections between John and Paul virtually demand that the judgment on Israel is likewise in Paul's mind in Romans 9-11.

With this in mind, note the following:

John was *The Voice in the wilderness,* preparing for the coming of the Lord in national judgment at the time when Israel's sins would be removed. This is undeniable (Isaiah 40:1-12–> Mark 1:1-3 / John 1:23). Salvation and judgment are conjoined.

John was *The Messenger* and *Elijah* who would prepare for the coming of the Lord in judgment of Israel for violating Torah - the application of the Law of Blessings and Cursings. This would be the time when the righteous, the remnant, would become the jewels in YHVH's crown. Once again, judgment and salvation are synchronous. This is undeniable (Malachi 3:1-6 / Mark 1:1-2). Yet, as noted, I have yet to find a commentator who makes these connections between John and Paul.

Did John "successfully" fulfill his role as *The Voice, The Messenger* and *Elijah*, to warn of the Great Day of the Lord? If he did, then he fulfilled his role in the "restoring all things."[94] At least it would have to be admitted that he initiated that restoration and that the consummation of the process would be the parousia as posited in Romans 11. (John certainly fulfilled his role as a martyr, helping to fill the measure of end times, eschatological suffering).

We could expand our discussion of John as *Elijah*, but, this is sufficient to establish the identity of John as the eschatological prophet beyond any dispute.

---

[94] Space forbids lengthy discussion of the "restoration of all things" but, see my *Like Father Like Son, On Clouds of Glory* book for an in-depth study of this fascinating issue. That book is available from my websites, Amazon, Kindle and other retailers.

When we conflate his identity as *The Voice, The Messenger* and *Elijah* together, we have indisputable evidence of the following:

☛ John was a last days prophet of God. He was in fact, a fundamentally important eschatological figure.

☛ The identification of John as a prophet of God, inspired by the Holy Spirit of God, serves as an indicator of John's eschatological role and function.

☛ He was the prophet of God designated to initiate the restoration of Israel - the fulfillment of the Abrahamic and Davidic Covenant promises - the restoration of Israel anticipated by Paul in Romans 11.

☛ As *The Voice, The Messenger* and *Elijah*, John heralded the coming Great Day of the Lord.

☛ That Day foretold by John was the Day of the Salvation of Israel, when the Lord would bring Israel's covenant history to its consummation, with the arrival of the New Creation - the kingdom. That Day would be the coming of the Lord for the salvation of Israel in Romans 11.

☛ The coming of the Lord heralded by John was to be a time of *national judgment on Israel for violating Torah*, but, at the same time, it would be the salvation of the righteous remnant, who would comprise, "God's special people."

☛ The coming of the Lord foretold by John was the same Day of the Lord anticipated by Paul in Romans 11:25-27, the time of Israel's salvation. This means that the coming of the Lord for the salvation of "all Israel" in Romans 11 was to be the coming of the Lord *in national judgment of Israel for violating Torah*. It was not to be an end of time, cosmos destroying event.

☛ John declared, emphatically, unambiguously and without equivocation, that the promised Day of the Lord was near. This means that when Paul wrote, the Day was even nearer. And of course, that is precisely what Paul said in Romans 13:11-14f:

> "And do this, knowing the time, that now it is high time to awake out of sleep; for now our salvation is nearer than when we first believed. The night is far spent, the day is at hand. Therefore let us cast off the works of darkness, and let us put on

the armor of light. Let us walk properly, as in the day, not in revelry and drunkenness, not in lewdness and lust, not in strife and envy."

I think language could hardly be clearer. Paul was patently looking for the imminent Day of the Lord, the time of Israel's salvation. As Nanos correctly says:

> "Paul certainly expected the final events (Romans 8:18f; 1 Cor. 15; 1 Thess. 4:13-18) in his own lifetime. When he speaks of the *pleroma* of the Gentiles who are to come in and of Israel's return, he is thinking in terms of years – not even decades, let alone centuries or millennia. The preconditions for the final events were well underway...Thus, when we read of Israel's trespass, failure, and rejection, we must remember that for Paul their duration was to continue for 20 years, not 2000. He cites Dunn (Romans, p. 18) – 'Paul seriously contemplated this outreach being achieved within his lifetime, as the last act before the end and the necessary preliminary to the salvation of Israel (1 Corinthians 4:9; Romans 11:13-32).'"[95]

Nanos does a fine job showing that the restoration of Israel was indeed taking place in the first century and that Luke chronicles that restoration. To be sure, the restoration was not a nationalistic, geo-political restoration. The NT writers defined that restoration in terms of the work of Christ through the power of his resurrection. Notice more from Nanos:

> "Luke sketched the outline of Acts around the striking success (not the rejection) of the apostolic mission to Israel which represented the restoration of Israel as promised (Acts 15:13-18) appealing constantly to the multitudes of believing Jews to highlight this point (Acts 2:41, 47; 4:4, 5:14; 6:1;, 7; 9:31, 42; 14:1; 17:10-12; 19:20; 21:20). ... "Further, these are Jews for whom the restoration of Israel is of utmost importance (Acts 1:6; 2:46; 3:1, 21; 5:12; 109f; 11:2; 15:1-8; 21:20-22:3f; 23:6;

---

[95] David Nanos *The Mystery in Romans*, (Minneapolis, Fortress, 1996) 278, n. 110. Nanos, like so many, charges Paul with a failed eschatology because he believes Paul was expecting the end of time.

24:14-21; 26:4-7; 28:20). Moreover, the Jews who do not accept the gospel or even oppose it are not pictured as rejecting some new faith or institution; rather, they are rejecting Abraham and Moses and the prophets, they are rejecting the hope of resurrection and the Messiah – thereby cutting themselves off from the promises to Israel (Acts 3:19-26; 13:46; 14:1-4; 17:3; 23:6-10; 24:14-21; 26:22-23)." (1996, 268).

So, the OT prophecies of the restoration of Israel were being fulfilled. God's promises did not fail. Israel was being called on to see the true nature of those prophecies. Yet, we are to believe that in spite of the fulfillment of those prophecies, the predictions of the consummation of what had begun *did fail!* How was God able to fulfill the amazing prophecies of the calling of the Gentiles and the restoration of Israel, *yet fail to bring about the parousia?*

Once we understand the true nature of the parousia being foretold by John, and continued by Paul, this troublesome problem disappears. Paul was not looking for a end of time event. We can establish this by looking at the prophecies of the salvation of Israel at the Day of the Lord that Paul quotes from in Romans 11.

DID PAUL ANTICIPATE A DIFFERENT DAY OF THE LORD FROM THAT FORETOLD BY JOHN?

To answer the important question posed by the title of this chapter, we need to examine the two major eschatological OT texts that Paul cites directly. We can also look at some other OT prophecies that are "echoed" by Paul.[96] This examination will reveal that Paul did not have an end of time parousia in mind. He was looking for the same Day of the Lord foretold by John as *The Voice*, *The Messenger* and *Elijah* - a day of national judgment on Israel.

It is all but universally agreed that Paul cites, echoes, quotes from Isaiah 27 and Isaiah 59 in Romans 11:26-27. What is fascinating is that many scholars who take note of these citations do not then connect the dots between Romans 11:25f and some other key eschatological texts that deal with Israel's "final" salvation, e.g. Daniel 9. Furthermore, as I have already noted, while they point out that Paul quotes from Isaiah 27 and 59, I have found extremely few who (Wagner being one) make the connection with Isaiah 40, which, like Isaiah 27 and 59 foretold the taking away of Israel's sin.

Isaiah 27

One of the texts that Paul cites directly is Isaiah 27. This chapter is part of what is known as the Little Apocalypse, due to its eschatological content and because the NT writers cite it so often in their predictions of the end. Isaiah chapters 24-27 comprise the Little Apocalypse. (We would add that chapters 28-29 are also intensely eschatological in nature and likewise cited repeatedly by Jesus and the Biblical writers). It is difficult to do justice to this text in a short space, but, I will make a few bullet points.

→ The entire Little Apocalypse is concerned with the salvation of Israel. This concept permeates these chapters. I will not chronicle every reference here, but, this idea is found in 24:14f; 25:9f; 26:1-2; 27:1f, 13; 28:16f, etc. Significantly,

---

[96] Paul's citation of Jeremiah 31 and the promise of the New Covenant is extremely important, but, because it does not deal with the "coming of the Lord" *specifically*, I have chosen not to discuss it here. In *reality*, the New Covenant promise is nothing less, and nothing other than, the promise of the New Creation. I develop this in a book on the Sabbath that I am currently trying to finish (2016). But, once again, I have simply chosen not to address Jeremiah here for brevity sake.

salvation is inextricably linked to the time of Israel's judgment as well in almost every one of these contexts. See the discussion below for more.

→ The promised salvation / resurrection would be at the coming of the Lord (24:21f; 26:20f) just like in Romans 11.

→ The promised salvation / resurrection would be at the coming of the Lord (24:21f; 26:20f) *in vindication of the blood of the martyrs* (Isaiah 26:20).

→ The promised New Creation would come after the destruction of the old *due to Israel's violation of Torah* (24:1-5). This is hugely important but mostly overlooked.

We should not overlook the fact that the Little Apocalypse is focused on the salvation of Israel. In Isaiah 26:21, that salvation would be at the coming of the Lord "out of His place." Is this not the coming of the Lord "out of Zion" in Romans 11:25f? If not, why not? Perhaps Isaiah 26:21 explains why Paul used the terminology of "out of Zion" in Romans. I have not found a single commentator to make this connection, but, the connections are powerful.

If the coming "out of His place" in Isaiah 26 is the coming "out of Zion" in Romans 11, this serves as *prima facie* proof that Romans 11 was fulfilled at the coming of the Lord in the judgment of Jerusalem for shedding, "all the righteous blood shed on the earth." And this matches the message of John, as *The Voice*, *The Messenger* and *Elijah* concerning the imminent judgment perfectly.

→ Israel's salvation would be accomplished *by means of judgment* (27:9).

> "Therefore by this the iniquity of Jacob will be covered; And this is all the fruit of taking away his sin: When he makes all the stones of the altar like chalk stones that are beaten to dust... Yet the fortified city will be desolate, The habitation forsaken and left like a wilderness."

It may be difficult for us to grasp but, the text is quite emphatic that Israel's salvation would come by means of her judgment and it is important to note once again, that this judgment would be when the martyrs were vindicated at the Day of the Lord.

Perriman comes close to the thesis of this book in his comments on Romans 11:13-26. He discusses the Gentile Christian antipathy against the Jews in light of the Jewish rejection of the Gospel and the coming salvation of Israel through judgment, as foretold by Isaiah:

> "Their rejection has led to the reconciliation of Gentiles to the God of Israel, but the swing in the direction of the nations can still be reversed, and that will mean 'life from the dead' - the restoration of Israel *following judgment* (Daniel 12:2-3; Hosea 6:1-2). Again, we have a hint that Paul expects a national return to God to happen - if it is going to happen at all - *immediately after the coming judgment.*"[97] (His emphasis).

I believe that what is at work in Isaiah (missed by Perriman and most commentators) is the doctrine of Blood Atonement based on Numbers 35:

> "Whoever kills a person, the murderer shall be put to death on the testimony of witnesses" (35:30). Six cities of refuge were provided for those who killed someone accidentally, or in passion, i.e. non-premeditated murder (35:9-15).[98]

---

[97] Andrew Perriman, *The Future of the People of God*, (Eugene, Or. Cascade Books, 2010)134. He adds, (p. 136): "The restoration that Isaiah (chapter 59, DKP) envisages, however, comes as a *consequence of judgment*." While Perriman correctly sees - as we are emphasizing - that Isaiah 27 and 59 foretold the judgment of Israel through judgment – and Paul believed it was imminent, he fails to make any connection with the avenging of the blood of the martyrs found in Isaiah. And, he has no discussion of the role of John as *The Voice, The Messenger* and *Elijah*

[98] Note how Peter "makes excuse" for the common people of Jerusalem in regard to Jesus' death in Acts 3:17f, "I know that you did it ignorantly..." He was saying that while they had committed a heinous crime, they did it in ignorance and thus, could now flee for refuge. (See Keener's discussion of "sins of ignorance" in Acts 3. (2013, 1102+). Interestingly, Keener makes no connection between the ignorance of the people in regard to the killing of Jesus and the law of Blood Atonement. The writer of Hebrews speaks of Hebrew Christians who had "fled for refuge" (Hebrews 6:18) by entering Christ and the New Jerusalem, the heavenly refuge. This reference to fleeing for refuge follows hard on the warning for them not to turn back to Judaism, because to do so was to "crucify Christ afresh" - thus, willfully taking their place with those guilty of the *purposeful* murder of Jesus and bringing the judgment of

When (first degree) murder was committed in Israel, the way - the only way - Atonement could be made was for the murderer to die. There was such as thing as "corporate guilt" in the mind of YHVH in regard to Israel as well (cf. Joshua 6:11f). When the leaders and the people of Israel sinned together, the nation was held accountable. Thus, in both Deuteronomy and in Isaiah, we find the time of judgment on Israel is the time when the martyrs – slain by the nation - would be vindicated. As Deuteronomy 32:43 says:

> "Rejoice, O Gentiles, with His people; For He will avenge the blood of His servants, And render vengeance to His adversaries; He will provide atonement for His land and His people."

Here is the doctrine of Blood Atonement at work. The "murderers" would receive vengeance. The martyrs who died at their hands would be vindicated; YHVH would save His people.

→ This judgment would be when Jerusalem and the temple was destroyed (24:10f; 25:1-2; 27:10f). The people that YHVH had created, a people of no understanding, would be destroyed and the altar of the temple turned to chalk stone (27:1-11).

Chapter 27 echoes the Song of Moses that predicted that in Israel's last days, the people of no understanding would be destroyed. This would be, like Isaiah 26:20f, the time when the martyrs would be vindicated (Deuteronomy 32:43).

→ While the fortified city would be desolated and the temple altar turned to chalk stone, the Lord would blow the great trumpet to gather His elect from the four winds (27:13).

In Matthew 24, we find Jesus' prediction of the impending judgment on Jerusalem. That judgment would fall on the "holy city" because of her blood guilt, the shedding of the blood of the prophets and saints of the Lord (Matthew 23:29f). In verses 29f, he described that event in typical Hebraic prophetic, hyperbolic language, as his coming on the clouds of glory. He says that at that time:

> "The Son of Man shall send forth his angels with the sound of the Great Trumpet, and they shall gather together the elect from

---

Blood Atonement on themselves.

the four winds."

This is a direct echo of Isaiah 27:13.[99] Thus, Isaiah 27 and Matthew 24 posited the salvation of the saints, their vindication and the judgment of their persecutors at Jesus' coming, a national judgment on Jerusalem, just as Malachi 3-4 demanded.

So, in Romans 11:26f, Paul foretold the salvation of Israel that would come at the Day of the Lord.

He said that salvation would be in fulfillment of Isaiah 27:9.

But, the salvation of Israel in Isaiah 27 would take place at the coming of the Lord in vindication of the martyrs and the judgment of Israel for her blood guilt (26:20f; See also Isaiah 4:1-4).

Therefore, unless one can prove that Paul was simply borrowing the terminology of Isaiah as a verbal prop in Romans 11, this means that Paul had in mind the coming salvation of Israel (the righteous remnant) in the national judgment of Israel. As Jesus said, all the blood, of all the righteous martyrs, would be vindicated at that time.

The hermeneutical question must be asked:

Since Paul appeals to Isaiah 27 as one of the sources for his expectation of the salvation of Israel at the Day of the Lord, and,

Since Isaiah 27 foretold the salvation of Israel at the time of the judgment of Israel for shedding innocent blood, and,

---

[99] Scholars are in general agreement that Jesus is echoing Isaiah 27:13. See John Nolland, *New International Greek Testament Commentary, Matthew*, (Grand Rapids, Paternoster, 2005)985. W. D. Davies and Dale Allison Jr., also connect Matthew 24:31 with Isaiah 27:13, as well as Romans 11. *International Critical Commentary, Vol. III, Matthew 19-28*, (New York, T & T Clark, 2004)362. I agree with those connections, but, unless we are willing to posit the failure of Matthew and Romans, then Jesus' statement in Matthew 24:34, that the gathering / salvation in view would take place in his generation, this demands the first century fulfillment of Romans 11.

Since Jesus posited the salvation of Israel, (in fulfillment of Isaiah 27:13) at the time of the judgment of Israel for shedding innocent blood (Matthew 23:29f / 24:29-34), then,

What is our basis for divorcing Paul's doctrine of the salvation of Israel from the time of judgment on Israel for shedding innocent blood - i.e. AD 70?

The salvation of Israel promised in Romans 11:26f occurred in AD 70.

Isaiah 40

It takes but a brief notice to realize that Isaiah 40 and Romans 11:25f speak of the same time and same event.

✔ Isaiah 40 spoke of the coming time when Israel's sins would be taken away. Paul spoke of the taking away of the sin of Israel.

✔ Isaiah posited the restoration of Zion and Israel, and that is unequivocally at the heart of Paul's message and hope.

✔ Isaiah 40, remember, is cited by Paul in Romans 10 & 11 to speak of Israel, her then current rebellion and the implied consequent judgment that was coming, as well as to remind of God's faithfulness to fulfill His promises to Israel. How then, would we divorce the coming of the Lord in Isaiah 40 from that in Romans 11?

✔ Isaiah said Israel's salvation / restoration would be at the coming of the Lord when He would have His reward with Him. Paul said Israel's salvation would occur at the coming of the Lord.

Does Isaiah 27 predict a different salvation of Israel from that foretold in Isaiah 40? If so, what is the proof for that? Where does Isaiah 27 delineate between the salvation of Israel to come at the Day of the Lord, from the salvation of Israel at the Day of the Lord in chapter 40? What is the difference between the taking away of Israel's sin in Isaiah 27 and that in Isaiah 40 - or in Romans 11? It is specious to attempt such a dichotomization. It is one salvation, at the same Day of the Lord.

This means that Isaiah 40 and Romans 11 spoke of the same event, the salvation of Israel. They both speak of that event as coming at the Day of the Lord. And of course, what cannot be missed is that John was *The Voice* to herald that impending Day of the Lord, and he manifestly declared that it was at hand. John was heralding the coming of the Lord in national judgment of Israel - the Day of Isaiah 27 - the Day of the coming of the Lord in judgment of Israel for shedding innocent blood. That was indubitably fulfilled in AD 70.

Isaiah 59

Isaiah 59 serves as the other OT prophecy specifically cited by Paul as a source of his anticipation of the coming salvation of Israel. As I have noted repeatedly, virtually all commentators agree that Paul quotes from Isaiah 27 and 59. Yet, as of this writing, while the literature holds almost unanimous testimony about this, there is likewise a 100% lack of development of the *context* of either Isaiah 27 or 59 and how those contexts should influence our understanding of Romans 11. It is as if the commentators simply say, "Yes, Paul quotes from Isaiah but, the context of those prophecies is not important for our understanding of Paul's eschatology." This is extremely unfortunate. I posit that the context of those OT texts - when conflated with the ministry of John - is normative, they serve as the *crux interpretum* for understanding Romans 11. With that in mind, let's look at the context of Isaiah 59.

Isaiah 59, Blood Atonement, and Israel's Salvation

Isaiah 59 naturally breaks itself into three divisions: *Accusation, Acknowledgment, Action*. Let us briefly explain each of these divisions.

• **ACCUSATION→** In verses 1-8, Jehovah accuses Israel of being almost hopelessly sinful. Among her sins, "Your hands are defiled with blood" (v. 3). Hosea, contemporary of Isaiah, described her blood guilt, "they break all restraint. With bloodshed upon bloodshed" (Hosea 4:2). Three times in verses 1-8 Isaiah points to Israel's internecine guilt. This three-fold accusation serves to intensify the reader's awareness of that blood guilt.

• **ACKNOWLEDGMENT→** In verses 9-15, Israel confesses her sin. Salvation is far from her, "justice is far from us, nor does righteousness over take us, we look for light and there is none, ...justice is turned back, and righteousness stands afar off, truth is fallen in the streets" (v. 9, 15).

• **ACTION→** Jehovah, "Saw it, and it displeased Him that there was no justice...therefore...He put on righteousness as a breastplate, and a helmet of salvation on His head; He put on the garments of vengeance for clothing, and was clad in zeal as a cloak. According to their deeds, accordingly He will repay. Fury to His adversaries, recompense to His enemies; the coast lands He will fully repay. So shall they fear the name of the Lord...The Redeemer will come to Zion and to those who turn from transgression in Jacob" (v. 16f).

Isaiah 59 then, another of Paul's sources of appeal for the salvation of Israel, is just like Isaiah 27, a prediction of the judgment of Israel for shedding innocent blood. This fits the context of Romans 11 quite well.

Romans 10-11 sets forth the recalcitrance of Israel toward the gospel (10:16f), the message of their salvation. We should not forget that in Matthew 23:31f Jesus said he would send his prophets and wise men to Israel and they would be rejected and persecuted. That is being echoed in Paul's lament over Israel's rejection of the gospel message.

In Romans 10:21, Paul quotes from Isaiah 65:2 to speak of Israel's rebellion, their rejection of the Word of the Lord. The significant thing about this is that in Isaiah 65, the prophet foretold that Israel was going to fill the measure of her sin and be destroyed. Israel's rebellion -*including the shedding of innocent blood* - would reach its height. Jehovah would come and destroy her. However, this destruction would result in, and be followed by, the new creation (65:6-19). This is Israel's salvation. This is Romans 11.

In the first century generation, as the gospel went forth, "to the Jew first, and then to the Greek" (Romans 1:16-17), the Jews refused to accept the message of a Torah free, Gentile equal, kingdom. *They killed the messengers who proclaimed that message.* Remember that Paul was writing in the midst of persecution (Romans 5, 8, 12) that was instigated by the Jews. Paul himself had been a persecutor of The Way, killing and imprisoning followers of Christ on the behalf of the leaders of Israel (cf. Acts 21-22; Galatians 1; 1 Timothy 1).

Thus, in Romans 10-11, Paul directly quotes from (or echoes) two (actually *several*) Old Testament prophecies of Israel's salvation, and those prophecies anticipated the Lord's judgment coming against Israel for shedding the blood of the righteous. This is significant in light of Matthew 23 as we have already suggested.

Jesus said Israel would fill the measure of her sin, the sin of shedding the blood of the righteous and be destroyed in his generation. The martyrs created by Israel's blood guilt, described in Isaiah, would be included in Jesus' promise that all of the martyrs all the way back to creation would be avenged in his generation. If they are included, and who could exclude them, then one cannot exclude the promises of Isaiah from the purview of Jesus in Matthew 23. Nor can one isolate and exclude the prophecies of Isaiah 27 and 59 – as cited by Paul in Romans 11 – from that interpretive equation.

Thus, when we consider the actual context of Isaiah 27 and 59, and we do not confine ourselves to the few words cited by Paul, it becomes increasingly clear and convincing that Paul was looking forward to the coming of the Lord for the salvation of Israel to be sure. But, he knew, based on those OT prophecies that he quotes, *that Israel's salvation would come at the time of her judgment for shedding innocent blood.*

When we accept this, there no need to point an accusing finger at Paul for a failed eschatology as so many scholars do. The fulfillment of his prophecy was in fact at hand, objectively and historically vindicating him as a prophet and apostle of Jesus. The Deliverer truly was about to come out of Zion- just as Isaiah 26:21 foretold.

An important note here by way of reminder. It is important to honor what scholars increasingly recognize, and that is that when a Hebrew writer or speaker cited a partial verse (as we have them divided) from an OT text, they were calling the mind of the reader / hearer to the broader prophetic context.

Tom Holland says,"The mere quotation of a short text had the affect of alerting the reader to the OT passage from which it had been taken. In this way these texts had a far greater meaning for the first readers of the NT than is normal today. Their knowledge of these passages meant that they automatically understood the passage of the NT that they were reading in the light of the OT passage out of which the quotation was drawn."[100] He adds, citing Dodd, that the early church knew the OT so well that when NT writer used a key word or two that, "the theology of the OT passage that the text (or words) was originally in was brought over into the passage in which it was now quoted." In other words, partial quotation of OT prophecies included the entire OT context. (2004, 27).

Andrew Perriman adds a similar thought:

> "The premise of this book has been that, generally speaking, when Old Testament quotations or allusions occur in the N T., they should be allowed to bring into focus the wider narrative or argumentative context from which they have been drawn. Peter[101] means us to see the coming judgment upon Israel's enemies that is foreseen by Isaiah or the Psalmist. It is hard to believe that he would have gone to such lengths to evoke those earlier historical manifestations of divine judgment if what he had in mind was something quite different."[102]

This quotation is particularly relevant in light of Paul's citation in Romans 10-11 of so many OT prophecies of the salvation of Israel at the time of her judgment for shedding innocent blood!

---

[100] Tom Holland, *Contours of Pauline Theology*, (Christian Focus Publications, Geanies House, Fearn, Ross-Shire IV20 1TW, Scotland, UK, 2004) 27.

[101] He is commenting on 2 Peter 3.

[102] Andrew Perriman, *The Coming of the Son of Man*, (Paternoster, London, 2005, 2006)125.

While we could multiple these citations and thoughts many times over, we will give but one more. Rikki Watts says,

> "In the absence of chapter and verse divisions, part-citations were apparently used as short hand references to larger contexts, and the same could reasonably be expected of allusions."[103] He adds: "As a number of scholars have noted, the technique of quoting the first section of a verse while the latter unstated section is actually in mind is not uncommon in rabbinic writings." (Ibid) He cites Jeremias from Kittel's TDNT 56:701 as supportive of this as well. (1997, 135).

So, if we accept *metalepsis* as a legitimate Hebrew hermeneutic, and employed by Paul in Romans, there is little doubt that when he cited Isaiah 27, 40, 59 and 65, no matter how brief those citations might be, he nonetheless had the wider prophetic context in mind. And that means that his concept of the salvation of Israel was inseparably tied to the impending national judgment on Israel for shedding innocent blood. That was in AD 70.

There is another key text that almost undoubtedly lies behind Paul's expectation of the taking away of Israel's sin, and that is Daniel 9:24-27.[104]

---

[103] Rikki Watts, *Isaiah's New Exodus in Mark*, (Grand Rapids, Baker, 1997)111.

[104] In preparation for the aformentioned debate with Dr. David Hester, I asked him when all the constituent elements of Daniel 9 were, or will be, fulfilled. His answer reveals a stunning ignorance of the relationship between the salvation of Israel, at the climax of her covenant history (cf. Isaiah 25:1-8; Daniel 12) and the salvation of "mankind." He stated that Daniel 9 is "irrelevant to the topic" of the second coming of Christ. He affirmed that since the Abrahamic Covenant predated the Mosaic Covenant, that it is unrelated to the fulfillment of Israel's Covenant, and that all Daniel 9 is concerned with was the termination of the "commonwealth of Israel." His abject failure to see that Daniel 9 predicted the resurrection, at the climax of Israel's history, is truly sad, but, common. See my book, *Seventy Weeks Are Determined...For the Resurrection*, for proof of the eschatological significance of Daniel 9.

9:24-27

> "Seventy weeks are determined For your people and for your holy city, To finish the transgression, To make an end of sins, To make reconciliation for iniquity, To bring in everlasting righteousness, To seal up vision and prophecy, And to anoint the Most Holy."

Daniel foretold the time of the putting away of the sin of Israel. Paul looked forward to the putting away of Israel's sin.

Daniel predicted the consummation of Israel's promises; Paul anticipated that climactic event.

Daniel 9 spoke of the "sufferings of Christ and the glory to follow" (Daniel 9:26f; cf. 1 Peter 1:11) while Paul, motivated by the passion and resurrection of Jesus the Messiah, spoke of the coming "glory" of the salvation of Israel.

Daniel posited the climax of his prophetic countdown at the "overwhelming flood" of the end times (which, we might note, would include vindication for the suffering of the Messiah)! Paul saw the consummation at the coming of the Lord.

Are these two different soteriological / eschatological events? Does Daniel speak of one salvation event, while Paul envisioned another, unrelated to Israel's prophetic countdown and schema? This is patently untenable since Paul says that Israel's salvation would be in fulfillment of God's covenant with Israel (Romans 11:27). Daniel 9 is clearly part of the prophetic matrix from which Paul is drawing. That has implications for the time and framework for the fulfillment of Romans 11, as we have already demonstrated from Isaiah and Malachi.

What is critical about this relationship is that the end of the seventy weeks is the destruction of the "city and sanctuary" in the time of the Abomination of Desolation (Daniel 9:26-27). There are no weeks, no prophetic countdown indicated beyond that event. Daniel was told, "Seventy weeks are determined on your people and on your city." The fate of the nation and the fate of the city are confined within that seventy week limitation.[105] If the fate of Israel, her

---

[105] See my *Seal Up Vision and Prophecy*, for a fuller discussion. That book is available from Amazon, Kindle, my websites

salvation, belongs within the seventy weeks, and if the seventy weeks cannot be extended beyond AD 70, then the salvation of Israel in Romans 11:25-27 belongs to that period. It had to be fulfilled no later than AD 70.

What we find then, in an examination of the texts that lie behind Paul's prediction of the salvation of Israel is that there are several common tenets and motifs that are, by and large, overlooked or ignored by the commentators.

☛ They all do in fact speak of the salvation of Israel.

☛ They all speak of the salvation at the time of the judgment of Israel.

☛ Almost all of them specifically posit that salvation at the coming of the Lord.

☛ Four of those underlying prophecies, Isaiah 27, 59, 65 and Daniel 9 specifically place the time of salvation, the climax of Israel's covenant history, at the time of *national judgment* on Israel. Not one of the underlying prophecies speak of an "end of time" event.

☛ Isaiah 27, Isaiah 59 and Daniel 9 all show that the reason for the judgment that was coming was *for shedding innocent blood*. Thus, the judgment and Israel's salvation is the time of the vindication of the martyrs.

This final point becomes incredibly important for understanding Romans 11:25f. The issue of martyr vindication is seldom, if ever explored in discussions of Romans 11. So, to that we turn.

---

and other retailers.

ROMANS 11 AND MARTYR VINDICATION

While many commentators mention the "suffering" that Paul discusses in Romans, few if any see it in the same vein that they do the motif of suffering even in other books such as 1 Peter, i.e. eschatological sufferings. In this application, the sufferings that Paul had in view really had no eschatological significance *per se*. Suffering is simply the lot of Christians in this world. I suggest this is an unfortunate oversight.

Cranfield sees the suffering in Romans as that which characterizes the Christian experience between the Cross and the parousia.[106] It is simply the lot of Christians to suffer until the end of time. Dunn takes a somewhat similar view, although he acknowledges that the suffering is related to the "suffering of Christ" that had an eschatological "tension" to it. In spite of this, Dunn still simply assigns the sufferings to the time between Jesus' resurrection and the end of the current age.[107] Hendrickson says, "The apostle is thinking of suffering in general; therefore, pain, (physical as well as mental), sickness, disappointment, unemployment,, poverty, frustration, etc.."[108] Pate expresses this view when he says that the sufferings of this present time, are an expression of life in, "this age" as opposed to, "the age to come."[109] Holland, like most commentators, sees the release from, "the sufferings of this present time" as reference to the end of

---

[106] C. E. B. Cranfield, *Romans, A Shorter Commentary*, (Grand Rapids, Eerdmans, 1985)193.

[107] James D. G. Dunn, *Word Biblical Commentary, Romans 1-8*, (Dallas, Word Publishers,1988)468.

[108] William Hendrickson, *New Testament Commentary, Romans*, (Grand Rapids, Baker Academic, 2002)265.

[109] C. M. Pate, *The End of the Age Has Come,* (Grand Rapids, Zondervan, 1995)62. He appeals to Isaiah 65 for the yet future coming of a literal New Heaven and Earth. He also says that Romans 8:18-22 is the clearest expression of this hope to be found. He says that the reference to "the suffering of this present time" and the statement "the glory that shall be revealed" are expressions of "this age" and "the age to come."

time when the entire created order is renewed in a "heaven on earth."[110] Longenecker joins these commentators in defining the, "sufferings of the now time" as, "a general reference that includes everything that believers in Jesus suffer, whether as finite and fallible humans under the curse of sin and depravity or as Christians in their witness for God and the Gospel."[111]

I must say that these comments raise some serious questions about the "victory" of the Christian, especially in light of what Paul said prior to Romans 8:18f. After all, in chapter 7 he gloried in the fact that Christ had given victory over the futility of life under Torah. In Romans 8:1-3, he exulted in the victory of the law of sin and death that Christ gives - as he spoke of, "the law of the spirit of life in Christ Jesus" (8:1-3). In the verses leading up to verse 18 he spoke of the wonders of being adopted as children of God. Yet, we are to believe that in 8:18f he laments the continuation of the Adamic Curse of life in Christ for the Christian? The sufferings of "this present time" means that Christians labor under the Curse until some proposed "end of time?" The Christian is to look on the normal course of human experience as living under "depravity"? Where then is "deliverance?" Where and what is salvation? Where is the victory?

It is unfortunate that so many commentators do not see the suffering in the book of Romans as related to the eschatological sufferings of the "end times." To miss this motif is to miss part of the purpose for the coming of the Lord in Romans 11:25f - the vindication of the suffering of the saints - *as promised in the very prophetic texts that Paul quotes from!* And we should not lose sight of the fact that Jesus identified John the Baptizer as a part of that body of martyrs to be vindicated (Matthew 17:10f). A quick survey of the epistle will quickly reveal that persecution - and the promise of vindication - was very much on Paul's mind.

Romans 2:1-9

> "Therefore you are inexcusable, O man, whoever you are who judge, for in whatever you judge another you condemn yourself; for you who judge practice the same things. But we

---

[110] Tom Holland, *Romans the Divine Marriage*, (Eugene, Or., PickWick Publications, 2011)274-275.

[111] Richard Longenecker, *The New International Greek Testament Commentary, Romans*, (Grand Rapids, Eerdmans, 2016)718.

know that the judgment of God is according to truth against those who practice such things. And do you think this, O man, you who judge those practicing such things, and doing the same, that you will escape the judgment of God? Or do you despise the riches of His goodness, forbearance, and longsuffering, not knowing that the goodness of God leads you to repentance? But in accordance with your hardness and your impenitent heart you are treasuring up for yourself wrath in the day of wrath and revelation of the righteous judgment of God, who "will render to each one according to his deeds": eternal life to those who by patient continuance in doing good seek for glory, honor, and immortality; but to those who are self-seeking and do not obey the truth, but obey unrighteousness—indignation and wrath, tribulation and anguish, on every soul of man who does evil, of the Jew first and also of the Greek."

Paul does not speak specifically of martyr vindication here, but, it is very much present in the background.

1. The apostle is clearly warning the Jews that they cannot judge the pagans without incurring God's wrath just because they have Torah and the Gentiles didn't (2:14f). After all, they were just as guilty of violating God's law as the pagans (v. 19f).

2. He refers to the wrath that was *coming*.[112] In chapter 1:18, he says the wrath of God was already coming (present active indicative) on the ungodly.[113] Paul

---

[112] Interestingly, Webb (2006) does not even address a connection between Paul's discussion of the coming wrath and John's message. Most other commentators likewise fail to see, or ignore the connections.

[113] In 1 Thessalonians 1:10, Paul likewise refers to the coming wrath. Jesus was (present active indicative) "delivering" them from that impending wrath. That is the wrath of 1 Thessalonians 2:14-16 - judgment on Jerusalem for shedding innocent blood. 1 Thessalonians 1:10 and Paul's reference to Jesus as "the deliverer" is a clear equivalent to Romans 11:25f. This places the salvation of Israel at the time of the avenging of the blood of the martyrs at AD 70 - just like Matthew 23, Isaiah 27 and 59. These texts are clearly parallel.

had the sense that the time of judgment had arrived or was hanging over their head. (See 1 Thessalonians 2:14-16). We should not overlook the fact that it was the Jews who were bringing that wrath on themselves by persecuting the church.

3. Paul said that at the coming wrath, it would be when YHVH would give "tribulation" (*thlipsis*) to the ungodly. This is a direct parallel to 2 Thessalonians 1, where Paul addressed the Thessalonian church, under tribulation (*thlipsis*). But he promised them that their suffering would be vindicated and they would receive "relief" (*anesis*) when the Lord Jesus is revealed from heaven" (1:7). The persecutors of the Thessalonian church were not the Roman authorities. In both Thessalonica and Rome it was the Jews.

Just as in 1 Thessalonians 2:14f, Paul was promising that God was about to judge Old Covenant Jerusalem for her internecine guilt of killing the prophets, of Jesus and Jesus' apostles and prophets – resulting in the filling up of the measure of her guilt.

Not only did Paul promise vindication and relief to the Thessalonians, but, he said: "It is a righteous thing with God to repay with tribulation, those who are troubling (*thlipsis*) you" (v. 5). *The persecutors of the Thessalonians were not the Roman authorities,* just as it was in Romans. It was the *Jews*. Paul, in both Romans and Thessalonians was saying that they persecutors would have the tables turned on them. The persecutors would become the persecuted! That is precisely what happened when Nero turned against the Jews and destroyed Jerusalem (cf. Revelation 17:16f).

This is where Perriman misses the mark. He repeatedly calls our attention to the imminence of the judgment in Romans. He emphasizes that Paul was not looking far down the hazy future. He tells us, quite eloquently at times, that both the Romans and the Thessalonians, "were surely led to believe that within their lifetime rest would be granted to them and their persecutors punished, "when the Lord Jesus is revealed from heaven." (1999, 116, 117). He even tells us that what was intended in Paul's promise was, "Wrath on Israel" (p. 119+). He links that coming wrath to the ministry of John the Baptizer and says that John, "had in mind just the sort of religious-political disaster that took place in AD 70" (1999, 118). While Perriman links that coming wrath to John and AD 70, in these early chapters of Romans, he fails to make any connection with the coming salvation of Israel in chapter 11.

So, how can it be argued on the one hand that Paul and the Romans expected the Day of the Lord against the persecutors in AD 70, and then, turn that same identical language and prediction into a prophecy of an event that was not - by any measure - imminent and coming soon? How can we turn Paul's prediction of impending wrath against those who were, *right then*, persecuting the Romans, into a prediction of wrath against someone not even persecuting them?

It needs to be emphasized again that Perriman acknowledges that Paul is speaking of the impending judgment of those who were, *when he wrote*, persecuting the nascent Roman church. But remember, when Paul wrote, *the Roman authorities were not in any way persecuting the church,* as the historical record shows! Are we to believe then, that Paul was predicting the destruction of Rome, for persecuting the Roman church (when they weren't doing that!) and he said that judgment was coming very shortly to punish their persecutors when that punishment was four centuries away? This stretches credulity a bit too far.

So, if Paul's "coming wrath" was the wrath about to come of John, and John's coming wrath was AD 70, how does Perriman (and a host of other commentators) then extrapolate four centuries beyond that admittedly imminent judgment to claim that Paul's prediction, "Will end in the overthrow of Rome as a power implacably hostile to the reconstituted people of God" (1999, 123).

So, to reiterate, if the wrath that was coming, and coming soon, against those who were persecuting the Roman church, this means that Paul did not have a far distant judgment of Rome in mind.

If the coming wrath was that foretold by John the Baptizer, then as we have seen, that means that Paul's prediction of the wrath to come at the Day of the Lord was the impending national judgment of Israel.

The only "wrath to come" as an expression of martyr vindication, that was truly imminent when Paul wrote, was the event foretold by John and by Jesus - the judgment of Jerusalem in AD 70.

Romans 5:1-3

> "Therefore, having been justified by faith, we have peace with God through our Lord Jesus Christ, through whom also we have access by faith into this grace in which we stand, and rejoice in hope of the glory of God. And not only that, but we also glory in tribulations, knowing that tribulation produces perseverance."

Paul is speaking here of the coming glory, the glory of chapter 8, and just as in that text, he posits that coming glory in the context of the "tribulations" that the Roman church was enduring. The glorification of the Romans, the vindication of their suffering, would be at the Day of the Lord. I think Perriman's comment in this regard is more than worth considering as it relates to the coming of the Lord in chapter 11. Commenting on what Paul expected in regard to the Day of the Lord he says:

> "One thing is clear: whatever the Day of the Lord might look like, it would have to be the sort of event that could plausibly be communicated to the church at Thessalonica, as Wright points out, by the Roman postal system (2 Thessalonians 2:1-2)" (2005, 117). Well, this means that the Day of the Lord being anticipated by Paul could not therefore, be an end of time, earth consuming, cosmos destroying event, for one could hardly read about such an event in the mail![114]

The point to be made here is that if the Day of the Lord was not an end of time event, but, as John the Baptizer foretold, a time of national judgment on Israel, then the coming of the Lord in Romans 11:25f is not at the end of the Christian age. It is not anywhere in the future. It occurred in AD 70 in the vindication of the martyrs, as foretold by Isaiah 27, Isaiah 59, by Daniel 9, by John the Baptizer as *The Voice, The Messenger* and as *Elijah*.

---

[114] See my *How Is This Possible?* for a fuller discussion of this important element. Scholars normally simply brush aside the fact that many believers in Thessalonica and Ephesus believed that the Day of the Lord had already come! Wright notes that it would have been impossible for the Thessalonians to have believed that the New Creation of Romans 8, the resurrection of 1 Corinthians 15 / 1 Thessalonians 4, etc. could have already happened. (N. T. Wright, *Paul*, Minneapolis, Fortress, 2005)56f). Thus, Wright recognizes the problem that if you hold to a literalistic recreation / end of time eschatology, that it would have been impossible for the Thessalonians to have believed it was in the past. However, Wright clearly holds that 1 Thessalonians 4 is a yet future, literal parousia. Of course, he is correct in one way. If in fact those texts predicted what Wright and most commentators say those texts foretold, i.e. a literal new creation, a literal, physical resurrection, etc.! But that is the point! The brethren in Thessalonica and Ephesus clearly did not hold that view of the Day of the Lord and the resurrection!

Only by divorcing John's message from Romans 11 can one posit a yet future coming of the Lord. Only by ignoring the context of tribulation and coming vindication in Romans, and then separating that discussion from Matthew 23, can one find a different coming of the Lord from that which occurred in AD 70. It is only by ignoring or discounting this pervasive theme in Romans, and its relationship to the rest of the Biblical corpus on martyr vindication that one can even begin to postulate that Romans 11:25f is in our future.

The word "tribulations" is from *thlipsis*, meaning pressure. The word is used 45 times in the NT, and with very few exceptions referred to persecution for the cause of Christ. This word, in the great majority of cases, does not refer to the normal human experience, such as cancer, heart trouble, financial distress, etc.. It is *persecution*. What should be noted is the same contrast between the then current tribulation and the expectation of glory.[115]

Romans 8:16-23

> "The Spirit Himself bears witness with our spirit that we are children of God, and if children, then heirs—heirs of God and joint heirs with Christ, if indeed we suffer with Him, that we may also be glorified together. For I consider that the sufferings of this present time are not worthy to be compared with the glory which shall be revealed in us. For the earnest expectation of the creation eagerly waits for the revealing of the sons of God. For the creation was subjected to futility, not willingly, but because of Him who subjected it in hope; because the creation itself also will be delivered from the bondage of corruption into the glorious liberty of the children of God. For we know that the whole creation groans and labors with birth pangs together until now. Not only that, but we also who have the first fruits of the Spirit, even we ourselves groan within ourselves, eagerly waiting for the adoption, the redemption of

---

[115] At work here is the "honor -v- shame" motif that was so powerful in ancient world, but seems almost lost on modern readers. See Randolph Richards, and Brandon J. O' Brien, *Misreading Scripture With Western Eyes*, (Downers Grove, IVP Press, 2012)113f, for an extensive discussion of the honor / shame motif in Hebraic culture. This is an extremely important concept for understanding the purpose of the parousia. Cf. 2 Thessalonians 1.

our body."

Many commentators, such as Wright, take note of Paul's emphasis on his "now time" versus the Old Covenant references to, "it shall come to pass" (2013, Vol. II, 556). However, some commentators such as Gentry claim that Paul's reference to the suffering of the "now time" had nothing to do with Paul's eschatological expectations. He says the suffering that Paul refers to is actually referent to the, "*internal* struggle of the Christian against *indwelling sin*, not the public buffeting of the Christian against *external* persecution" (*Dominion*, 2009, 472, his emphasis). Wright essencially concurs in his YouTube series on Romans 8. Hendrikson also agrees claiming that the suffering Paul refers to is the suffering resulting from sin (2002, 264). This is untenable.

Gentry and Hendrikson fail to grasp that Paul is addressing the futility of man under Law, *specifically under Torah* (Romans 7:6f). Paul is *not* discussing the futility of the Christian experience! Is the redemption in Christ so ineffective, so weak, so lacking, that Paul had to describe the Christian life as the "suffering of the now time"? No, Paul exults in the *victory* over the indwelling sin: "I thank God through Jesus Christ our Lord...There is therefore, no condemnation for those in Christ" (Romans 7:25-8:1f).

In addition to all of this, Gentry ignores the words for suffering and groaning that Paul uses. Those are words that do not refer to internal anxiety. They are words that denote external persecution. How Gentry can overlook this and even suggest that Romans 8 is a discussion of *Christian futility* is disturbing. His claim is mere desperation.

Wright is emphatic that Paul was saying that the time for the fulfillment of Israel's hope had arrived. And yet, Wright and others then turn around and tell us that those OT prophecies have not yet been fulfilled because we are still waiting on the redemption of creation.[116]

---

[116] This is a common practice. Joel McDurmon, president of American Vision has this to say about the "sufferings of this present time": "The phrase 'the present time' (*ton kairon de touton*, dkp) is an obvious eschatological/ prophetic reference. To what particular 'time' did Jesus refer? ...Jesus refers to *this time*– that is, His and His audience's time – not some time of judgment in the future. Whatever he's talking about, it refers to the people he was talking to." *Jesus V Jerusalem*, Powder Springs, Ga American Vision, 2012)34.

However, if the "glory that is about to be revealed" is the redemption of creation and, "the redemption of the body," and if that time of redemption is the time of the vindication of the "sufferings of this present time" it is specious to extrapolate the anticipated redemption beyond that time of vindication - AD 70. And in this, we find the inconsistency of Wright, McKnight and a host of others.

Wright is adamant that the vindication of the martyrs occurred in the judgment of Old Covenant Jerusalem in AD 70. That was the time of the coming of the Son of Man. It was the parousia. It was the arrival of the kingdom of God! He says commenting on Daniel 7:13f that it:

> "Has nothing to do with a figure 'coming' from heaven to earth. Despite the widespread opinion that this is what it 'must' mean in the gospels, there is no reason to suppose that on the lips of Jesus, or in the understanding of the earliest traditions, it meant anything other than vindication."

He then comments on Jesus before the Sanhedrin, as he quotes from Daniel:

> "Jesus' response, then, resonates with ironic power. Now, at last, when it can no longer be misunderstood, he can retell the story of Daniel 7 in his own revised version. He is claiming to be the representative of the true people of God. Like the martyrs on trial before the pagan tyrants, he is refusing to abandon the ancestral faith and hope, even if it costs him his life. ...He therefore declares that Israel's god will vindicate him; and that vindication will include the destruction of the Temple which has come to symbolize and embody the rebellion of Israel against God, her determination to maintain her national exclusivism at the cost of her vocation." (1996, 524).

He also comments on Matthew 16:27-28:

> "The whole of the story, of judgement for those who had not

---

However, McDurmon, in our debate mentioned above, continually affirmed that we are still waiting on the redemption of the body and physical creation. This is a gross oversight – or rejection - of the imminence that permeates the text. Yet, this is a common view.

followed Jesus and the vindication for those who had, is summed up in the cryptic but frequently repeated saying "the first shall be last, the last first. In other words, when the great tribulation came on Israel, those who had followed Jesus would be delivered; and that would be the sign that Jesus had been in the right, and that in consequence they had been in the right in following him. The destruction of Jerusalem on the one hand, and the rescue of the disciples on the other, would be the vindication of what Jesus had been saying throughout his ministry" (1996, 338).

McKnight agrees with Wright in positing the destruction of Jerusalem as the time of the vindication of the sufferings of Jesus and his followers. Commenting on Matthew 16:27-28 he says:

"It is reasonable, then, to argue that this vindication took place when Jerusalem was sacked by Rome as God's punishment for covenant faithfulness. Jesus therefore predicted a vindication of himself and his followers before the death of the disciples. This view fits admirably with the context (Mark 8:34-38) and gives adequate ground for Mark's insertion of the logion before his account of the transfiguration. In the previous context, Jesus promises the disciples that, though they would suffer like him, they would be vindicated by God. and just as Jesus was to suffer the ignominy of a humiliating death at the hands of the leaders in Jerusalem, so he would be vindicated. The disciples need to be assured of Jesus' vindication, and this is precisely how the transfiguration ought to be understood – as proleptic vindication." (1999, 136).

The question is appropriate: Was the suffering of Jesus and that of his disciples not part of Paul's, "the sufferings of this present time"? If not, why not? If it was part of the warp and woof of the eschatological narrative of end times sufferings, how is it possible to divorce Romans 8 or Romans 11 - the promised "glory about to be revealed" and the salvation of "all Israel" - from the vindication that was coming in AD 70? If, as we have seen, Paul has John's impending "wrath about to come" in mind as the time of the vindication for "the sufferings of this present time" then the evidence is all but coercive and points inexorably to the fact that "the glory about to be revealed in us" was the time of the vindication of their suffering - in AD 70.

I think DeMar has correctly caught Paul's intent:

> "The New American Standard translation does not catch the full meaning of this passage. Following Robert Young's Literal Translation of the Bible, we read, 'For I reckon that the sufferings of the present time are not worthy to be compared with the glory about to be revealed in us.' Whatever the glory is, it was 'about to be revealed' (see Revelation 2:10; 3:2, 10; 10:4; 12:4; 17:8). Peter tells his readers that the 'Spirit of glory and of Christ rests on you' (1 Peter 4:14). This was a present condition, not something that the people in Peter's day would have to wait for a future rapture."[117]

The sad reality is that far too many commentators, as we have demonstrated, simply turn Paul's reference to suffering into a vague prediction of the plight of Christians throughout the entire, two millennia so far, span of the Christian age.[118] In order to do that, however, it must be demonstrated that the suffering that Paul had in mind is totally unrelated to that spoken of by Jesus in Matthew 23.[119] It must be shown that the "glory" had nothing to do with John as one of

---

[117] Gary DeMar, *Last Days Madness*, (Powder Springs, Ga., American Vision, 1994)191. DeMar seems not to realize the implications of his own comments. If the "glory" was not far off, then the redemption of the body was near, and that falsifies any futurist eschatology.

[118] Hays, like the commentators cited above, says "Paul's point in Romans 8:35-36 is that Scripture prophesies sufferings as the lot of those (i.e. himself and his readers) who live in the eschatological interval between Christ's resurrection and the ultimate redemption of the world." *(Echoes*, 1989, 58). But, this means that Hays, like those other commentators, has to either ignore, or "elasticize" those multitudinous temporal statements into meaninglessness. And, he has to ignore the role of John as Elijah, who was to "restore all things."

[119] It would likewise have to be demonstrated that Jesus' three parables about the vindication of the martyrs at his coming are totally unrelated to Paul's discussion of the impending vindication of the martyrs in Romans 2 / 8 / 12 / 13 / 16! Was Paul indeed discussing a different set of martyrs from those Jesus discussed in Matthew 21-22 & Luke 18? Was he discussing a different Day of the Lord in vindication

the end times martyrs to be vindicated. It must be shown that, "the wrath to come" that Paul posited as "coming" (present active indicative - Romans 1:18 / 2:1-9) had nothing to do with John's "wrath about to come." But where is the distinction? One would likewise have to ignore the powerful words used by Paul to describe the then current suffering and then show a distinction between the "glory about to be revealed" in Romans 8, and the coming of Christ to be glorified (and bring glory) in 2 Thessalonians 1.

As we have shown, Paul uses the word *thlipsis* in Romans to speak of the tribulation that the Romans were enduring. He likewise employs the word "*stenazo*" and as Perriman says, "The language of 'groaning' in Romans 8:23 (*stenazo, stenagmos*), strongly suggests the experience of those who are oppressed by the enemies of God" (2006, 110).

Paul also utilized the word *pathemata*, which Balz-Schneider tell us means: "the sufferings to which Christians and especially the apostles are subject in this world and which would result primarily from persecution (thus, 2 Corinthians 1:16-17; Colossians 1:24; 2 Timothy 3:11; 1 Peter 5:9; Hebrews 10:32; cf. the more precise definition in 10:33.)."[120] It should be more than obvious that "the suffering of this present time" was not a reference to the "Christian experience" i.e. the common lot of Christians as human beings, throughout time.

This is confirmed by Paul's victory statement in Romans 8:33f. His references to suffering, to persecution, to sword and peril, cannot be viewed as expressions of the plight of Christians - i.e. the normal human experience. Paul and his contemporary brethren were being persecuted for their faith. Those persecutions were "the sufferings of the now time" and should not be ignored in our exegesis of Romans 8:18f.

Furthermore, one would have to totally mitigate or discount the temporal delimitations found in Romans 8, that demand an imminent fulfillment.

---

of the martyrs? Where is the evidence for that?

[120] Horst Balz and Gerhard Schneider, *Exegetical Dictionary of the New Testament,* Vol. 3, (Grand Rapids, Eerdmans, 1993)1. The word is used some 16 times in the NT, and with very few exceptions, it refers to the suffering of persecution.

When Paul spoke of the glory that was to be revealed, he did not simply say that it was "coming." He said it was "about to be revealed." He used the word *mello*, with the infinitive. The *Blass-DeBrunner Greek Grammar* says that when mello is used in the NT with the infinitive that it "indicates imminence."[121]

Perriman takes note of the imminence in Romans 8:18f: "The thorough-going eschatological character of the argument is brought out in the second half of Romans 8. In the first place, the sufferings of the *present* time are contrasted with the glory that is *about to be* (*mellousan*) revealed in the 'sons of God at the redemption of their bodies (8:18)."[122]

Gentry commented on the meaning of *mello* in Revelation 1:19: "When used with the aorist infinitive - as in Revelation 1:19 - the word's predominant usage and preferred meaning is: 'be on the point of, be about to.' The same is true when the word is used with the present infinitive, as in Rev.3:10. The basic meaning in both Thayer and Abbott-Smith is: 'to be about to."; emphasis added.).[123]

Both Moo and Dunn agree that *mello* indicated that Paul expected the realization of the "glory" imminently. Moo, discusses Paul's use of *mello* and agrees that it, "might stress the imminence of the revelation of this glory." (1996, 512, n. 19). Similarly, Dunn, says, "It is natural to hear in the *mello* the note not only of certainty (see 8:13) but of imminence" (1988, Vol. 38, 468). We could add a plethora of citations of scholars commenting on other texts where *mello* is used,

---

[121] *Blass-DeBrunner, A Greek Grammar of the New Testament and Other Early Christian Literature,* (Chicago, University of Chicago Press, 1961)181.

[122] Andrew Perriman, *The Future of the People of God*, (Eugene, Ore. Wipf and Stock, Cascade Books, 2010)117.

[123] Kenneth Gentry, *Before Jerusalem Fell: Dating the Book of Revelation* (Tyler, TX: Institute for Biblical Economics, 1989)141-142. In a revision of this work, Gentry draws back from this position, but his "justification" for doing so is unconvincing. I suggest that Gentry "saw the train coming," because the word *mello* is used by Paul in Acts 17:30-31; 24:14f to speak of the "about to be" judgment and the resurrection! If Gentry followed his comments on *mello* in Revelation, he would have to abandon his futurist eschatology, and he has demonstrated no willingness to do that.

but will refrain from that. There is no question that *mello* powerfully indicated imminence.[124] Thus, Paul anticipated the "redemption of the body" very soon.[125] But, *mello* is not the only word that he used to assure the Romans that their "sufferings of this present time" were to be short lived before the "revelation of the sons of God."

Paul also used the word *apokaradokeo*. This word powerfully conveys the idea of eager anticipation and expectation of what is coming.[126] Moo says, "The word 'eager expectation' suggests the picture of a person craning his or her neck to see what is coming" (1996, 513). The great grammarian, A. T. Robertson agreed: "to watch eagerly with outstretched head."[127]

---

[124] I suggest that when *mello* is used with other words of imminence, such as in Romans 8, words like *apekdekomai* and *apokaradodeo*, that the imminence factor in *mello* is emphasized and strengthened.

[125] Dr. David Hester, like many commentators who allow their presuppositions to rule their exegesis, rejects the objective imminence of the Biblical language. He says the church, "looks for a speedy consummation at the return of her Lord," even stating, "If the church loses her sense of the shortness of time and her expectancy of the end, it is proof that she has lost the gospel of Jesus Christ." He then chided me for believing in the *objective first century nearness* of the end: "You seem to bind Christ to a schedule, while Christ is beyond time." So, like other commentators, they talk about the end being near, but, near in their vocabulary is so elastic and stretchable, that it means nothing! This is as false as false can be. See my *Who Is This Babylon?* book for a thorough refutation of this claim. Hester has no grasp of Proverbs 13:12– "Hope deferred makes the heart sick!"

[126] Longnecker (2016, 717f) gives scant attention to the power of this word and the other words of imminence in Romans 8:18f. His focus in his commentary is on identifying "the creation" as both the sentient and non-sentient creation, coupled with his expectation that material creation will be restored to Edenic perfection. This seems to have guided his exegesis, instead of actually allowing the force of the linguistics to come into full play.

[127] A. T. Robertson, *Word Pictures in the New Testament, Vol. IV.*, (Nashville, Broadman, 1933)375.

Balz and Schneider comment on *apokaradokeo*: "the majority of fathers understand *apokaradokeo* as an intensification of *karadokia* and thus, an especially strong expression of expectation." .... "it remains most probable that with *apokaradokia* Paul intends to give expression to the element of earnest and eager longing. The preposition *apo* thereby strengthens the intensive character of the expression." (Vol. 1. 1990, 132).

Paul also used the word *apekdekomai*, which means, "an eager expectation" (cf. The use of *apekdekomai* in Hebrews 9:28 especially in light of Hebrews 10:37). This is not the, "it will happen one day by and by," kind of waiting that modern Christianity demonstrates and teaches. Paul wanted his audience to *expect* the parousia.[128]

Strengthening the imminence of Paul's language in Romans 8 is the direct connection between the "redemption of creation,"[129] the OT predictions of the

---

[128] We will not discuss here the many almost fantastical attempts to either mitigate or somehow counter the multitudinous statements of the imminence of the end that are found in the NT. The indisputable fact is that God can tell time, and has communicated to man objectively about time. It is specious in the extreme to make the old cliche that God does not see time like man does, in order to avoid the difficulty. After all, the God that supposedly does not see time as man does, Jesus said He knew, "the day and the hour" of the end. Likewise, Paul said God "has appointed a day" which means God knew the calendar and operated on the calendar in regard to His promises! These are declarations that the Father knows full well how to tell time!

[129] I will not develop it here, but Paul's reference to the "birth pains" also demands that Paul expected the eschatological consummation very soon. The "birth pains" is reference to the Messianic Woes, tenet that was prominent in the OT and rabbinic thought, as part of the end times drama that would lead directly to the Day of the Lord. For Paul to say they were in the "birth pains" was to say the resurrection was near. See Jesus' referent to the birth pangs in Matthew 24:8. Sadly, Longenecker (2016, 725) seeks to mitigate this connection saying that Paul's used the language of the birth pangs "until now" as a reference to "mundane, nontheological" time, not eschatological time. This is not supported by the text or context. Romans 8 is intensely eschatological. To ignore Paul's references to "the now time" does a disservice to exegesis.

"restoration of all things" - and the ministry of John the Baptizer as *Elijah*. Once again, we are in virtually uncharted territory. I have found no commentator who sought to harmonize Romans 8 with the ministry of John as *Elijah*.

I am convinced that part of the reason for this is that at least some commentators realized that John was predicting an impending national judgment on Israel. However, those same commentators believe that the "restoration of all things" must include the physical restoration of earth to an Edenic utopia. Thus, while the OT prophecies and the Jewish story line was that Elijah was to "restore all things" and while Jesus said that John was Elijah, he clearly did not bring about that material restoration. Therefore, John failed in his eschatological mission. His mission is not relevant to the discussion of Romans 8, it is assumed.

However, if John's message of the Day of the Lord was fulfilled in the national judgment of Israel, meaning that he did in fact fulfill his role as *The Voice, The Messenger* and *Elijah*, then perhaps it is time to re-evaluate the literalistic concept of the resurrection and the "restoration of all things."

John did predict the Day of the Lord, and that Day was in AD 70. But, that Day was likewise, in the eschatological narrative, the time of the kingdom[130] the resurrection, the restoration. So, I suggest that if the Day of the Lord took place *as John predicted*, then work of the "restoration of all things" likewise took place, and it is time for Bible students to re-align their concepts of the restoration of all things.

When Jesus said that John was Elijah who was to come and "*restore* all things." The word for *restore* is a cognate of *apokatastasis* found in Acts 3. This is, "the restoration of all things" spoken of by all the OT prophets. This is the restoration of the kingdom that the disciples asked about in Acts 1:6.[131]

---

[130] According to Jesus, in the events of the fall of Jerusalem, the kingdom and redemption - always inextricably tied to the resurrection - took place (Luke 21:28-32). Thus, in the mind of Jesus, AD 70 and the consummation are tied, and that means that in the mind of John they were synchronous and essentially synonymous as well.

[131] One of the most commonly held views among non-Dispensationalists is that in Acts 1, the disciples were still unclear as to the nature of the kingdom, and maintained a literalistic, nationalistic expectation. I think this is untenable in light of the fact that Jesus had

The most commonly held view is that John, like Jesus, actually failed to bring his ministry to fulfillment due to his martyrdom. This fails to see that as Wright has noted in regard to Israel's unbelief and rejection of the gospel chronicled in Romans 10, that Israel's unbelief - resulting in the death of "Elijah," as well as the Atoning work of Jesus - was God's plan all along (2013, 1178+).

I think it legitimate to ask: If John properly understood the nature of the Day of the Lord (as many scholars admit) as a time of national judgment on Israel, and not a cosmos wide, time ending event, then how do we say that he totally misunderstood *the nature of the resurrection and the kingdom*? The Day of the Lord, the resurrection and kingdom are inseparably linked temporally as well as conceptually. So, how did John get the Day of the Lord right, but, the resurrection and kingdom so wrong? A simple listing of the predictions and promises that John got right should convince us - at least should challenge us - to think carefully before charging him with a false prediction of an "end of time."

John *understood* that he was *The Voice* and *The Messenger*. He got it right.

John *understood* that the Spirit would be poured out shortly. He got it right.

John *understood* that the establishment of the kingdom was imminent. He got it right.

John *understood* that the time of the harvest was present. Jesus confirmed that (John 4:35). Thus, John got it right.

John *understood* that the Day of the Lord was to be the impending national judgment on Israel. He got it right.

In light of everything *that John got right*, we ask again, upon what basis do we charge him with a failed eschatology, and a misunderstanding of the nature of the judgment, kingdom and resurrection?

---

    instructed them concerning the kingdom for forty days, opening their eyes to understand the scriptures (Luke 24:24f; 45f; Acts 1:4). If, after having their minds opened, and if, after forty days of that enlightened instruction, they still did not "get it" then perhaps Jesus should have gotten another set of apostles to carry on the task of kingdom proclamation!

As Jesus said, "It was necessary that the Christ should suffer" (Luke 24:46). Part of the offense of the gospel to many was that Israel's restoration, Israel's glory, Israel's salvation, was *supposed* to be accomplished through the martyrdom of John and by Jesus (not to mention the suffering of Jesus' "apostles, prophets and wise men"). The vindication of the suffering of all of the martyrs was to be, as foretold by Paul's foundational texts of appeal for Israel's salvation, at the coming of the Lord - salvation and judgment are joined. Did John not also know that his martyrdom was related to the eschaton? How could he know of Israel's OT prophecies and not know the connection? After all, he was a prophet, full of the Spirit from his mother's womb.

So, when we examine Romans 8, the promise of the restoration of all things at the vindication of, "the sufferings of this present time," we are remiss to ignore the critical role of John as Elijah, *a martyr of God*. Simply put:

☛ Romans 8 is about the "restoration of all things."

☛ That restoration would be accomplished at the time of the, "adoption, to wit, the redemption of the body."

☛John, as Elijah was the herald of the "restoration of all things" at the Day of the Lord. Thus, John was a herald of the resurrection - which is nothing other than "the restoration."

☛John said the Day was near.

☛The Day that John proclaimed, as *The Messenger and Elijah*, was national judgment on Israel.

☛That Day would be the time of the vindication of the suffering of, "the now time" in Romans 8:18f.

☛The Day of the Lord in vindication of the suffering of "the now time" of Romans 8 came in the national judgment of Israel in AD 70 - (Matthew 23). It did come soon. John was vindicated as a prophet.

☛ Therefore, the "restoration of all things," and the "glory" (versus the shame of suffering) arrived in AD 70.

That means that the promised "restoration" - no matter what our concept of that might be[132] - was to occur in the national judgment of Israel in fulfillment of Malachi 3-4. That is the Day that John / *The Messenger* / *Elijah* proclaimed.

I think it is evident then that Paul posits the restoration / redemption at the time of martyr vindication, and his use of so many powerful indicators of imminence should not be ignored by modern exegetes, in spite of traditional prejudices that claim he was speaking of the restoration of material creation.

Another critical factor to consider about Romans 8 is that Paul was anticipating the consummation of Israel's eschatological hope. His hope was "the redemption of the body" which of course, he said was found in Moses, the Law and the prophets" (Acts 24:14f). This means that where ever we posit the fulfillment of Romans 8, it must fit within a context in which Israel remains as God's covenant people.

Dunn took note of this: "Paul is clearly talking about the fulfillment of Israel's promises." (1988, 467). This is explicitly stated in Romans 11:27, where Paul, citing Isaiah 59, says that *Israel's salvation would be in fulfillment of His covenant with them*: "This is my covenant with them, when I take away their sin." Israel's salvation would only come by means of the fulfillment of God's covenant with Israel.

I fail to see how anything could more clearly establish the truth of the concept of *Torah to Telos* than what Isaiah / Paul says about Israel's salvation. God would consummate Israel's salvation history *in fulfillment of His covenant promises to her*. That salvation would occur at the coming of the Lord. Thus, God's covenant with Israel would stand firm until the coming of the Lord. This is *prima facie*, *Torah To Telos*.

---

[132] Gary DeMar comments on the need to honor the imminence of "the glory about to be revealed": "The New American Standard translation does not catch the full meaning of this passage. Following Robert Young's Literal Translation of the Bible, we read, 'For I reckon that the sufferings of the present time are not worthy to be compared with the glory about to be revealed in us.' Whatever the glory is, it was 'about to be revealed' (see Revelation 2:10; 3:2, 10; 10:4; 12:4; 17:8). Peter tells his readers that the 'Spirit of glory and of Christ rests on you' (1 Peter 4:14). This was a present condition, not something that the people in Peter's day would have to wait for a future rapture." (*Madness*, 1994, 191).

Those paradigms that say - as both Amillennialism and Postmillennialism does - that Israel is no longer God's covenant people, and yet, they posit the fulfillment of Romans 8 and Romans 11 in the future, are patently illogical. If Israel's salvation is yet future, *then Israel remains God's covenant people, and we thus have a Two Covenant doctrine in Paul.* Yet, Paul and the rest of the NT writers had one (covenant) hope and that hope sprang from Moses, the law and the prophets.[133]

Wright castigates the Two Covenant doctrine as ultimately being anti-Semitic:

> "The two-covenant position says precisely what Paul here forbids the church to say, namely that Christianity is for non-Jews."[134] Yet, logically, to affirm a future resurrection, a yet future new creation, a yet future parousia, is to affirm that Israel's promises found in Torah, remain valid. God's covenant with Israel - every jot and every tittle - remains in effect. This is in fact, a Two Covenant Doctrine. Moo likewise rejects the two covenant idea noting from Romans 11 that: "There is only one tree." (1996, 725).

But, if, as is clear, Paul was anticipating the fulfillment of Israel's covenant promises, Israel's eschaton, does this not take us back to Deuteronomy 32, as well as the ministry of John and his expectation of the Great Day of the Lord? Does this not posit the climax of Israel's covenant history in the arrival of the

---

[133] Dispensationalism teaches, sometimes implicitly, sometimes explicitly, that there will yet be (if there isn't already) a Two Covenant reality. Many leading Dispensationalists (e.g. Thomas Ice and others) deny that the promised New Covenant of Jeremiah 31 has been established. It will not be made until the Second Coming and in the Millennium. That covenant will demand animal sacrifices, temple worship, physical circumcision, festal pilgrimages, etc.. Yet, all of those things are forbidden for Christians under the Gospel! Thus, Christians have one covenant, Israel has another in the Millennium. The practical - not to mention the theological - contradictions in this paradigm are manifold, as I show in my book, *The New Covenant: Fulfilled or Future?* Available on Amazon, Kindle, my websites and at other retailers.

[134] N. T. Wright, *Climax of the Covenant*, (Minneapolis, Fortress, 1993)253+.

New Creation? How do we honor the eschatological narrative of the Song and Paul's emphasis on the (first century) fulfillment of Israel's promises, and then extend the fulfillment of Romans 8 & 11 far beyond the end of Israel's covenant in AD 70 - to a supposed end of the Christian age? After all, Hebrews affirmed, 2000 years ago, that Torah, God's distinctive covenant with Israel, was "nigh unto passing" (Hebrews 8:13). The extrapolation of the passing of Torah, or the fulfillment of Torah, into the distant future clearly creates a Two Covenant theology.

We need to be very clear at this juncture. The Abrahamic Covenant preceded Torah (Galatians 3). Those promises to Abraham were subsumed / assimilated into Torah and continued on.[135] But Paul is very clear that God's promises to Abraham would not and could not be fulfilled *through* the Law of Moses. Instead, the Law of Moses was the "school-master" to lead to Christ, the promised Seed, through whom the promises would be received (Galatians 3:18f).

The key point is that the Abrahamic promises of the New Creation, resurrection life, salvation, would come, not at the end of the Christian age, but, "at the time appointed by the Father" (Galatians 4:1-4) - which would be at the end of the Mosaic Covenant: "After the faith has come, we are no longer under a school-master" (Galatians 3:24f). Torah would endure until the time of the inheritance! Thus, Israel's salvation - the reception of the Abrahamic promises - would come at the end of Torah. This is *Torah to Telos*.

So, when today, it is suggested that Israel's salvation is yet future, that it will not occur *until the end of the Christian age*, this is a gross miscarriage of covenant understanding. It is through the New Covenant of Messiah that the promises of Abraham are realized. But, to reiterate, when a person says that we are waiting on Israel's salvation, they are thereby implying that Torah remains valid, and that the Gospel likewise is in force– a Two-Covenant Doctrine.

Torah is not, however, the Gospel of Christ, and the Gospel of Christ is not Torah. The Gospel is the fulfillment of God's promises to Abraham and to Israel. Paul affirmed that covenant transformation was taking place through his

---

[135] Zechariah, John's father, saw during his own prophetic declaration of the mission of his son, that the Abrahamic covenant promises were to be fulfilled through John's ministry (Luke 1:72f). He saw the predictions of Israel's salvation as a continuation of that covenant, as well as the fulfillment of all the prophets who ever spoke.

ministry (2 Corinthians 3:16-4:1-2). But, he also said that the Old Covenant Law of Moses was "nigh unto passing," meaning that "the ministration of death" was nigh unto passing. This means that the "better resurrection" of life promised to Abraham was about to be revealed. We are not, today, waiting for the termination of Torah so that the Inheritance might be our's. What is more, we are not waiting for the end of the Gospel age so that we can receive the promises of Abraham. We are, through faith in the promised Seed of Abraham, participants in the Inheritance. Torah has passed.

There is a final connection to make. Paul's "redemption of creation" is patently the restoration of all things foretold by Peter in Acts 3. I know of no commentators that deny this. This being true, I suggest that we are, once again, firmly within the context of the fulfillment of John, *The Messenger* of Malachi 3. Here is why.

In Acts 3:19f, Peter called on Israel to "repent, and be *converted*" (from *epistrepho* - literally, "turn again"). We can, I posit, hear an echo of Malachi 3:7 in that sermon. This is true because John, as *The Messenger* was to call on Israel and offer the Lord's invitation: "Return *(from epistrepho, LXX)* to me, and I will return *(epistrepho)* to you."

A quick note here: The motif of returning to the Lord so that He might "return" to Israel is common in the OT. It is found in Joel 2:12-14; Zechariah 1:3; Hosea 5-6, and other texts. In each case, YHVH had "departed" from Israel *by withdrawing covenant blessings*. In one case, Ezekiel 10, the Shechinah Glory departed the temple. The promise was always made that if / when Israel repented, the Lord would "return" to her. What is to be noted, and what is consistent with the nature of John's message as *The Messenger*, is that in the OT, neither the departure or the return of the Lord was ever a bodily, physical presence, departure or return. This has a direct bearing on our understanding of the promise of Christ's parousia - and Romans 11.

In Malachi 3, Adonai was inviting Israel to repent and to turn back to Him by turning away from their sins, the sins of verses 5f (violation of Torah). His invitation was both gracious and foreboding. Repentance would lead to the restoration of covenant blessings (cf. Malachi 3:18f). Failure and refusal to turn back to Him would lead to the judgment of verse 5f - national judgment. One way or another, YHVH would "come" either in blessings or in judgment, but, He *was* coming! So, in Malachi 3 we have the call "repent and turn again." That was John's message as *The Messenger*.

In Acts 3, Peter called on Israel to "repent and turn again."[136] Was Peter making an offer different from John as *The Messenger*? No, John was *The Messenger*, offering the invitation and prospect of the "return" of YHVH of Malachi and that powerfully suggests that the promise of the parousia in Acts 3 must be viewed within the purview of John's message of the imminent kingdom / judgment.[137] If this connection is valid, the nature of the parousia and the nature of the restoration of all things is firmly established as being the restoration of covenant relationship in Messiah - not the restoration of material creation.

And there is another, very direct link between John as *The Messenger* and *Elijah* and Acts 3.

Peter spoke of, "the restoration of all things spoken of by all the prophets." This patently puts us into the realm of the anticipation of the hope of Israel – the message of John as Elijah - who was to call Israel to "obey the Law of Moses." It tells us that Peter's eschatological hope was grounded in Torah and God's promises to Israel. That hope is called the "restoration of all things."

The word "restoration" is from *apokatastasis*. The disciples used a verbal form of this word when they asked Jesus, "will you at this time *restore* the kingdom to Israel" (Acts 1:6). This word and this hope is directly linked with the mission and message of John as Elijah.

It should be remembered that as Jesus and the disciples came down from the Transfiguration Mount that Jesus told the disciples not to tell anyone what they had seen. Their response was to ask Jesus why the scribes spoke of the coming

---

[136] We cannot miss the fact that in Malachi the Messenger / Elijah would call on Israel to "obey the Law of Moses" (Malachi 4:4f). In Acts 3, Peter tells Israel that obedience to Torah meant acceptance of Jesus as Messiah.

[137] Note also that John urged his audience to repent in light of the impending judgment, "the wrath about to come." In Acts 3, Peter told his audience that if they would repent, the Lord would grant them, "times of refreshing (*anapsuxeos*). F. F. Bruce says this word indicated, "Repentance would bring the people of Jerusalem a respite from the judgment foretold by Jesus, as it brought the Ninevites a respite from the destruction announced by Jonah" (F. F. Bruce, *New International Commentary on the New Testament, Acts*, (Grand Rapids, Eerdmans, 84, n. 38). So, John and Peter were offering the same thing.

of Elijah. Jesus said the scribes were correct and, "Elijah must come first and *restore* all things" (Matthew 17:12– He used a cognate of the same word found in Acts 1 and Acts 3). He informed them that Elijah had already come, and they realized that he was referring to John the Baptizer.

So, John, as Elijah, had the mission and message of, "the restoration (*cognate of apokatastasis*) of all things." After Jesus' resurrection and after forty days of inspired instruction about the kingdom, the disciples asked Jesus if the time had come for the restoration (cognate of *apokatastasis*) of the kingdom. Then, in Acts 3, Peter called on his audience to repent so that the restoration (*apokatastasis*) of all things would come at the parousia. The parallels between John, as *The Messenger / Elijah* and Acts 3 are more than impressive then.[138]

The Messenger / Elijah (Malachi 3-4) would call on Israel to repent and turn again (*epistrepho*) to the Lord, so that He would turn back (*epistrepho*) to them (Malachi 3:7).

The Messenger / Elijah, (Malachi 3-4), i.e. John the Baptizer, would call on Israel to repent and turn again, "lest I come and smite the earth with a curse" (Malachi 4:4f). John warned his audience to repent to avoid, "the wrath about to come" (Matthew 3:7).

Peter called on his audience to repent and turn again (*epistrepho*) so that the promised "restoration (*apokatastasis*) of all things" could be consummated at the parousia. So, just as John, as *The Voice, The Messenger* and *Elijah* had declared the imminence of the kingdom / restoration of all things at the Day of the Lord, Peter directly echoed Malachi and the ministry of John. Consider then the following:

---

[138] Once again we can see the "disconnect" in the literature in regard to the connections between John's message and the rest of the NT teaching on eschatology. F. F. Bruce alludes to the fact that the apostles asked about the "restoration of Israel" in Acts 1:6, and that it is possible to see Acts 3:19f as related to that restoration. However, he never investigates those connections and never addresses the potential implications of conflating John's ministry with Acts and the story of the salvation of Israel. He does not even mention any relationship between John, the restoration of Israel and Romans 11. (F. F. Bruce, *New International Commentary on the New Testament*, (Grand Rapids, Eerdmans, 1990) in loc.

The redemption of creation in Romans 8 is the restoration of all things in Acts 3 - where Peter echoed Malachi and the ministry of John as *The Messenger* and *Elijah*.

Elijah was to come and, "restore (*verbal form of apokatastasis*) all things." The disciples came to realize - and modern exegetes need to know - that John was *Elijah*, (who had preached the imminence of the kingdom - *which was the promised restoration*). After forty days of kingdom instruction from Jesus they asked if the time had come for the promised restoration to be realized.[139]

In fulfillment of John's promise made in Matthew 3, the apostles were baptized in the Spirit, meaning that the kingdom was being inaugurated,[140] and the Day

---

[139] The disciples were not, in spite of common claims by commentators, (e.g. F. F. Bruce, *New International Commentary on the New Testament, Acts*, (Grand Rapids, Eerdmans, 1990)35f), chided for their eager expectation of the kingdom. In fact, they were given to know that the time was very, very short, because they were told to go into Jerusalem where they would receive the promise of the Spirit - *the promise made by John the Baptizer!* (And thus, John's message as eschatological prophet continued beyond his martyrdom. His message was: coming wrath / reward / kingdom and Spirit. These are the motifs / themes in Acts 1 and following). In prophecy, the establishment of the kingdom would be empowered by the Spirit (Joel 2-3 / Isaiah 32 / Ezekiel 37:12f). So, when Jesus told the disciples they would receive the empowering Spirit in just a few days, that was a powerful answer to their question about the "restoration of the kingdom"! Jesus had, as we have seen, opened their eyes to understand the scriptures, and he had instructed them for forty days about the kingdom (the kingdom that both John and Jesus had proclaimed was near). I propose that the disciples were now, after all of that instruction, keenly aware of the true nature of the kingdom, and knew that the time was upon them. As Pao says: "An understanding that suggests that the disciples misunderstood the nature of the kingdom must be rejected in light of Acts 1:3." David Pao, *Acts and the Isaianic New Exodus,* (Grand Rapids, Baker Academic, 200)95, n. 141.

[140] Remember that according to Ezekiel 37, YHVH would pour out His Spirit to "raise Israel from the dead" i.e. to end her exile by giving the New Covenant of peace. On Pentecost, the Spirit was poured out, the New Covenant began to be proclaimed, and the promised forgiveness of sin (of Isaiah 40 / Daniel 9) began to be

of the Lord was not far off.[141] Thus, Peter urged his audience: "Save yourselves from this untoward generation" (Acts 2:40).[142]

As in chapter 2, in chapter 3:19f, Peter called on his audience to repent and turn again to the Lord so that the restoration of all things at the parousia would be fully realized. Peter was promising the fulfillment of the invitation of Malachi 3:7 - the fulfillment of John's message.

The message of Acts 3, therefore, was the message of John, *The Messenger and Elijah*, who promised the imminent coming of the Lord in either blessing (the restoration) or judgment (The message of Malachi 3-4 and John).[143]

This means that the promised coming of Christ in Acts 3 was the imminent coming of Christ promised by John, as *The Messenger* and *Elijah*.

---

offered. It would be realized fully at the parousia (Romans 11:26f).

[141] See Keener's discussion of the relationship between the kingdom and the eschatological Spirit. He observes, "the disciples would have every reason to understand these two themes as inseparably linked" (Craig Keener, *Acts: An Exegetical Commentary*, Vol. I, (Grand Rapids, Baker Academic, 2012)682. I agree, but, the promise of the kingdom and the Spirit *belonged to John's ministry*. Thus, the discussion of those related themes in Luke and Acts must be viewed as extensions of John's message and influence.

[142] The outpouring of the Spirit and the gift of tongues were eschatological signs of the nearness of the Day of the Lord. See my *Into All The World, Then Comes the End*, for a discussion of this. The book is available from my websites, Amazon, Kindle and other retailers.

[143] Although these connections seem firm, I have found little discussion of John's mission in Acts 1-3, except for fleeting allusions. Keener has not a word about John in his massive volume on Acts 3-14 (Vol. II). He does have a discussion of John as Elijah in Vol. I that contains some excellent reference material on how the ancients viewed Elijah (2012, 713+). Yet, he does not develop the significance of John's ministry as it relates to the restoration of all things, and makes no mention at all of any relationship to the salvation of Israel in Romans 11.

If, as seems indisputable, Malachi 3-4 and John as *The Messenger* and *Elijah* does in fact lie behind Acts 1-3, it means that the, "redemption of creation" in Romans 8, and the coming salvation of Israel in Romans 11, must be viewed as *the coming day of national judgment proclaimed by John.* This demands, once again, a "re-calculation" of the current theological understanding of the parousia of Christ, "restoration of all things" and the "redemption of creation."

Romans 10 - They are Without Excuse

Romans 10 does not explicitly chronicle persecution of the church, but, it does speak eloquently of Israel's rejection of the gospel. Taken in the context of the rest of the epistle, as well as the prophetic background that Paul quotes from and applies to that rejection, there can be little doubt that persecution was present. Israel did not simply say, "No" to the gospel; they persecuted the, "apostles, prophets and wise men" sent by Jesus.

Not only that, Paul's citation of Isaiah 40, as described earlier in this work, shows that Paul was pointing the accusing finger at his beloved nation, telling them that they were without excuse for their recalcitrance.

But, there is a powerful underlying theme of persecution (even if it is implicit) in Romans 10 if we are attuned to it. In Romans 10:21f, Paul quotes from Isaiah 65:1-2, twice, to establish two things: First, the justification for his Gentile mission was that God had called, but Israel spurned His call. Second, to speak of Israel's rebellion against YHVH and the fact that their unbelief would lead to the filling up of the measure of their sin (cf. Isaiah 65:6f).This hearkens us back to the filling up of Israel's sin, foretold in the Song of Moses (Deuteronomy 31:29) and Matthew 23.

Paul not only appeals to Isaiah but, once again, to the Song of Moses, as he speaks of his Gentile mission and his hope for the salvation of Israel (Romans 10:19 / 11:11). Hays is surely correct to note that:

> "Deuteronomy provides a fundamental theological resource for Paul's attempt to explain the puzzling experience of his own missionary activity. Gentiles believe; Jews do not. What is happening here? Deuteronomy offers Paul not only the explanatory narrative pattern (covenant election, Israel's unfaithfulness, God's judgment followed by God's ultimate gracious act of reconciliation / new creation), but also the 'jealousy' theory, based on Deuteronomy 32:21, as an

explanation of God's surprising decision to bring many Gentiles to salvation before reclaiming unfaithful Israel."[144]

In other words, Paul calls on the Song of Moses for the justification of his Gentile mission. In this we can see a connection with the message of John. When the Pharisees and Sadducees came to him (ostensibly to be baptized to escape the "wrath about to come,"[145] John warned them:

> "But when he saw many of the Pharisees and Sadducees coming to where he was baptizing, he said to them: "You brood of vipers! Who warned you to flee from the coming wrath? Produce fruit in keeping with repentance. And do not think you can say to yourselves, 'We have Abraham as our father.' I tell you that out of these stones God can raise up children for Abraham. The ax is already at the root of the trees, and every tree that does not produce good fruit will be cut down and thrown into the fire." (Matthew 3:7-10).

We have here, in "Reader's Digest" form, Paul's, "they are not all Israel that are of Israel" (Romans 9:3f) - the idea that God was able to call both Gentiles as well as those in Israel to be His people - to create children from "stones."[146]

---

[144] Richard Hays, *Conversion of the Imagination*, (Grand Rapids, Eerdmans, 2005)181.

[145] The coming of the Sadducees to be baptized tells us a good bit about the nature of the "wrath about to come." The Sadducees did not believe in life after death. So, if they did not believe in a Day of the Lord that would send people to an eternal hell, it is patently clear that they were not coming to John to avoid such a thing! But, if they understood, based on the consistent OT descriptions of the Day of the Lord, that it would be a time of *national judgment*, this helps explain their willingness to at least entertain the idea of submission to John's baptism.

[146] I am convinced there is more going on with John's reference to raising up children from stones that is normally recognized. I wrote three articles addressing this. The first is found here: http://eschatology.org/index.php?option=com_content&view=article&id=1134:god-is-able-of-these-stones-to-raise-up-children-of-god-1&catid=23:new-articles

So, Paul justified his Gentile ministry by citing Deuteronomy 32 - which foretold the calling of the Gentiles due to Israel's rebellion. God had, from the very beginning of Israel's history, predicted Israel's last days rejection of His calling.[147] As a result, those, "who were not a people" would become the children of God. John and Paul were, in essence if not specifically, telling their audiences that the time had come. And this posits the fulfillment of Paul's eschatology firmly within the framework of the first century. Paul was not preaching a message that was different from John. He was, to be sure "fleshing it out" a good bit, but, it was the same message. When we honor that connection, we cannot posit the fulfillment of Paul's eschatology beyond the first century.

The Song - along with Isaiah 65 and a host of other OT prophecies - foretold Israel's rejection of God, just as Paul describes in Romans 10. That rejection would include the persecution of the righteous remnant. Yet, YHVH promised that in Israel's last days, He would, "avenge the blood of His saints" (Deuteronomy 32:43). That puts the salvation of Israel in AD 70.

We must remember that in Matthew 23, Jesus chronicled Israel's internecine history and said that the measure of her sin that had been accumulating through the centuries, would reach its zenith in his generation. That cup of sin would be filled in Israel's persecution of Jesus' "apostles, prophets and wise men." Well, in Romans 10, Israel was rejecting Jesus' apostles and prophets. Those apostles and prophets were being persecuted and slain:

> "Who shall separate us from the love of Christ? Shall trouble or hardship or persecution or famine or nakedness or danger or sword? As it is written: 'For your sake we face death all day long; we are considered as sheep to be slaughtered.'" No, in all these things we are more than conquerors through him who loved us. For I am convinced that neither death nor life, neither angels nor demons, neither the present nor the future, nor any powers, neither height nor depth, nor anything else in all creation, will be able to separate us from the love of God that is in Christ Jesus our Lord." (Romans 8:34-39).

---

[147] This indisputable fact falsifies the Dispensational claim that the Jewish rejection of the offer of the kingdom was unplanned and led to the un-predicted, unforeseen, establishment of the church for the calling of the Gentiles.

Here is a clear-cut expectation (and exultation) in the knowledge that their suffering was to be vindicated.

When we also add into the equation what Paul said in 1 Corinthians 4:9, then we will realize that we cannot divorce Paul's discussion of Israel's unbelief in Romans 10 from the first century *sitz em leben*[148] of persecution of the church. Paul's comments in 1 Corinthians 4:9 have been perplexing to the commentators, but it is mostly because of the presuppositional views that demand a yet future, end of time eschaton. Note what the apostle said:

> "For I think that God has displayed us, the apostles, last, as men condemned to death; for we have been made a spectacle to the world, both to angels and to men."

These are stunning, challenging words! Was Paul a self-deluded apocalyptic messenger like those mentioned in Acts 5? Was Paul an ego-centric, delusional apostle of Jesus? After all, as many commentators have noted, there have been countless martyrs who have suffered for their faith since the death of the apostles and Paul. But, that is not the point. The point is the filling up of the measure of eschatological suffering (Matthew 23 / Revelation 6:9f).

Robertson says Paul's language suggests, "There is a great pageant in which the Apostles form the ignominious finale, consisting of doomed men who will have to fight in the arena till they are killed."[149]

This passage, 1 Corinthians 4:9, conflates with Jesus' prediction in Matthew 23 in a powerful way, and is, we aver, directly related to Paul's reference to, "the sufferings of the now time." That ties the entire discussion to the martyrdom of John as well. Jesus emphasized that the measure of sin would be filled by Israel when he sent his *apostles* to her and she killed them. In Corinthians, Paul says the *apostles* had been set forth by God, *last of all*, as men condemned to die.

---

[148] This term means the "life situation" or as we would express it, "the real world situation," of the first century as Paul and the NT writers described what was happening to them. Far too often, modern Bible students seem not to even understand the concept of original audience relevance.

[149] Robertson and Plummer, *International Critical Commentary*, First Corinthians, (Edinburgh, T and T Clark, 1978)85.

As already noted, Paul does not mean that he and the apostles would be the last to ever suffer martyrdom. He meant that *the eschatological measure of suffering* would be filled by their death, and then God's eschatological Wrath - the Day of the Lord – would come. Just as Revelation 6:9-11 promised the martyrs vindication when the full number of martyrs was reached, Paul posited the apostles as the pivotal players, *and he emphatically*, as the last ones to die. To extend the filling of the measure of the "afflictions of Christ" into a distant future is to ignore Paul's emphasis on his distinctive role, and, it ignores the limitations set by Jesus.[150]

We must see also, as noted elsewhere in this work, that in Revelation 6:17, John directly cites Malachi 3 when he queries "who shall stand before Him" in reference to the impending vindication of the martyrs at the Day of the Lord. So, Paul said the martyrdom of the apostles would fill the measure of eschatological martyrdom. When the measure of last days martyrdom was full, the Great Day of the Lord, when no man could stand before Him would come. That Great Day of the Lord, when no man could stand, was to be the time of national judgment of Israel, when all the blood of all the righteous, all the way back to creation would be avenged (Malachi 3:1-6; Matthew 23:29f). This patently dates Revelation to pre-AD 70, and demands a first century fulfillment of the salvation of Israel, since John, *The Messenger*, who heralded that Great Day, was also *The Voice* who proclaimed the impending salvation of Israel.

The eschatological nature of Paul's task is seen in the word θλιπσις, (*thlipsis*), examined above. In response to the disciples' question about a sign of the end, Jesus promised that they would be delivered up to "tribulation" (Matthew. 24:9, 21; cf. Daniel 12:1). This word is never used of Christ's expiatory work.

I think Munck's assessment of the apostle to the Gentiles points us in the right direction. Take note of some of his comments:

---

[150] In my debate with James Jordan (October, 2004), Jordan agreed that the martyrs in Revelation 6-19 were pre-70 martyrs and that God's wrath was consummated in the judgment of Old Covenant Israel. However, he insisted that Revelation 20 suggests a different set of martyrs to be filled up *beginning in AD 70* and consummated at the end of the current Christian age. As I noted, this creates a disjunction in Revelation. John sees no further than the judgment of Babylon in his vindication of the martyrs and that was in AD 70.

"It cannot be sufficiently stressed that with Paul it is not a matter of a call to apostleship in general, but of a clearly defined apostleship in relationship to the Gentiles. His personal call coincides with an objective eschatological necessity, namely God's plan that the gospel is to be preached to the Gentiles before the end of the age."[151]

"The call to the other apostles has an eschatological character, as they are to prepare the way for the coming of the Messianic age; but, in Paul's case the apostolic consciousness reaches a greater intensity than in the case of any other apostle or any Old Testament prophet. In a way he is called to play the part of the prophetic herald in the sense of Jewish apocalyptic thought." — "Paul regards himself as the one on whom the arrival of the Messianic age depends" (41).

"Paul is not only the one who knows what God's plan is and can tell of it, but the one by whose action this fulness is to be brought about." .... "Paul's work was more important than that of all the apostles who went to the Jews and were turned away by that impenitent nation. Where their work failed, the way of salvation provided for Israel will become a reality through Paul's work for the Gentiles. This also means that the apostles work is more important than that of all the figures in Old Testament redemptive history, because he has been appointed by God to fill the key position in the last drama of redemption" (43).[152]

---

[151] Johannes Munck, *Paul and the Salvation of Mankind*, (Richmond, John Knox, 1959)40. While Munck made these comments about Paul's self consciousness, ultimately, Munck believed that Paul's eschatological hope failed.

[152] I am convinced that Munck is right in his assessment of Paul and his eschatological role. To emphasize this, I posit that the "fullness of the Gentiles" was Paul's personal stewardship to accomplish (Colossians 1:24-27). This adds further credence to the thesis of this work, that the salvation of Israel had to be accomplished in the first century. I will not develop that here, but, I discuss it in-depth in my *Who Is This Babylon?* work, which is available on my websites, on Amazon, Kindle and other retailers.

Dunn says: "Paul understood his apostleship in eschatological terms as the last act on the stage of this world before (as we would say) the final curtain (particularly 1 Corinthians 4:9). It was because Paul saw himself as a (*the*) major actor in the final drama of God's reconciling purpose that he could also see his all too real sufferings as somehow bringing to completion what was still outstanding of the sufferings of Christ."[153]

Paul's claim to be the final, pivotal player in the eschatological schema magnifies the ubiquitous New Testament problem of the *naherwartung* – the imminent expectation of the parousia. Given Paul's view of himself[154] as the critical "last days" figure, Green's posit that, "There was a sense of imminence of the Return, which was not however, associated with temporal proximity,"[155] is untenable. Paul patently believed that the end was near. The end was tied directly to the completion of his ministry (Romans 13:11f; 2 Timothy 4:16f). It was likewise tied to the promise of the imminent vindication of those first century persecutions at the hands of Israel, who had become the enemy of God.

If Paul played a role as pivotal, end-time martyr in the fulfillment of eschatological expectation this forces us to look at Romans 11 within the temporal purview of Paul's ministry. His ministry - and his suffering - were eschatological to the core.

---

[153] James D. G. Dunn, *The New International Greek Testament Commentary*, (Grand Rapids, Eerdmans, 1996)114+. Dunn was alluding to Colossians 1:24f where Paul said that he - distinctively he - had been given the stewardship of filling up the measure of the suffering of Christ. This plays directly into the martyrdom motif in Romans 8.

[154] Some (e.g. W. D. Davies, *The Gospel and the Land*, Berkeley, University of California Press, 1974) 208+) maintain that in his early ministry Paul believed the end was near but that later in life he expressed more uncertainty. If, however, he saw his ministry as vital to the eschatological schema this posit is wrong. (See also Dunn, 1996, 116).

[155] Michael Green, *Evangelism in the Early Church*, (Grand Rapids, Eerdmans, 1970)268.

Many commentators recognize the eschatological nature of Paul's afflictions. Yet, the Biblical testimony concerning *Israel's* central role in filling the measure of that suffering and sin is ignored.[156] Surprisingly, not one commentator consulted correlates Paul's statement in 1 Corinthians 4:9 or Colossians 1:24 to Matthew 23. Only two correlate Colossians with Revelation and 1 Thessalonians 2: 14-16, and that was only in passing. Further, the Baptizer's martyrdom and its role in the end time schema is all but ignored. Yet, all these texts contain the identical motif.

Paul's pivotal role as end time martyr, in light of *Israel* as the key player in that persecution, sheds light on the nature of the eschatological "wrath to come" (Romans 2 / 5; 1 Thessalonians 1:10 / 1 Thessalonians 2:14-16) so eagerly anticipated by the apostle. It likewise adds emphasis - and provides parameters for - Paul's expectation of, "the glory about to be revealed," in contrast to, and as vindication of, "the suffering of the now time." But, if Paul's role was pivotal, then assuredly, John's role was as well, for he was also an end time martyr. John and Paul were rejected by Israel, and like their master, martyred by Old Covenant Israel.

So, while martyrdom is not specifically mentioned in Romans 10, it nonetheless is very much present. It most assuredly is present, as we have seen, in the chapters before chapter 8, and it is also present in the passages afterward. When we correlate what Paul said about filling the measure of martyrdom and what Jesus said about martyrdom and the filling up of the measure of eschatological suffering, it points us directly to the judgment of Old Covenant Jerusalem in AD 70.
So, Paul's discussion of Israel's unbelief and rejection of the gospel in Romans 10 carries with it the powerful, even if implicit, story of eschatological martyrdom. And his citations of the Song of Moses and Isaiah 65 confirm that.

---

[156] Dispensational writers are guilty here (Postmillennial and Amillennial writers likewise ignore this issue). In Millennialism especially, Israel is the "innocent victim" in the end times, being persecuted by the proposed Man of Sin. Yet, when we look closely at the passages of appeal, it is invariably Israel that is guilty of persecuting the followers of Christ! It is always, without exception, Israel that is the persecutor, not the victim of persecution by a pagan entity. This is incredibly important, but seldom noted.

Paul is not just capriciously, arbitrarily or carelessly citing Deuteronomy, Isaiah or other OT prophecies, as some scholars have suggested. He was not just "proof-texting." He was not simply lifting terms and phrases out of the OT that conveniently sounded good in his discussion, but which in reality had nothing to do with his discussion. Paul was saying that what those OT prophets foretold was being fulfilled. He was living in the days foretold by Deuteronomy and by Isaiah.

Hays notes the tendency of a lot of NT commentators: "Most NT scholars have tended to assume that Paul merely exploited the OT as a collection of oracular proof texts, without regard for the original context; thus, the idea that Paul read any individual OT book as a literary or theological unity has seldom been entertained" (2005, 25).

But, this kind of approach to not only Paul, but Jesus and the rest of the NT writers flies in the face of their declarations that they were in fact living in the days, and witnessing the events, foretold by the OT prophets (see Matthew 13:17; Acts 2:15f / 3:23f, etc.).

Beale asks, in discussion of how the NT writers used the Old:

> "Should not those with a high view of scripture begin with the assumption that the NT interprets the OT contextually and with hermeneutical integrity? Accordingly, if an OT passage quoted in the NT is a prophecy in its original context, would not a NT author also see it as a prophecy, and would he not see it as a beginning fulfillment if he identifies the prophecy with some reality in his own present time?) ... "Possibly a NT writer could use the OT analogically, but, the weight of the prophetic context of the OT passages tilts toward the notion of fulfillment, if there is no clear evidence to the contrary in the NT context. If this is a correct hermeneutical approach, then the prophecies discussed in this chapter about Israel's land being widened to include the whole earth have an already-not yet fulfillment in the NT."[157]

---

[157] Greg Beale, *A New Testament Biblical Theology*, (Grand Rapids, Baker Academic, 2011)772.

If these comments are correct, and they clearly are, then Paul envisioned himself living in the very day of the fulfillment of the Song, Isaiah and all of Israel's promises. That meant he believed firmly that *Israel's salvation was at hand*, and would take place at the coming of the Lord in vindication of the martyrs. There can be no doubt about when that was.

Romans 12:10-19

> "Be kindly affectionate to one another with brotherly love, in honor giving preference to one another; not lagging in diligence, fervent in spirit, serving the Lord; rejoicing in hope, patient in tribulation, continuing steadfastly in prayer; distributing to the needs of the saints, given to hospitality. Bless those who persecute you; bless and do not curse. Rejoice with those who rejoice, and weep with those who weep. .... Repay no one evil for evil. Have regard for good things in the sight of all men. If it is possible, as much as depends on you, live peaceably with all men. Beloved, do not avenge yourselves, but rather give place to wrath; for it is written, "Vengeance is Mine, I will repay," says the Lord.

Paul was extremely concerned about the plight of the Roman church enduring tribulation.[158] Observe the content of his *paranesis*.

1. He urges them to persist in prayer. This hearkens us back to Luke 18, where Jesus told the parable of the importunate widow. He had warned his disciples that times of persecution were coming, therefore, they ought always to pray. His discussion there centered on the prayer of the martyrs, "who cry out to Him day and night (v. 7). But, Jesus promised, "He will avenge them speedily" (v. 8 - *en taxei*, meaning soon, speedily, shortly[159]).

---

[158] Moo says, "we have no evidence that the Roman Christians were at this time going through any special time of persecution." He concludes from this that Paul was issuing a "general command" for Christians of all ages. (1996,780). But this position is an overt denial of the language of the text that affirms that the Romans *were* being persecuted!

[159] The term *en tachei* does not, in spite of some who say to the contrary, emphasize rapidity of action instead of the imminence of

If Paul was, as Dunn suggests, (1988, 743) echoing Luke 18, do we not have the right to suggest that Paul had the same imminent judgment for the vindication of the suffering saints in mind that Jesus promised? If so, Paul had the impending judgment of Israel in mind.

2. Paul urged them to not retaliate against those who were persecuting them (Keep in mind that it was *not* the Roman authorities) and assured them, "Vengeance is mine, I will repay' says the Lord." This is a direct quote of Deuteronomy 32:35[160] and as such, puts Paul's promise of vindication squarely in the context of the soon coming judgment of Old Covenant Jerusalem - just as John, *The Voice*, *The Messenger* and *Elijah* had proclaimed.

Wright calls the Song of Moses, "a vital chapter in this great story" of Israel (Vol. 1, 2013, 77). Wagner cites Mendenhall who calls the Song, or more correctly the entire book of Deuteronomy, "the bible of the prophetic movement" (2003, 201, n. 242). What he means by this is that Deuteronomy lies behind and serves as the fountain from which the message of the prophets flowed.

Hays tells us, "Deuteronomy 32 contains Romans *in nuce*."[161] Wagner calls our attention to how extensively Paul draws on the Song of Moses in Romans[162] (as well as in other of his epistles). In fact, Wagner indicates that Deuteronomy 32

---

occurrence. That claim is not supported by the instances of its use in the NT. See my detailed examination of the term in my *Who Is This Babylon?* The book is available on Amazon, Kindle, my websites and other retailers.

[160] The identical verse from the Song is quoted in Hebrews 10 where the saints were being persecuted. The author cited the Song twice, and then promised, "And now, in a very, very little while, (*micron, hosan, hosan*) the one who is coming will come and will not tarry." Very clearly, the author expected the imminent fulfillment of Deuteronomy 32, the prediction of the vindication of the martyrs in Israel's last days. And it did happen as predicted.

[161] Richard Hays, *Echoes of Scripture*, (New Haven and London, Yale University Press, 1989)164.

[162] Wagner lists no less than five citations of the Song in the book of Romans: (32:21 / 32:35 / 32:43 / 32:4 / 32:21f. (192, n. 216).

was paradigmatic for Paul's view of the end times:[163] "The Song addresses events that will befall Israel 'at the end of days' (31:29; 32:20), the time period in which Paul believes that he and his readers are now living"[164] (2002, 193).

So, if Paul envisioned himself living in the last days foretold by the Song of Moses, and if he was anticipating the fulfillment of the Song's prediction of the vindication of the martyrs in those last days, this is determinative that Paul had the impending judgment of Israel in mind in Romans 12:17f.[165] But of course, that would mean, since judgment and salvation go hand in hand, that Paul believed the salvation of "all Israel" in Romans 11 was likewise to take place in AD 70.

Romans 13:11-12

> "And do this, knowing the time, that now it is high time to awake out of sleep; for now our salvation is nearer than when

---

[163] It is significant that while many commentators take note of Paul's citation of the Song of Moses, I have found extremely few who have examined the implications of that citation. Wagner comes closest, yet does not fully develop it. If Paul meant to convey that the Song was about to be fulfilled in the vindication of the suffering of the Roman brethren, it meant that he had in mind the consummation of Israel's covenant age. This demands that we must interpret Romans 12 - indeed, the entirety of Romans - within that covenant context.

[164] For whatever value it might be, Josephus also believed that the Song of Moses was being fulfilled in the first century events: "Moses recited to Israel a poem of hexameter verse, which he has moreover bequeathed in a book preserved in the temple, containing a prediction of future events, in accordance with which all has come and is coming to pass, the seer having in no whit strayed from the truth." (*Antiquities*, 4:303).

[165] This scenario also strongly suggests that Paul has "re-defined" Israel. For him, the true Seed (cf. Romans 9:3f) were those of faith, who had accepted Jesus as Israel's savior / deliverer. But, in that scenario, those of Old Covenant Israel then became the enemy of God through their rejection of Jesus and his gospel. They essentially became the pagans who would be defeated at the coming of the Lord. Compare what Peter had to say about the identity of "the people" in Acts 3:21f.

we first believed. The night is far spent, the day is at hand. Therefore let us cast off the works of darkness, and let us put on the armor of light."

Is this not the salvation of Romans 11:25-27? It is certainly the anticipation of the coming of salvation. It is the promise of salvation at the day of the Lord, just as in Romans 11. Is it not the vindication of the suffering of "this present time" of Romans 8? Is this not the arrival of the New Creation, the redemption of "creation"?

Paul said something quite stunning here. He said the Romans knew the time of the parousia! This falsifies the most common claim made by those who reject the imminence of the Day of the Lord in the first century. It is maintained that, "Since Jesus did not know the day and the hour of his coming, (Matthew 24:36) then none of the NT writers could know the time." How could Paul then, say that the Romans knew what "hour" (*hora*) it was, and how could he say (correctly) "the night is far spent, the Day has drawn near"? Furthermore, how could John so confidently say, "Little children, it is the last hour"? (1 John 2:18).

Those who appeal to Matthew 24:36 to negate or nullify the force of Paul's language and that of the other NT writers who unequivocally affirmed the nearness of the end, fail to consider the chronological time line of revelation. Here is what we mean.

When Jesus uttered the words in Matthew 24:36 they were appropriate due to his Incarnation.

Jesus told his disciples that he would go back to the Father who would send the Spirit, and the Spirit would reveal to them, "things to come" (John 16:7-13).

Every epistle that we have was written after the disciples received the revelatory Spirit.

In those letters, the writers affirmed, through the Spirit sent by the Father who knew the day and the hour, that the end was near.

This means that when Paul told the Romans, "the night is far spent, the Day is at hand" he was not denying Matthew 24:36. He was however, speaking from the perspective of one to whom the Father had revealed the time. The fact is that it is anachronous to apply Matthew 24:36 to the post-Pentecost writings of the men who received their knowledge of the time of the end from the Father who knew the time.

Perriman suggests:

> "What especially demands an explanation is the proximity to some decisive eschatological moment implied by the imagery of the approaching day and the explicit assertion that "salvation is nearer to us now than when we first believed" (13:11). The nearness of this 'salvation' however, it is to be understood, must be measured in relation to a period of time of no more than twenty years" (2005, 115).

To reiterate the citation of Nanos is appropriate (even in light of the fact that he posited a failed final eschatology at the feet of Paul):

> "Paul certainly expected the final events (Romans 8:18f; 1 Cor. 15; 1 Thess. 4:13-18) in his own lifetime. When he speaks of the pleroma of the Gentiles who are to come in and of Israel's return, he is thinking in terms of years– not even decades, let alone centuries or millennia. The preconditions for the final events were well underway.....Thus, when we read of Israel's trespass, failure, and rejection, we must remember that for Paul their duration was to continue for 20 years, not 2000. He cites Dunn (Romans, p. 18) – 'Paul seriously contemplated this outreach being achieved within his lifetime, as the last act before the end and the necessary preliminary to the salvation of Israel (1 Corinthians 4:9; Romans 11:13-32)." (*Mystery*, 1996, 278, n. 110).

Milton Terry offers this for those who attempt to mitigate the language of imminence:

> "When a writer says that an event will shortly and speedily come to pass, or is about to take place, it is contrary to all propriety to declare that his statements allow us to believe the event is in the far future. It is a reprehensible abuse of language to say that the words immediately, or near at hand, mean ages hence, or after a long time. Such a treatment of the language of

Scripture is even worse than the theory of a double sense."[166]

There really is no justification for denying the objective imminence of Paul's eschatological expectation.

Romans 16:20

In the NT, Satan is viewed as the great adversary and persecutor of the saints. He withstood Jesus (Matthew 4) tempting him to sin. Peter wrote his first epistle amidst the, "fiery trial that is among you" (1 Peter 4:12) and encouraged the saints to "Be sober, be vigilant, for your adversary the devil, as a roaring lion, walks about, seeking whom he may devour" (1 Peter 5:8). Likewise, the book of Revelation constantly points the accusing finger at Satan as the persecutor of the saints (Revelation 2:10; chapter 12; chapter 20), and his final defeat is at the Great Assize.

There is a connection in 16:20 that I find compelling, and yet, as with the connections between John the Baptizer and Romans 11, so far, I have not found a single commentator who makes the connection.

The link is with Isaiah 27:1-5:

> "In that day the Lord with His severe sword, great and strong, Will punish Leviathan the fleeing serpent, Leviathan that twisted serpent; And He will slay the reptile that is in the sea. In that day sing to her, "A vineyard of red wine! I, the Lord, keep it, I water it every moment; Lest any hurt it, I keep it night and day. Fury is not in Me. Who would set briers and thorns Against Me in battle? I would go through them, I would burn them together. Or let him take hold of My strength, That he may make peace with Me; And he shall make peace with Me."

There is little doubt that Isaiah speaks of the restoration of Israel here. It is the time of her salvation (cf. Isaiah 25:9-10; 26:1-3; 27:2f). So, the time of Israel's salvation is the time of the crushing of Satan – which is Romans 16:20. (And,

---

[166] Milton S. Terry, *Biblical Hermeneutics: A Treatise on the Interpretation of the Old and New Testaments* (New York: Phillips & Hunt, 1883), 495–496.

needless to say, the destruction of Satan in Revelation 20).

Where does Isaiah place that salvation? It would be "in that Day" when:

> "The Lord comes out of His place To punish the inhabitants of the earth for their iniquity; The earth will also disclose her blood, And will no more cover her slain."

This is the Day of the vindication of the martyrs of God! Isaiah says, "in that Day," the Day of the Lord's coming, Satan, that old serpent, would be crushed.

If Isaiah 27 (not to mention Genesis 3:15) lies behind Paul's promise in Romans 16, this once again places Romans and the promise of Israel's salvation in the framework of the AD 70 judgment of Old Covenant Israel, for shedding innocent blood.

When Paul speaks of the imminent crushing of Satan, it is a periphrastic manner of saying the Romans saints were about to be vindicated from, "the sufferings of the now time." This is the promise that fulfillment of Jesus' prediction of the vindication of all the martyrs was now at hand. And that would be in the judgment of Jerusalem in AD 70.

The commentators agree that Paul is sounding an eschatological note here. However, as just noted, I have not, as of this writing, found a single commentator that links Paul's comments to the Day of the Lord in Isaiah 27 / 59 and the time of the vindication of the martyrs.[167]

Dunn confirms the eschatological content of Romans 16:20:

> "The hope of Satan being "crushed under foot' is part of a larger eschatological hope for the final binding or defeat of the

---

[167] Cline, in a lengthy article on the crushing of Leviathan, sees that destruction of Satan as the time of the vindication of the martyrs. He posits that at the "end of time." Incredibly, in his entire discussion of the crushing of Satan and martyr vindication, he says not a word about Matthew 23 or Romans 16:20- or John. Meredith Cline, "Death, Leviathan, and Martyrs: Isaiah 24:1-27:1" in, "A Tribute to Gleason Archer," ed. by Walter C. Kaiser, Jr. and Ronald R. Youngblood. Chicago: Moody Press, 1986)229-249.

angelic power hostile to God...That there is an influence from Genesis 3:15 is probable, but not necessarily direct and quite likely through the influence of Genesis 3:15 the entire strand of Jewish hope (Ps. 91:13). It is hard to diminish the strong eschatological note here, and the note of imminence implied in the *en taxei*."[168]

While he acknowledges that Paul was speaking of the eschaton, Dunn avoids any serious discussion of the problem posed by that objective imminence and he does not propose a solution to the problem. He makes no connection between Romans 16, Isaiah 27, the crushing of Satan and the time of the vindication of the martyrs.[169]

Gentry offers this succinct comment,"Romans 16:20 hearkens back to the Adamic Covenant." (1992, 113). He likewise makes no connection with Isaiah 27 or the vindication of the martyrs.

Holland hints at the issue in Romans 16:20, and I think properly assesses the context and framework of fulfillment:

> "The use of the definite article with Satan *(ton Satanan)* found elsewhere in the NT (Matthew 12:26; Luke 10:18), suggests this is a description or title rather than a name. It is 'the Satan.' But, what does Paul mean by this? He could be referring to those he sees as the servants of Satan, who seek to undermine the work of God among the Romans. If this is correct, then Paul expects these troublemakers to come under some form of judgment. In Revelation 3:9, the apostle John records the words of the Jesus to the church at Philadelphia, 'I will make those who are the synagogue of Satan, who claim to be Jews though they are not, but are liars– I will make them come and to fall down at your feet and acknowledge that I have loved you.' Paul

---

[168] James D. G. Dunn, *Word Biblical Commentary, Romans 9-16, Vol. 38b*, (Dallas, Word Publishers, 1988)905.

[169] Dunn is not alone in not connecting the dots with Isaiah 27 and the promise of martyr vindication with Romans 16. In a survey of over 20 commentaries in my Logos Bible study program, I did not discover even one that made that connection.

has already compared the unbelieving Jewish community with Pharaoh (Romans 9:17-18). This picture given in Revelation is of the apostate Jewish nation serving the will of the state as it persecuted the church. (He cites Wright, *Perspectives* as corroboration). This situation could be reflected here, and if so, then the fall of Jerusalem in AD 70 would have been a significant blow to this unholy alliance."[170]

If Isaiah 27 serves as the fountain of Paul's promise of the salvation of Israel at the Day of the Lord in vindication of the martyrs, then once again, the thesis of this work is confirmed. It demands that the Day of the Lord for the salvation of Israel was the Day foretold by Jesus in Matthew 23 - AD 70.

Of course, all of this ties in with John's ministry and message. John was *The Voice* to declare the coming salvation of Israel at the Day of the Lord (Isaiah 40). The salvation of Israel would be at the Day of the Lord when Leviathan, that old serpent (the Devil) would be crushed (Isaiah 26:1-4; Isaiah 27:1-3). Isaiah 26:19-21 positively posits that at the time of the resurrection and vindication of the martyrs - and the time of the destruction of the city and temple.

So, Israel's salvation would be at the crushing of Satan.[171] The crushing of Satan would be at the time of the vindication of the martyrs. The vindication of the martyrs would be in the judgment of Old Covenant Jerusalem. Paul anticipated the crushing of Satan very shortly. That crushing of Satan would be the salvation of Israel in Romans 11:25f.[172] Therefore, the salvation of "all Israel" of Romans 11:25f was to be at the judgment of Old Covenant Jerusalem - the time of the

---

[170] Tom Holland, *Divine Marriage*, (Eugene, Ore., Pickwick, 2011)478.

[171] The crushing of Satan is patently the fulfillment of Genesis 3:15, which demonstrates that the Adamic problem was conflated / subsumed into the story of Israel, and the solution to that problem would be at the end of Torah.

[172] Here is the "good news - bad news" for Israel. She had become the adversary, Satan, and was about to be crushed. The righteous remnant would be saved: "Behold, therefore, the goodness and the severity of God!" (Romans 11:22).

crushing of the persecutor, Satan.[173]

Since John was *The Voice* to announce the Day of the Lord – the time when Israel's sin would be taken away (Isaiah 40:1-2), and since the time when Israel's sin would be taken away is Romans 11:25f – at the Day of the Lord - then John's message and ministry should be determinative for placing Romans 11 in the proper context, and that was imminent when John ministered and Paul wrote. Only by creating a bifurcated narrative about Israel's last days salvation at the Day of the Lord can one separate Paul's promise of the impending crushing of Satan and his discussion of the salvation of Israel - in fulfillment of John's message.

What we see then, in this brief survey of Romans and the promise of martyr vindication is that, while many commentators totally pass over how prominent this theme / issue is in the epistle, from the first of the book to the end, Paul is focused on that promised time of vindication. And he posits that vindication, the time of the "manifestation of the sons of God" at the coming of the Lord out of Zion, in fulfillment of God's Old Covenant promises found in the Song of Moses in Isaiah 26-27, Isaiah 59, 65-66 and other texts. It is helpful to note that this motif of suffering and the promise of imminent vindication / relief is found throughout the NT and that promised vindication is invariably posited at the judgment of Old Covenant Israel and coming very soon. We will list some of those texts here.

In Jesus' parabolic teaching, as well as his prosaic teaching, the promise of martyr vindication is prominent and invariably he spoke of the first century judgment of Old Covenant Jerusalem.

☛ **Matthew 21 and the Parable of the Wicked Vineyard workers.**
They killed the servants sent to them. They killed the Master's Son, and He would come and miserably destroy them. The Jerusalem leaders understood

---

[173] Needless to say, as suggested, this has a direct bearing on the dating and application of Revelation since the Apocalypse addresses the impending, imminent destruction of Satan, that old Serpent, the persecutor of the saints. That destruction would be at the Great Day of the Lord when no man could stand before Him (Revelation 6:12-17) a direct citation of Malachi 3:1-2, which leads us directly back to John as The Messenger, and his message of impending national judgment of Israel!

"that he spoke of them" (Matthew 21:40f).

☛ Matthew 22 and the Parable of the Great Wedding Banquet.
Those who had been invited mistreated and killed the servants sent to them. The Master of the Wedding sent out his armies, killed those wicked men and burnt their city.

☛ Matthew 23:29f
Jesus' discussion of Israel's internecine history climaxes with his prediction of the impending judgment that would occur in his generation. He said that all of the righteous blood, of all the righteous shed on the earth, all the way back to Abel,[174] would be judged and avenged in that catastrophic event. This text should be the guiding light through the often hazy task of eschatological discussions, because the theme of martyr vindication permeates many, if not most, of the major eschatological predictions.

☛ Luke 18:1-8
This text correlates perfectly with Matthew 23 and the promise that the martyrs would be vindicated "speedily." It is specious to try to avoid the objective imminence of Jesus' promise, especially when one conflates Luke 18 with Matthew 23.

☛ 2 Corinthians 4:8-16f
In verses 8f, the apostle described the apostolic suffering at the time but then promised, "Our light affliction, which is but for a moment, works in us a far more exceeding glory." Needless to say, this is the identical, "suffering of the

---

[174] Many commentators seek to depreciate the scope and significance of the judgment of Jerusalem in AD 70, by claiming it was strictly a "local judgment on the Jews." But, when one honors Jesus' language that claim is found to be totally specious. When one realizes that the martyrs that he mentions are the same martyrs found in Hebrews, where the writers gives the same "list" of martyrs, it is untenable to claim that the judgment of AD 70 was local with no "universal" implications. And since when did the geographical size of an event determine its meaning in God's eyes? Was not the crucifixion - and resurrection!! - not even more "local" than the destruction of Jerusalem? Would those who argue that the judgment of the city was insignificant due to its limited geographical nature thus argue that the Passion of Jesus was an even more insignificant even, given its even more "local" and unknown nature?

now time," versus the, "glory about to be revealed" in Romans 8.

The date of 2 Corinthians is generally thought to be circa 55-57 AD, meaning that it was not Roman persecution that Paul had in mind.

☛ Philippians 1:6, 28; 4:5
Paul promised that the Lord would perfect his work in them at the parousia, thus, they were to not be terrified by their adversaries (their persecutors) because, "the Lord is at hand."

The date of Philippians is generally thought to be circa 61 AD, meaning that it was not Roman persecution that Paul had in mind.

☛ Colossians 1:24-27
Paul's language in this text has perplexed the commentators for centuries. He said he- he *personally* and *emphatically* - was, "filling up in my flesh what is lacking in the afflictions (*thlipsis*) of Christ." When we view his comments through the prism of 1 Corinthians 4:9 and Matthew 23, the enigma disappears. He realized that he and the other apostles were the crucial, climactic players - the last in the Triumph Parade of martyrs - in God's end times schema. His language demands, since he and the apostles were the consummation of filling the measure of suffering,[175] that the promised vindication of that suffering, per Deuteronomy 32, was to be in Israel's final end (Deuteronomy 32:43).

The date of Colossians is generally thought to be circa 62 AD, meaning that it was not Roman persecution that Paul had in mind.

☛ 2 Thessalonians 1:7-12
This text, when viewed properly, powerfully communicated the reality of the first century persecution in contrast to the promise that the Thessalonians - not some far distant church - would be vindicated, "when the Lord Jesus is revealed from heaven." Language could hardly be more clear, emphatic and

---

[175] Take note of how Paul's comments in 1 Corinthians 4:9, and the dating (pre-Neronian persecution) and context of that suffering (i.e. at the hands of the Jews) plays into our understanding of Revelation. There, "Babylon" killed the apostles and prophets of Jesus (Revelation 18:20, 24). Her cup of sin was full (Revelation 17:6f), and judgment was about to fall.

unambiguous.[176]

The date of 2 Thessalonians is generally thought to be circa AD 51-53 AD, meaning that it was not Roman persecution that Paul had in mind.

Hebrews 10:32f
The author speaks of how the Hebrews brethren had suffered the loss of their goods, suffered ostracism and shame for their faith. However, just as Paul did in Romans 12, the author quoted from Deuteronomy 32 to promise that the Lord would avenge them at the Day of the Lord. Given the "Jewish" context and content of the book, and its provenance, we are safe to conclude that it was Jewish persecution that was taking place. Thus, it was entirely appropriate that the Song be cited. The promise of the imminent vindication of their martyrdom at the Day of the Lord was promised in the Song. And now, it was to be fulfilled "in a very, very little while, and the one who is coming will come and will not tarry" (v. 37).

Are we to suppose that the promised vindication of suffering that is promised in Hebrews is to take place at a different time, against different persecutors, from that which Paul promised in Romans? Is the "heavenly" inheritance, the "great reward" of "the promise" in Hebrews 10:35-39, a different glory, a different promise from the, "glory about to be revealed" in vindication of the, "suffering of the now time" in Romans 8? Where is the evidence to support such a view? Since both Paul in Romans 12 and Hebrews cites the same identical prophecy of the last days vindication of the martyrs in Israel's last days, I think we are logically compelled to posit fulfillment at the end of Israel's Old Covenant age.

The date of Hebrews is generally thought to be circa 63 AD, meaning that it was not Roman persecution that Paul had in mind. Furthermore, the intensely "Jewish" nature and context of the book suggests that it was not Roman persecution that the author had in mind.

James 5:6-10f
James writes to those being oppressed by the wealthy, and urges them to endure that persecution, "until the coming of the Lord" because ,"the parousia has drawn near" (James 5:6-8). Indeed, echoing Matthew 24:32, he tells them, "The

---

[176] See my book, *In Flaming Fire*, for an in-depth analysis of this text. The book is available on my websites, Amazon and other retailers.

Judge is standing right at the door."

The date of James is widely thought to have been written as early as 49 AD, meaning that it was not Roman persecution that James had in mind. Like Hebrews, James is concerned with issues that are related to Israel and the church's relationship with Jerusalem.

I Peter 1:5f

Peter's first epistle strongly echoes the message of Malachi (And Hosea). The reality of persecution is dominant in the epistle.[177] But, just as in each of the texts above, there is likewise the indisputable promise that the suffering saints would be avenged after they had suffered "a little while" (1 Peter 1:5f). The measure of suffering had to be, and was being, filled up (1 Peter 5:9), thus hearkening us back to Matthew 23 and 1 Thessalonians 2:14-16 and Revelation 6:9f.[178]

If Romans is concerned with the imminent martyr vindication at the coming of the Lord and if 1 Peter is about the imminent vindication of the martyrs at the coming of the Lord, how do we posit two different Days of the Lord separated by two millennia?

Peter assured his suffering audience that Jesus was, "ready (*hetoimos*) to judge the living and the dead" (1 Peter 4:5). He stated, in words too clear and emphatic to negate, "The end of all things has drawn near" (4:7). He tells them that the "appointed" time (*kairos*) for that promised *telos*, (*the* judgment[179]) had arrived (1 Peter 4:17).

---

[177] See Mark Dubis, *Messianic Woes in First Peter, Suffering and Eschatology in 1 Peter 4:12-19* – Studies in Biblical Literature, Vol. 33, (New York, Peter Lang, 2002), for an excellent discussion of how pervasive the theme of suffering and martyrdom is in 1 Peter.

[178] I am convinced that Revelation was written prior to 1 Peter and that Peter cites Revelation a good bit. I develop this in my *Who Is This Babylon?* book.

[179] Take note of Peter's use of the *anaphoric article* in verse 17, which means that Peter was affirming, unmistakably, that the time had arrived for the judgment of the living and the dead of verse 5.

I will not develop it here, but, there is a direct correspondence between Romans 8 and Paul's discussion of the, "suffering of the now time" versus the, "glory about to be revealed" and 1 Peter. As a matter of fact, a person could (and I currently am - 2016 - working on a MSS) create a parallel chart demonstrating those numerous, perfect parallels. When this is done, the overwhelming sense of imminence cannot be denied. And, given the pre-Neronian dating of both Romans and 1 Peter, the declarations of the imminent vindication of the suffering in both epistles points us directly to the fulfillment of Matthew 23 - AD 70.

The date of 1 Peter is generally thought to be circa 64 AD, meaning that it was probably not Roman persecution that Peter had in mind.

There is one final thought to offer here. 1 Peter cites Isaiah 40:6-8 as he writes to the "diaspora" (1 Peter 1:1). Isaiah 40 is a text about the "salvation of Israel" her "return from exile" - the focus of the ministry of John as *The Voice*. Peter's citation of Isaiah and his application of that text, indicates that he believed the restoration of Israel as promised by Isaiah - and *The Voice* - was taking place.

Dubis says that Peter,

> "Makes a remarkably bold claim here, and this should not be missed. By repeating Isaiah 40:8's use of *rhema*, First Peter draws a link between the *rhema* (word, DKP) of Isaiah 40 and the *rhema* of the gospel. In other words, when 1 Peter speaks of the *rhema* that was preached to them in the gospel, First Peter has in mind the specific *rhema* of Isaiah 40, namely the promise of restoration from exile. Thus, 1 Peter equates the good news of what has happened in Christ with Isaiah 40's glorious hope of Israel's restoration. For Peter, then, the long anticipated restoration of Israel has found (and, at the parousia, yet will fully find[180]) its realization in the readers of 1 Peter themselves. Identified as Israel, the readers currently experience Israel's

---

[180] Like most commentators, Dubis acknowledges that Peter spoke of the parousia as imminent. But, since he sees the parousia as an "end of time" event, he tacitly suggests Peter was wrong. This ignores the nature of the salvation that he agrees was underway and how that is related to John's message of the Day of the Lord as national judgment on Israel.

exile, but they will yet (and already are) experiencing Israel's eagerly expected restoration." (2002, 53).

Dubis fails to mention the fact that this promised restoration is exactly what was promised by John, as *The Voice of Isaiah 40*. He does not mention John's ministry as *The Messenger* that demanded that the consummation of the restoration at the parousia must therefore be posited at the time of the national judgment of Israel. He likewise fails to connect 1 Peter and the concept of the restoration of Israel based on Isaiah with Romans where, as we have seen, Paul likewise cites Isaiah 40 in his discussion of the salvation of Israel. This failure to connect John and with Paul is common.

Revelation 6:9-17
Little needs to be said here. Few commentators doubt that Revelation is focused on the martyrs and their vindication at the Day of the Lord. What is commonly overlooked however, is the direct connection between Revelation and the Old Covenant promises of that vindication in Israel's last days, (Deuteronomy 32–> Revelation 19:2) not to mention the inseparable connection to Jesus' ministry.[181] Very often, the connection between the salvation of "all Israel" in Romans 11 and John's discussion of the salvation of those out of the twelve tribes is also overlooked. Yet, these are patently the same issues and promises.

I suggested above that Revelation was written prior to 1 Peter. While this is currently a minority view, there is strong inter-textual evidence to support this. Not only that, but, the internal evidence of Revelation is more than sufficient to prove this.

---

[181] As I discuss in my *Who Is This Babylon?* in Jesus, Paul and Revelation, we have the identical pattern concerning martyrdom and the identity of the entity guilty of that pattern. In Jesus (Matthew 21-23) and Paul (1 Thessalonians 2:14-16) it was Old Covenant Jerusalem that had killed the prophets, she killed Jesus, and would kill the apostles and prophets of Jesus. In Revelation, it was "Babylon" that had killed the prophets (16:6), Jesus (11:8) and the apostles and prophets of Jesus (18:20-24). I fail to see how we can create a total bifurcation between Jesus, Paul and John and suggest that it was somehow Rome that John was accusing of that horrible blood guilt.

There was clearly Jewish persecution against the church at work in the Apocalypse (Revelation 2:9f; 3:9f; 11:8; 12; 14).[182] Unless one can clearly and definitively divorce John's extensive discussion of martyr vindication from Jesus' and from Paul's focus on the guilt of Old Covenant Jerusalem, and somehow also show that John's discussion of the salvation of "all Israel" in Revelation 7 & 14 is not related to Romans 11, then I suggest that these connections not only prove that Revelation was written prior to AD 70, but, they show that John, like Jesus predicted, and like Paul said, Satan, the great persecutor, was about to be crushed very shortly.

What we see in each of these texts is that it is patently obvious that *it was not Roman persecution of the church that was in view*. This is significant because if / since it was not Roman persecution of the church taking place, then neither Jesus nor Paul were promising the judgment of Rome for persecuting the saints. This can hardly be over-emphasized since it is common among scholars to say that especially in the Pauline literature, and Revelation, the focus was on relief from some supposed Roman persecution.[183]

Some years ago, Harnack said, "Unless the evidence is misleading, they (the Jews, DKP), instigated the Neronic outburst against Christians; and as a rule, whenever bloody persecutions were afoot in later days, the Jews are either in the background or the foreground"[184] That historical assessment has been strengthened through the years.

---

[182] For an in-depth *apologia* for the early dating of Revelation, see Kenneth Gentry's, *Before Jerusalem Fell*, Revised, (Fountain Inn, South Carolina, Victorious Hope Publishing, 2010).There appears to be an increasing number of scholars who now espouse the early dating, and that view was dominant in the 19th century.

[183] Cornelius Vanderwaal says: "Revelation, like the rest of the New Testament, contains a running polemic against the Jews and their rejection of Christ. It shares this theme with many of the early Christian passion homilies, which were testimonies against the Jews. The thesis that Revelation is directed against Rome is indefensible on scholarly grounds." Cornelius Vanderwaal, *Hal Lindsey and Biblical Prophecy*, (Ontario, Paideia Press, 1981)122.

[184] Adolph Harnack, *Mission and Expansion of Christianity*, Harper and Brothers, 1961)57.

Wright is certainly correct to say, "Persecution of Christians did not in fact, initially come from pagans." He continues, "In fact, the earliest and best evidence we possess for serious and open hostility between Jews - especially Pharisees – and the nascent Christian movement is found in the earliest period for which we have evidence, namely in the letters of Paul. He, by his own admission, had persecuted the very early church with violence and zeal" (1996, 374).

Gibbons said that the cause of the Neronian persecution, which began in approximately AD 64, was the Jews.[185] But, the fact is that prior to that - in Jesus' references to persecution - and in Paul, Peter, James and John, the persecution in view took place prior to the outbreak of the Neronian persecution, and sprang from Jewish resistance to the gospel.[186]

So, when we come to Romans and Paul's discussion of, "the sufferings of the now time," versus the, "glory about to be revealed," and the persecution the church was enduring, it is anachronistic to project that situation into a post AD 64, post AD 70, context. Paul was writing in the context of, and writing about, Jewish persecution of the church.

This should, therefore, give a bit of pause in the current theological discussions about Romans 11:25-27. That text, while not specifically mentioning martyr vindication, nonetheless contains the idea and the promise. The OT prophecies that Paul quotes, Deuteronomy 32, Isaiah 27, 59, 65 as we have shown, promised the salvation of Israel at the time of the judgment of Israel for shedding innocent blood.

As noted, few scholars (I have yet to find even *one*) give even passing notice to this motif and its critical role for understanding Romans 11. As we have seen, Holland and Perriman speak of the impending coming wrath of the Lord in

---

[185] Edward Gibbon, *Rise and Fall of the Roman Empire*, Vol. I, (New York, The Modern Library, Random House)459f.

[186] We find in Acts 19 the record of a local outburst of persecution, i.e. that instigated by Demetrius the silversmith. But, this was not an organized or widespread persecution as indicated by Paul's own testimony about Jewish persecution.

Romans,[187] yet, neither man develop the prophetic background and how it related to the promise of martyr vindication.[188]

Paul was not addressing the issue of suffering and martyrdom in a timeless vacuum. As we have seen, that motif is found in virtually all of his epistles, and it is in the epistles of the other NT writers. Paul was being faithful to the message of his Master who had promised that his followers - inclusive of his, "apostles, prophets and wise men" - that they would be persecuted by the Jews who would hate them for his name sake. That persecution would fill the eschatological measure of sin and suffering. But Paul, like Jesus, promised that the Jewish persecutors would themselves receive tribulation, "when the Lord Jesus is revealed from heaven" (2 Thessalonians 1:7f). It is an unfortunate failure of the exegetes and commentators to not see these connections.

In this survey of suffering and martyrdom in Romans we have established the following:

1. Paul was anticipating the fulfillment of John's message of "the wrath about to come" (Romans 2; 5). If the connection between Johns "wrath about to come," and Paul's discussion of impending wrath is valid - and I fail to see how it is not - that demands that Romans 11:25-27 (Not to mention the eschatological promises in chapters 8-16) were fulfilled in the national judgment of Jerusalem in AD 70.

---

[187] Yet, as we have seen above, Perriman wants to extrapolate that vindication all the way to the fall of Rome in the fifth century. But, this imputes guilt to Rome when Paul wrote, which is anachronistic, and extends the vindication for four centuries, well beyond the temporal demands of the text.

[188] Interestingly, Holland insists that it is important, "to give careful attention to Paul's use of Isaiah 59" (2011, 384). Yet, in his discussion, he says not a word about Isaiah's three-fold accusation against Israel for shedding innocent blood and the subsequent threat of the coming of the Deliverer in vengeance on the persecutors and salvation for the remnant. Hendrikson (2002, 383) likewise discusses Paul's citation of Isaiah 27 and 59 but completely ignores the indisputable fact that Isaiah posited Israel's salvation at the time of her judgment for shedding innocent blood.

Honoring the connection between John's message as *The Voice, The Messenger* and *Elijah*, who foretold the salvation of Israel at the time of the judgment of Israel demands that we view the salvation of Israel in Romans 11 (in the entire epistle) as the time of national judgment on Israel. John's message was Paul's message. Yet, as we have noted, the commentators completely fail to even mention any connection between John's ministry and message, and Romans 11.

2. Paul's citation of Isaiah 27 & 59, predictions of the salvation of Israel at the time of the vindication of the martyrs, at the coming of the Lord, is virtually *prima facie* proof that his longed for salvation of "all Israel" was to be fulfilled in AD 70.

We can surely ponder the hermeneutical question of how one can ignore the motif of martyr vindication at the coming of the Lord in the very prophecies to which Paul appeals for his eschatological hope of Israel's salvation. If Paul was expecting the fulfillment of Isaiah 27 & 59 in Romans 11, then he was patently looking to the events foretold by Jesus in Matthew 23 - the vindication of all of the blood of the martyrs, all the way back to creation.

3. Paul unequivocally posited the vindication of the Roman's suffering in fulfillment of Deuteronomy 32, which is a prediction of martyr vindication in Israel's last days – not the end of time.

4. We have shown how paradigmatic Matthew 23 must be considered in light of the vindication of the martyrs motif in Romans and the rest of the NT corpus.

5. Paul's expectation of imminent vindication / relief for that pressing first century suffering is echoed repeatedly throughout his epistles and the rest of the NT corpus, including in Peter, James and Revelation.

6. In all of Paul's epistles, and in the other NT epistles, the persecution that was occurring was *prior to any Roman persecution.* This excludes any suggestion that Paul had in mind some distant, unknown persecutor[189] - or even the Romans.

---

[189] The tradition in which I was raised posited the fulfillment of 2 Thessalonians 2 as a yet future coming of the Lord to destroy the Roman Catholic pope, who will, supposedly, regain the incredible authority that the pontiffs possessed in the middle ages. When he regains that power, he then turns on the "true church" and instigates a horrible, unparalleled persecution against the true believers. At the

He - and the early church - was being persecuted by Jerusalem. Paul wrote all of his epistles in which he spoke of the then on-going persecution and promised imminent vindication at the coming of the Lord - before the Roman persecution began! Why is this fact overlooked by the commentators, who seem to be in some kind of rush to lay guilt for that early persecution at the feet of Rome? Chronologically, that is untenable.

It was to Jerusalem that God had always sent His prophets. It was to Jerusalem that Jesus sent his, "apostles, prophets and wise men" (Luke 11:49f). It was of Jerusalem that Jesus said, "it is not possible that a prophet perish outside of Jerusalem" (Luke 11:31-33). It was in Jerusalem's (Israel's) last days that God would avenge the blood of His elect (Deuteronomy 32:43).

If we allow that the salvation of Romans 13:11f is the same salvation in chapter 11:25f, it demands that "All Israel" was saved within Paul's lifetime (through the consummation of his ministry).

When we harmonize that information with the theme of martyr vindication, it posits that salvation at the judgment of Old Covenant Jerusalem.

When we join Paul's discussion of coming salvation with John's ministry, we cannot avoid the conclusion that the salvation of Israel at the coming of the Lord was to be in AD 70.

---

zenith of that persecution, Jesus appears out of heaven and destroys him. There is simply no textual justification for this view. It violates the imminence of the text. It ignores the then on-going persecution. It ignores the fact that Paul said the Son of Perdition was already alive. There is no justification, anywhere in scripture, for that doctrine.

JOHN, *THE VOICE, THE MESSENGER* AND *ELIJAH*:
REVELATION AND THE SALVATION OF "ALL ISRAEL"

I have suggested that the book of Malachi - and thus, the mission of John as *The Voice, The Messenger* and *Elijah* - plays a significant role in Revelation. One thing is certain and that is that as *The Voice*, John's mission was about the salvation of Israel. His own father saw that, and rejoiced in it (Luke 1). So, when we come to Revelation and read of the 144,000 out of the twelve tribes of Israel, coming through the Great Tribulation and being led to the New Creation, we are firmly on the ground of the work of John, *The Voice*, but also, as *Elijah*.

Revelation 7 and 14 are about the salvation of Israel.[190] Thus, Revelation is John's contribution to our understanding of Romans 11. This being true, since Revelation depicts the salvation of the *remnant* (the 144,000) this suggests, does it not, that Romans 11 is about the salvation of the remnant and not, as many propose, the salvation of the numeric majority of Israel?

Unless Paul is expanding on the remnant motif in Romans 11, telling us that while throughout God's dealings with Israel it was invariably a remnant that was saved, but that now, at the eschatological consummation *all* Israel would be saved, then we must view Romans 11:25f as a prediction of the consummation of the process that had already begun. After all, in chapters 9-11, up to verses 25f, his entire discussion has been focused on the salvation of the *remnant*. So, does he suddenly abandon that discussion to say that after all, the entirety of Israel would be delivered?

Contra such a suggestion, I propose that Romans 9-11 and Revelation present the same narrative, the same concern for the salvation of Israel, the totality of the *remnant* of Israel. And let me return to a brief discussion of Isaiah 27 & 59 in this connection.

---

[190] Some try to identify the twelve tribes as the church, unrelated to ethnic Israel. However, the identification of the twelve tribes negates this. See also Romans 11, where Paul asked "Has God cast off His people whom He foreknew?" (11:1). His answer is a resounding "No" and his evidence is that he himself was part of the righteous remnant, as a member of the tribe of Benjamin. He is using the tribal heritage and association prosaically, just as in Revelation. To be sure, Paul, and the 144,000 were all followers of Jesus as Messiah, thus making them "spiritual Israel" but they were also "Israel according to the flesh" (Romans 9:1-3).

As we have noted, Paul draws directly on Isaiah 27 and 59 for his prediction of the salvation of "all Israel." What is glaringly missing from the literature is that in both Isaiah 27 and 59, it is the remnant that is saved. Notice that in Isaiah 27, we find the destruction of the city and the temple, along with the destruction of the people that YHVH had created. However, at the sounding of the Great Trump, the righteous would be gathered. This is patently the salvation, not of "all Israel" but, the salvation of all the righteous remnant.

Likewise, in Isaiah 59, the Lord would come in judgment of those who had shed innocent blood, and give, "Fury to His adversaries, recompense to His enemies." Yet, he would bring salvation, "to those who turn from transgressions." Once again, this is undeniably the salvation of the remnant, not "all Israel."

So, this raises another serious hermeneutical question. Paul, in his discussion of the fate of Israel in his day, spoke of the impending judgment on the nation, and the salvation of the remnant. Then, he predicted the salvation of "all Israel" and his support for that was taken on Isaiah 27 & 59. But, Isaiah 27 & 59 did not predict the salvation of the entire nation. They did not predict the salvation of the majority of the nation. Both Isaiah 27 & 59 predicted the salvation of the remnant at the time of the coming of the Lord in judgment of the nation.

So, the question of hermeneutic is: where does Paul change the concept from the salvation of the remnant, foretold in those OT prophecies, to the salvation of "all Israel"? He said that the salvation of "all Israel" would be in fulfillment of those two prophecies, but, those two predictions did not foretell the salvation of the nation, the majority, the whole of Israel! So, how can it be argued that Romans 11 predicted the salvation of "the mass of ethnic Israel" – in fulfilment of Isaiah 27 / 59 - when neither Isaiah 27 or 59 foretold the salvation of the majority of Israel?

Paul's reliance on Isaiah, and their indisputable prediction of the salvation of the remnant, leads me to conclude that in Romans 11:26-27, Paul's reference to the salvation of "all Israel" was a prediction of the consummation of the salvation of the remnant, the process that was already underway, but, as Paul affirmed, would not be prolonged (Romans 9:28).

I want now to show how John's ministry impacts our understanding of not only Romans, but of Revelation, and thereby demands an early dating of Revelation and fulfillment in AD 70, in the vindication of the martyrs.

We need only briefly to note that Revelation 7 & 14 are, like Romans 11, about the salvation of Israel. After all, the 144,000 are out of the twelve tribes of Israel and they are redeemed to God from men. They are led to the Water of Life in the New Creation (Revelation 7:14f –> 22:1f).

I must note a stunning claim on the part of Gentry. Contra all church history and in stark contrast to all creeds,[191] Gentry now claims that: "Despite initial appearances, Revelation 21-22 does not speak of the consummate new creation order."[192]

The problem for Gentry and his new position is that it violates what Paul had to say. There is no support for the (stunning) claim that the New Creation of Revelation 21-22 is not, "the consummate new creation." To see how radical and groundless Gentry's new position truly is, we need to develop how John anticipated that New Creation and how it relates to the consummative salvation of Israel. Keep in mind that Gentry, and a host of other commentators - posit Romans 11 as a yet future, "end of human history" event. Yet now, he is suggesting (by implication) that the salvation of Israel in Revelation is not related to that!

---

[191] I call attention to this amazing rejection of creedal theology because Gentry has often condemned the preterist view because it is "non-creedal." Yet now, Gentry is espousing a view that is *unknown* in all creeds and particularly in the Westminster Confession.

[192] Kenneth Gentry, *Navigating the Book of Revelation*, (FountainInn, SC., GoodBirth Ministries, 2010)177. It might be argued that a careful reader of Gentry could see this dramatic change coming. After all, he earlier took the view that the marriage of Christ depicted in Revelation 21 took place in AD 70 (2009, 367). The implications of Dr. Gentry's new position are staggering, but we cannot fully develop them here.

Let me repeat: Revelation 7[193] & 14 are about the salvation of Israel. The salvation of those out of the twelve tribes demands this. Their salvation would be the fulfillment of Isaiah 49 as evidenced by the fact that one of the elders before the throne describes the 144K and their reward:

> "Therefore they are before the throne of God and serve Him day and night in His temple. And He who sits on the throne will dwell among them. They shall neither hunger anymore nor thirst anymore; the sun shall not strike them, nor any heat; for the Lamb who is in the midst of the throne will shepherd them and lead them to living fountains of waters. And God will wipe away every tear from their eyes" (Revelation 7:15-17).

Take note of the constituent elements of the promise:

1. The 144K would be before the Throne of God.

2. They would be in the temple of God. In Jewish thought and in scripture, the Messianic temple of God would be fully established at the parousia of Messiah.

3. They would no longer hunger or thirst. If Gentry sees this as a metaphoric, spiritual reality fulfilled in AD 70, where will he go to prove a yet future, literal reality and fulfillment?

4. They would be led to living waters. Needless to say, the living waters are in the New Creation (Revelation 22:1f). But once again we ask, if Gentry posits this as spiritually fulfilled in Christ and his body in AD 70, what texts would he then appeal to for a literal fulfillment of the prophecy? Upon what basis would he posit the salvation of Israel foretold in Romans at the so called end of time, while at the same time saying that the salvation of Israel in Revelation was fulfilled in AD 70?

---

[193] I find a direct connection between the prophecy of Isaiah 40:1-2 and the taking away of the sin of Israel, the 144,000 who washed their robes and made them white in the blood of the Lamb and the redemption of Zion. This may not be a direct "echo" but, there is enough similarity to at least cause us to consider it. If the connection is valid, then we find a direct link between John's ministry and Revelation.

5. The *Great Shepherd* would lead them to these blessings.

6. There would be no more tears.[194]

The question we ask at this juncture is: Is the salvation of Israel foretold in Isaiah 49 a different salvation, to be accomplished at a different time, from that foretold and heralded by *The Voice of Isaiah 40*? If it is not different, then what we have in Revelation is the anticipation of the climax and fulfillment of John's message. The answer to this is to be found in a common motif from both chapters.

We have a direct link between Isaiah 40 and Isaiah 49 here. Isaiah 40:10f describes Jesus as *the shepherd* who would come and hold his sheep in his arms, just as Isaiah 49 describes Messiah as the *Great Shepherd*. So, Isaiah 40 & 49 describe the same salvation of Israel under the metaphor of the Great Shepherd. John was *The Voice* heralding that salvation. Thus, the salvation of Israel in Revelation 21-22, being the fulfillment of Isaiah 49, was to be fulfilled within the purview of John's, "the kingdom of heaven has drawn near" - and be related to the time of the national judgment of Israel. (See also 1 Peter 5:1f in light of the imminent parousia of 1 Peter 4:7, 17).

Now, if / since Gentry sees Revelation 7 & 14 fulfilled in Revelation 21-22 and that was in AD 70, he has a severe problem. Revelation 7 & 14 are prophecies that are drawn directly from Isaiah 49 as we have seen. But as just shown, they are directly related to Isaiah 40 as well, and thus, to the Baptizer's ministry. But, this being true, as we have shown, Romans 11 is drawn from and dependent on Isaiah 40 and John's ministry as well. So, both Isaiah 49 & *chapter 40* foretold the salvation of Israel - in other words, *the fulfillment of Romans 11:25f.*

---

[194] Many Postmillennialist / Dominionists grant that the New Creation of Revelation 21-22 arrived in AD 70. In my debate with Joel McDurmon, I documented that he took this position. I then noted that in that New Creation, there is no more "the death," no more "the curse" and thus, I posed the question, if, in the New Creation that arrived in AD 70, those things were overcome and removed, what more do we need to look forward to? McDurmon never attempted an answer, because neither he or any other Dominionist has an answer. Revelation 21-22 describes the consummate solution to the Adamic Curse. If you posit, as Dominionists do, the arrival of that New Creation in AD 70, you have thereby negated any futurist eschatology. See the book of my debate with McDurmon for more.

So, if Isaiah 40 / 49 were fulfilled in AD 70 – as necessary in Gentry's application of Revelation 21-22 to AD 70 - then, unless Romans 11 foretold a different salvation of Israel from that foretold in Revelation, of logical necessity *Romans 11 was fulfilled in AD 70.*

If Isaiah 49 is a prophecy of the salvation of Israel and was fulfilled in AD 70, where is the delineation between Isaiah 49 / Revelation 7 & 14 and the salvation of Israel in Romans 11:25f? Did the Old Testament foretell two distinct last days, Messianic salvations of Israel, different in nature, separated in time by so far 2000 years?

There is strong contextual support for this argument. In Romans 13:11f, Paul said, "and now is our salvation nearer than when we first believed." This salvation would arrive at the full arrival of "the day" which was imminent. The question is valid, is this not the salvation of Israel of chapter 11? In both chapter 11 and chapter 13 the promised salvation would arrive with the parousia - the Day of the Lord, which falsifies the claim of Hester that Paul did not have a specific coming of the Lord in mind in Romans 11. Unless Hester can prove that Romans 11 and Romans 13 speak of different salvations, to come at different times, at different comings of the Lord, then patently, Paul had a very specific coming of the Lord in mind.

The salvation of Israel in Romans 11 and 13 is the salvation of Israel in Revelation 7 & 14,[195] which was likewise imminent. But if the salvation of Romans 13 is the salvation of chapter 11, then Gentry - (not to mention other Postmillennialists who agree that the salvation of the remnant in Revelation 7 / 14 occurred in AD 70) - has surrendered the creedal view of Romans 11. I fail to see how one can divorce the "salvation" of Romans 11 from the salvation of Romans 13 - or Revelation.

---

[195] The salvation of Israel in Romans 13:11-13 and Revelation is the "salvation" to arrive at Christ's second appearance in Hebrews 9:28. After all, that salvation in Hebrews would, just as in Romans and Revelation, be in fulfillment of God's Old Covenant promises to Israel found in Torah (Hebrews 9:6f; 10:1-2). Hebrews 10:37 emphatically says that Jesus' coming would be in a "very, very little while" and without delay. This demands that the fulfillment of Romans 11 was very, very near.

For brevity let me ask a couple of other questions that can serve as food for thought and further development at a later time:

1. Is the time of the vindication of the martyrs - at the Day of the Lord for the salvation of Israel - in Revelation a different Day of the Lord for the salvation of Israel, at the time of the avenging of the blood of the martyrs as foretold in Isaiah 27 and 59?[196]

2. Is the time of the vindication of the martyrs in Revelation a different vindication of the martyrs than that foretold by Jesus in Matthew 23, as well as in his parabolic teaching?

3. Is the Great Day of the Lord of Revelation 6:12-17, for the vindication of the martyrs, the Day when no one could stand before Him, a different Day of the Lord from that in Malachi 3:1-3 – the Day when no man could stand before Him?[197] If they are the same Day, then since Malachi 3 is, as we have demonstrated above, the Day of the Lord *in national judgment of Israel for violating Torah*, this is *prima facie* evidence that Revelation was written prior to AD 70. It likewise proves that Revelation was about the impending, at hand, judgment of Old Covenant Jerusalem.

4. Is the time of the fulfillment of the Song of Moses in Revelation 19:2 the prophecy of the avenging of the martyrs *in Israel's last days*, a different fulfillment of the Song from that anticipated in Romans 12 and Hebrews 10?

5. Is the coming of the Lord of Revelation 19, the Lord decked out in his royal apparel, coming in judgment and vindication of the martyrs, a totally different coming of Lord decked out in royal battle array, from that in Isaiah 59? The correlations between Isaiah 59 and Revelation 19 are quite impressive to say the

---

[196] Does not the image of Messiah decked out for the Holy War against "Babylon" in Revelation 19, call to mind the Messiah in Isaiah 59 as he would come in judgment of Israel for shedding innocent blood? If that connection is valid, it once again demands an early dating of Revelation and application to AD 70.

[197] The image or language of "standing" at the Day of the Lord is highly suggestive of a historical Day of the Lord - never an "end of time" event. See Nahum 1:1f; Ezekiel 13:5; Jeremiah 46:15, 21, etc..

least, but, seldom explored.[198]

6. Is the time when the Lord would lead His flock and carry them in His arms of Isaiah 40:10f a different time of His leading them to living waters in Isaiah 49 –> Revelation 7 & 14? If Isaiah 40 and 49 speak of the same time, the salvation of Israel at the coming of the Lord, then since John was *The Voice* heralding that Day of the Lord as near, this demands that Revelation was to truly have been fulfilled imminently.

7. Is the time when the Lord would rule in His kingdom, the time of the salvation of Israel in the kingdom (Isaiah 40:10-12), a different time of the rule of the Lord and His Messiah from that in Revelation 11:15f and 19? If not, since John (and Jesus) said, "the kingdom of heaven has drawn near," and since the kingdom would fully arrive at the time of the destruction of the city, "where the Lord was slain" this demands a pre-AD 70 dating of Revelation. It likewise demands that Revelation was concerned about the fulfillment of Israel's promises, and the imminent destruction of Jerusalem in AD 70.

8. Is the coming of the Lord to His temple - the Messianic Kingdom temple in Malachi - a different Kingdom temple from that in Revelation? If not, then John's ministry delimits fulfillment of that temple promise to the coming of the Lord in national judgment of Old Covenant Israel.

9. Is the time of the opening of the books when the righteous remnant would be the "jewels[199] in the crown" of the Lord, a different judgment and rewarding of the righteous when the books would be opened in Revelation 20?

---

[198] Isaiah 59 helps define Paul's "all Israel" in Romans 11. In Isaiah, salvation is undeniably for, "those who turn away from ungodliness in Jacob"– i.e. the remnant. So, if Isaiah is Paul's prophetic source for his hope of the salvation of "all Israel," then since Isaiah expressly defines those to whom salvation would be given as the *remnant*, is this not determinative for the definition of "all Israel" in Romans?

[199] See our earlier discussion of the word translated as "jewels." It is *segulla* and means special possession and carries some amazing connotations.

10. Is the Great Day of the Lord's wrath foretold by Elijah / John a different Great Day of the Lord's wrath in Revelation 6 / 16 / 18-19? If not, then John's ministry and message confines the fulfillment of the Great Day of Wrath to the time of national judgment on Israel for violating Torah.

Each of these constituent elements (and this list could be expanded) spring from Isaiah 40 and Malachi. They thus belong to the ministry and message of John the Baptizer as *The Voice*, *The Messenger* and *Elijah*. John in Revelation is patently repeating the message of John the Baptizer.[200]

All of the elements here are *prima facie* demonstration and validation of *Torah to Telos*. The eschatological consummation is tied directly to the fulfillment of God's promises to Old Covenant Israel. Torah would endure until the *Telos*.[201]

These correlations also mean that the Biblical story of eschatology is not about the end of time, or the consummation of the New Covenant age. It is about the climax of the Old Covenant history of Israel. John the Baptizer, as *The Voice*, *The Messenger* and *Elijah*, stood as the "pivot point" of the ages.

He was *The Voice* to prepare for the coming of the Lord for the salvation of Israel, the time of the taking away of Israel's sin through Messiah. This is the salvation of Israel in Romans 11.

---

[200] J. Massyngberde Ford, a NT scholar, at one time posited (but later abandoned it I believe) the view that John the Baptizer actually wrote the Apocalypse. See the *Anchor Bible Commentary on Revelation* (New York, Doubleday, 1975). While I do not accept that view of the authorship of Revelation, the parallels between the Baptizer's ministry and Revelation are more than impressive.

[201] Several commentators have noted that Revelation, with its repeated seven-fold judgments, echoes Leviticus 26 and the Law of Blessings and Cursings. If this be the case, and a careful reading of Revelation shows that John is clearly alluding to those passages, this is powerful proof that Revelation is about the impending judgment on Jerusalem, for those are Mosaic Covenant sanctions. They thus have nothing to do with literal Babylon, the Roman Catholic church, paganism, or some future persecuting power that will eventually come on the scene etc..

He was *The Messenger* to prepare for the coming of the Lord to the Messianic temple, the time of national judgment on Israel.

He was *Elijah* to prepare and warn the people of the impending wrath about to come, the wrath that would lead them to the resurrection harvest and the everlasting kingdom, where ethnic origins would no longer avail. He was to prepare them for the New Creation.

John's ministry, then, is fundamentally and critically important to our understanding of Biblical eschatology, and certainly for our understanding of Romans 11. To ignore his relationship with Romans 11, *as virtually all scholars* do, is to deprive ourselves of a *crux interpretum* for a proper understanding of that great text. It is time to correct this oversight.

WHAT KIND OF COMING OF THE LORD DID JOHN, JESUS AND PAUL ENVISION / EXPECT / PREDICT?

I believe the foregoing material has already answered this question, but, perhaps it would be good to spend a few moments developing this a bit more. Many commentators take it for granted that Paul in Romans 11 predicted the end of time, earth burning (or at least an earth *renovating*), event.

Once we understand the message of Malachi, the message of *The Messenger*, who is *Elijah* – and thus *John* – then the eschatological message takes on a totally different flavor. John never predicted the kind of eschatological consummation assumed by the commentators.[202] And I would suggest that if / since John did not predict such an event, that neither did Jesus or his followers.

The NT writers repeatedly cite Malachi, *(not to mention Isaiah)* as the source of their eschatological expectation. Malachi's message was John's message *as Elijah*. I would also say that John's message was Jesus' message and Jesus' message was that of Paul - this is axiomatic. Thus, to know what John said about the end time expectation becomes determinative for understanding what the other NT writers understood about the end times. It tells us what Paul was expecting in Romans 11.

John's "wrath about to come," including the time of the harvest, was national judgment on Jerusalem, *covenantal judgment*. That judgment would also be the time of the Kingdom – "the kingdom of heaven has drawn near," said John. This agrees perfectly with the conflation of judgment and the kingdom rule in Isaiah 40.

---

[202] As I have noted, commentators commonly ascribe error or failure to John, Jesus and the apostles in regard to their eschatological expectations. Baldwin (1972, 252) says "Whatever may have been the truth about John's understanding of his role, he believed that the Messianic age was being ushered in and that only through a process of testing by fire could anyone escape final judgment (Matthew 3:11, 12). He undoubtedly knew the message of Malachi and was profoundly influenced by it. In the life of Jesus the expectation of John was not fulfilled. An interval separated the first and second comings and the day of grace was extended to delay final judgment." The view presented herein prevents such ascriptions of failure and delay.

The idea that neither John nor Jesus anticipated the end of the time-space continuum is increasingly accepted by numerous scholars. This is more than fascinating and significant. If neither John or Jesus predicted such a thing, then why does the theological world cling so tenaciously to a doctrine of, "the end of time" and the, "end of the world"?

What I will do now is share with the reader just a few citations from the world of scholarship in which leading commentators acknowledge that neither John or Jesus predicted, "the end of time,"[203] or the end of the physical creation.[204]

Commenting on "the Day of the Lord" in Thessalonians, Wright says,

> "I have no hesitation in saying that, had Paul been alive in the year we call AD 70, when the convulsions in Rome during the Year of the Four Emperors were quickly followed by the destruction of Jerusalem, he would have said, 'That's it. That's the Day of the Lord.' I think that this is precisely what the notorious passage in 1 Thessalonians 2:16 is referring to; God's

---

[203] There are of course, scholars who insist that John, Jesus and the NT writers did predict an "end of time" eschaton. E.g. Edward Adams, *The Stars Will Fall From Heaven*, Library of New Testament Studies 347, (London, T and T Clark, 2007, in which he rejects the views of N. T. Wright. See also: *The Apocalyptic Jesus, A Debate*, between Dale Allison, Marcus J. Borg, John Dominic Crossan, and Stephen Patterson, (Santa Rosa, Ca., Poleridge Press, 2001).

[204] It might also be noted that even some of the early church writers affirmed "the end of the world" in a distinctly covenantal sense, even though they, like modern commentators, also then posited the future end of time. Origen said: (emphasis added): "We do not deny, then, that the *purificatory fire and the destruction of the world* took place in order that evil might be swept away, and *all things be renewed*; for we assert that we have learned these things from the sacred books of the prophets…And anyone who likes may convict this statement of falsehood, if it be not the case that the *whole Jewish nation was overthrown within one single generation* after Jesus had undergone these sufferings at their hands. For forty and two years, I think after the date of the crucifixion of Jesus, did the destruction of Jerusalem take place." (*Contra Celsum*, IV, xxi-xxii; Ante-Nicene Fathers, Vol. IV)505, 506.

wrath has come upon them *eith telos*, in a climactic and decisive way." (*Paul*, 141). (See his comments again above where he says John anticipated the imminent judgment on Israel).

In another work he adds:

> "Paul here reflects the early Christian tradition, going back to Jesus himself, according to which Jerusalem was to be destroyed, and according to which that destruction was to be interpreted as the wrath of God against his sinful people. In the same Thessalonian correspondence, Paul asserted that the wrath of God had indeed come upon them 'to the uttermost' (1 Thess.2:16.) It is this awareness of an imminent end to the way the Jewish world had looked for so long, rather than an imminent end to the space-time universe, that drove Paul on his mission with such urgency. From his own point of view he lived in an odd interim period: judgment had been passed on Jerusalem, but not yet executed. There was a breathing space, a 'little time' in which people could repent, and in which the message of Jesus could spread to Gentiles as well as Jews (though it always remained, for Paul, 'to the Jew first'). When Jerusalem fell, Jews on the one hand would undoubtedly blame those who had reneged on their Jewish responsibilities, including those Jewish Christians who, like Paul, had been enjoying fellowship with pagans and regarding it as the Kingdom of God and the true expression of the covenant God made with Abraham."[205]

As noted above, McKnight says:

> "He (Jesus, DKP) did not see beyond the destruction of Jerusalem but connected both the final judgment and the final deliverance with that event. In other words, like Jewish prophets of old, Jesus saw the next event, in his case, the destruction of Jerusalem – as the end event of history." (1999,

---

[205] N. T. Wright, *Jerusalem in the New Testament*; Originally published in *Jerusalem Past and Present in the Purposes of God*. P. W. L. Walker, (2nd ed., Carlisle, Paternoster, 1994, PDF file)53–77.

130).²⁰⁶

> "Jesus prophesied of the destruction of Jerusalem as the climactic event in Israel's history that would end the privilege of Israel in God's plan. He also attached to this the final resolution of Israel through the images connected with remnant and redemption."

He goes ahead to say that Jesus did not fail, yet, the disciples lived beyond 70 expecting that one day God would, "bring all of ordinary history to a closure that would feature Israel as God's people and Jesus as his Messiah."... (1999, 138).

> "I will argue that Jesus saw no further than A.D. 70 and that he thought everything would be wrapped up in conjunction with that catastrophic event for Israel. In seeing the future this way, Jesus was not mistaken; rather, he envisioned the future very much like the Jewish prophets of the Israelite tradition did and not all that different from the way of contemporary Jewish prophets" (139).

Mark Nanos adds his testimony,

> "Within the mainline Jewish writings of this period, covering a wide range of styles, genres, political persuasions and theological perspectives, there is virtually no evidence that Jews were expecting the end of the space-time universe...What then did they believe was going to happen? They believed that the present world order would come to an end – the world order in which pagans held power, and Jews, the covenant people of the creator god, did not." (1996, 61, n 70).

---

[206] Note that McKnight acknowledges that Jesus did not see beyond AD 70, but, then he claims that Jesus posited "the end event of history" at that time. Later, McKnight seeks to salvage Jesus from a failed eschatology by claiming that Jesus' prediction was true, therefore we do not need to charge him with a failed eschatology. So, on the one hand, Jesus was right (AD 70 fulfilled his prediction). Yet, on the other hand, his prediction assuredly did fail, because he saw AD 70 as the "end event of history". The only tenable position is to simply say, "His predictions did not fail. He did not envision the end event of history. He did envision the end of Israel's world and of their covenant history."

R. T. France says,

> "The unwary reader is in danger of assuming a note of finality in the future hope of the Old Testament that is in fact foreign to it. The "eschatology" of the Old Testament prophets was not concerned with the end of the world, but with the decisive act of God which will bring to an end the existing order of things in the world, and inaugurate a new era of blessing, of a totally different order."[207]

Brown, commenting on the language of Christ's coming in Matthew 24:29f, concurs that this language is from the O.T. and that there is no justification for taking it literally. It is metaphoric language to describe Jehovah's powerful intervention into history, not to end history.[208] Likewise, Reiser says the Jews did not look for the end of time or the end of earth. They believed in renewal, but after the end, life on earth went on.[209]

Joseph Mayor points out that the dominant view of ancient Rabbis was that the world / creation is permanent and will never pass away.[210] He cites Ps. 148:4-6 and 104:5 as supportive texts that the ancients appealed to.

I fully agree with these assessments. What few of these same scholars note, however, is John's role in that eschatological expectation. What is also done by these same scholars is to admit to the first century fulfillment of the Day of the Lord, but then, due to presuppositional views of the "real" end, and the "real kingdom" they then posit another, yet future, literal coming of Jesus at the end

---

[207] R. T. France, *Jesus and the Old Testament*, (Grand Rapids, Baker, 1982)84.

[208] Colin Brown, *New International Dictionary of New Testament Theology*, vol. 2, (Grand Rapids, Regency Reference Library, Zondervan, 1986)35f.

[209] Marius Reiser, *Jesus and Judgment*, Fortress, 1997)148.

[210] Joseph Mayor, *The Epistle of St. Jude and the Second Epistle of St. Peter*, (Eugene, Or., Wipf and Stock Publishers, 1907/2004)162, n. 2.

of human history.²¹¹ The problem is, that if Jesus' eschatology and that of his followers was in fact the same as that proclaimed by John, *there is not another Day of the Lord to be found anywhere in the NT.*

John clearly did proclaim both salvation – the kingdom – as well as judgment and he said fulfillment had drawn near. Furthermore, our examination of the texts that foretold his ministry and the texts lying behind Romans 11 have informed us that the coming Day of the Lord that *The Messenger / Elijah /* John proclaimed was to be *a day of national judgment on Israel*, when the righteous remnant would be saved.

So, John was not anticipating an end of time, cosmos destroying event. He did proclaim the coming of the Lord for the salvation of Israel. That Day was to be the time of national judgment of Israel. But, that is the coming of the Lord in Romans 11. To express it another way, if the salvation of Israel proclaimed by John was to occur at the time of national judgment on Israel is the salvation of Israel foretold in Romans 11, then all speculation about a future salvation of national Israel are specious and unsubstantiated.

The coming of the Deliverer out of Zion, in fulfillment of those OT texts that foretold John's ministry and the salvation of Israel, was to be a time of *national judgment of Israel* – for shedding innocent blood. And there can really be no doubt about when that was.

To understate the case tremendously, if what we are proposing here is accurate, the implications for the religious Zionist movement are devastating and fatal. In fact, all end time speculation based on the idea of a yet future coming of the Lord for the salvation of Israel at the "second coming" are negated. It matters

---

²¹¹ Other scholars all but overlook any first century, national judgment as the fulfillment of John, as Elijah, and his eschatological prediction. Verhoef, for instance, suggests that John foresaw the first and second comings of Jesus and that the ultimate fulfillment of his prediction was the end of time. Pieter A. Verhoef, *The New International Commentary on the Old Testament*, (Grand Rapids, Eerdmans, 1987)295. Interestingly, Verhoef agrees that Malachi was predicting covenantal judgment on God's covenant people. Yet he extrapolates that to a yet future end of the Christian age coming of Christ– *which demands that Torah remains valid until that time.* This hardly agrees with the powerful *naherwartung* – the sense of imminence - in John's message.

not whether that be Amillennialism, Postmillennialism or Dispensationalism. Any doctrine positing a future for national Israel based on Romans 11 falls in light of John's ministry. All claims that national Israel has a divine right to the land, in anticipation of that supposed future salvation of Israel, are falsified.

At the risk of redundancy, let me put this another way.

As *The Voice* John was the herald of the taking away of Israel's sin (Isaiah 40:1-2) and kingdom at the Day of the Lord.

As *The Messenger*, he would declare the impending national judgment on Israel for violating Torah and the arrival of the Messianic temple.

As *Elijah*, he would prepare for the Great And Terrible Day of the Lord, the time of the kingdom and resurrection.

In light of these realities, it is difficult to over-emphasize his eschatological role. It means that he was the herald of the coming of the Deliverer out of Zion for the salvation of Israel! But, since John's message was one of national judgment on Israel, that demands that Romans 11 was fulfilled at the time of national judgment on Israel in AD 70.

The implications of this are, needless to say, stunning, for to re-state, I have not found even one commentator who has made the connection between John and the coming of the Deliverer in Romans 11.

PAUL, *JESUS AS THE DELIVERER* AND JOHN'S MESSAGE OF THE WRATH TO COME

A brief look at the message of John concerning the wrath about to come, and the message of Paul the apostle confirms what we have seen so far. We have already noted that in Romans 2 and 5 Paul specifically references the coming wrath. Jesus would deliver the Roman saints from that. But, we need to look closer.

John warned of "the wrath about to come" the imminent kingdom and the harvest.

From the time of John's ministry until the apostle Paul, that wrath had not fully come. National, covenant judgment on Jerusalem did not been poured out.[212] This is a critical element that is far too often ignored or overlooked. So, if the national judgment for the salvation of Israel had not fallen when Paul wrote his epistles, does this not at least *suggest* that Paul was anticipating the fulfillment of John's "wrath about to come" in his ministry? Or, should we believe that Paul simply ignored John's message and proclaimed another, far distant, unrelated "wrath to come"?

Before proceeding to that, let's remind ourselves once again of the prophetic texts that underlie both John's ministry as well as Paul's prophecy of the coming of the Deliverer for the salvation of Israel.

Isaiah 26-27 – Isaiah predicted coming wrath at the Day of the Lord. The fortified city would be desolated, the altar turned to chalk stone, and the people that YHVH had created would be forgotten because of their blindness and

---

[212] There had been, however, to major events, prior to the writing of Thessalonians, that may well have served as signs to the nation of that impending catastrophe. Josephus relates that under the Procurator Cumanus, circa 48-52 AD, there was a riot in the Temple area of Jerusalem. Over 30,000 people were trampled to death in one day. Earlier, between 39-41 AD, occurred the infamous incident in which Caligula commanded that his statue be erected in the Temple at Jerusalem. This incident brought the nation to the brink of war. (Josephus, *Antiquities*, Bk 19, Wars Bk. II, chap. 10), These events could have been the basis of the claims of the false teachers who said the Day of the Lord had already come (2 Thessalonians 2:1f).

refusal to heed His word (27:10-12). So, we have coming wrath at the time of the salvation of Israel, and, it would be at the time of the vindication of the martyrs (26:20-21). This is patently a time of national judgment on Israel / Jerusalem. Should we ignore this in our investigation of Romans 11?

Isaiah 40 - The prophecy of *The Voice*, who would announce the salvation of Israel, the taking away of her sin and the kingdom. This would be the time of judgment (wrath to come) / reward, at the redemption of Zion. John unquestionably fulfilled his role as he announced the kingdom, the harvest and the wrath about to come. And, Paul cited Isaiah 40 twice in Romans 10-11. He patently had the same time of Israel's salvation in mind.

Isaiah 59 - As we have seen, it would be Israel's guilt in shedding the blood of the saints that would incite the coming of the Lord in vengeance. That time of recompense would also be when the Lord would be the Deliverer for those who would "turn away ungodliness from Jacob." We thus have both judgment and reward in the same text. And we need to be reminded once again that Isaiah serves as one of the key sources for Paul's eschatological expectation of the salvation of Israel in Romans.

Malachi 3 -*The Messenger* would warn of the impending national judgment on Israel for violating Torah. This is patently about "wrath to come." Yet, in v. 15f, it would also be when the Lord would bless those who remembered Him - the righteous remnant.

Malachi 4 - *Elijah* would announce the coming of the Great and Terrible Day of the Lord, the time of covenant wrath on Israel for violating Torah. John's message in Matthew 3 is an undeniable echo of Malachi 4:1-6.

In each of the background source texts that Paul appealed to in Romans 11, coming wrath is an intrinsic element of the prophecy That wrath was coming to avenge the blood of the martyrs - for violating Torah.

In each of the prophecies of the ministry of John, as *The Voice*, *The Messenger* and *Elijah*, coming wrath is inseparably tied to the time of salvation.

In Isaiah 59 the Deliverer *(roumai*, LXX) would come, and he would deliver his people from that coming wrath. We should not forget that in Romans 11:22f, Paul discusses "the severity of God" and proceeds to make the promise of the "Deliverer" coming out of Zion in fulfillment of Isaiah 59. It cannot be denied therefore, that lying near the surface of Paul's promise of coming salvation, there is also the threat of the wrath to come.

In an earlier epistle, the apostle had said Christ was *delivering* (*roumenon*, present participle) the Thessalonians from "the wrath" (1 Thessalonians 1:10). Contextually, the coming wrath in chapter 1 points to the wrath that was hanging over the heads of the nation of Israel for their bloody history of killing the prophets, of Jesus, and now, of his apostles and prophets (1 Thessalonians 2:14-16). Then, once again in chapter 5:9, the apostle assured his audience that Christ had delivered them from that impending wrath.

F. F. Bruce makes the connection between Romans 11, 1 Thessalonians 1 and Paul's claim that the Thessalonian saints were being, (present participle), delivered. He says:

> "The present tense of *ruomenon* carries no implication of realized eschatology with it. .. The participle plays the part of a *nomen agentis'* our deliverer' (Romans 11:26, in a quotation from Isaiah 59:20 LXX, where *ho roumenos,'* 'the Deliverer,' is practically a divine title."[213]

While Bruce makes the connection between Thessalonians, Romans 11 and Isaiah 59, he, like other commentators, says not a word about *why* the wrath was coming in Isaiah 59. He says not a word about the nature of the wrath that Christ was to deliver them from. And, he does not mention the role of John as *The Voice*, *The Messenger* and *Elijah* proclaiming that coming wrath.

Best differs somewhat from Bruce, insisting that we honor the verbal tenses. Commenting on the "coming wrath" Best says:

> "How quickly this anger approaches is not said but if it were regarded as infinitely remote it would hardly be described as approaching (emphatic in position in the Greek)."[214]

---

[213] F. F. Bruce, Word Biblical Commentary, 1 & 2 Thessalonians, (Waco, Word Publishing, 1982)19+.

[214] Ernest Best, *The First and Second Epistles to the Thessalonians,* (Peabody, Mass, Hendrickson, 1986)84.

Bruce insists that the present indicative of "who is delivering us" indicates that, "the deliverance is taking place even now before the return of Jesus." Like most commentators, Best posits the coming wrath as the time of Christ's second coming, making no connection with 1 Thessalonians 2. He sees no evident link between the coming wrath and the prophetic background of Romans 11. He does not mention the ministry and message of John.[215]

Paul's reference to the coming wrath in Thessalonians is, I suggest, part of a consistent doctrine that he continued to discuss in Romans. There, Paul mentioned the coming wrath (1:18f). He expounded on it a bit more in chapter 2, a text that plainly warned Jews of that coming wrath. In chapter 5:9, he says Christ would deliver (*sothesometha*) the Romans from that coming wrath. Romans 5:9 is a reiteration of 1 Thessalonians 5:9.

We need to be reminded once again at this juncture that John's impending "about to be" wrath had not fallen when Paul wrote 1 Thessalonians - or Romans. But, in 1 Thessalonians 2:14f, he says God's wrath was hanging over Israel's head for shedding innocent blood. And this hearkens us back to Isaiah 27 & Isaiah 59 where Israel's salvation would also be at the time of wrath on Israel for shedding innocent blood. And for this, we have the explicit and emphatic words of Jesus in Matthew 23 where he predicted the wrath that was coming on Jerusalem for her bloody guilt. So, upon what basis do we divorce Paul's referent to the wrath to come from that foretold by John or from Jesus' discussion?

Is it possible that in Romans 11, Paul is not only drawing on Isaiah, but, he is also echoing what he had written in Thessalonians, and in the earlier chapters in Romans? And the question also becomes: Is Thessalonians an echo of Matthew 3:7 – and John's message: "Who has warned you to flee from the wrath about to come?" How can we delineate between Matthew 3, 1 Thessalonians 1:10 and 1 Thessalonians 2:14-16?

---

[215] As of this writing, I have found only one commentator who linked 1 Thessalonians 1:10 with chapter 2 and the coming wrath on Israel, and that is Adam Clarke, as noted above. One would think that if he made that connection he would then link that to John's ministry, but, in his Thessalonian commentary, he does not do so. There is an almost unquestioned assumption in the literature that Paul was referencing the "end of time" coming of the Lord.

The connection is confirmed once again when we turn to Matthew 3 and look at John's message.

John's Mission - as *The Voice* - was to prepare for the coming of the Lord for the salvation of Israel.

John's message was that the Day of the Lord – the time of the salvation of Israel - was at hand - truly imminent in the first century.

John's Day of the Lord for the salvation of Israel is the Day of the Lord of Romans 11.

Therefore, the Day of the Lord of Romans 11, being the Day of the Lord for the salvation of Israel proclaimed by John as *The Voice* – was imminent.

The Day of the Lord that John - as *The Voice* – heralded, was the Day of the Lord that he proclaimed as *The Messenger* (Malachi 3:5-6).

The Day of the Lord of Malachi 3:5-6 was a time of national judgment on Israel for violating Torah.

Therefore, the Day of the Lord of Romans 11 was the Day of the Lord - national judgment - against Israel for violating Torah.

From the evidence above, it seems very clear that neither John, nor Jesus, nor Paul or the rest of the NT writers anticipated a literal, bodily, physical coming of Jesus out of heaven, as a 5' 5" Jewish man, riding on literal clouds to bring human history to an end. Rather, he like the Old Covenant prophets before him, looked for and predicted a "historical" Day of the Lord - covenantally climatic- but, of the same nature as those previous Days of the Lord (cf. Isaiah 64:1-4). While the dominant view in Christianity remains to be an expectation of a "rapture," and the end of human history, it simply does not fit the evidence.

If we accept the role of John as *The Voice, The Messenger* and as *Elijah*, and his normative, determinative eschatological role, the traditional paradigms cannot be sustained.

Only by ignoring the nature of the Day of the Lord that John preached can we maintain a literalistic view of the coming of Christ.

Only by altering, distorting and re-defining the Day that he preached can we posit the traditional view of the Day of the Lord.

There is no textual support for either ignoring, distorting or re-defining the Day that John preached.

PAUL AND THE LITTLE APOCALYPSE

As we noted above, there is wide scholarly agreement that Isaiah 24-27, called the Little Apocalypse, had a great influence on the eschatology of the NT writers. This seems particularly true in Paul's case. In a brief scan, I discovered that Paul quotes from the Little Apocalypse no less than seven times in Romans 8-11.[216] What is so significant about this is that Isaiah 24-29 contains no less than six (I think more, actually) predictions of the salvation of Israel, but, in every occurrence that salvation is posited at the time of the judgment of Jerusalem.

1. Isaiah 24 - We find the establishment of the kingdom in v. 20 at the time of the punishment of the wicked. That kingdom arrives at the time of the judgment of "the people" and "the city" that sits in the midst of "the land" (v. 10-12.[217] Compare Ezekiel 5:8-9). The entire chapter is about the coming judgment of Israel becausem "they have broken the everlasting covenant" (v. 5).

2. Isaiah 25:6-9 - The Messianic Banquet and the resurrection, the salvation of Israel takes place when the city and the temple would be turned over to foreigners (verses 1-3). It should hardly be necessary to note that Paul quotes from Isaiah 25:8 in his discussion of coming resurrection in 1 Corinthians 15.

3. Isaiah 26:1-3, 19f - We find the resurrection: "your dead shall live"– but, this is undeniably posited at the time of the Messianic Woes, commonly called the

---

[216] Wagner (2003, 343) has Paul citing the Little Apocalypse eight times, with the majority of those citations being in Romans 9-11. Like several other scholars, he does not list Isaiah 26 as lying behind Romans 8:18f, but to me, this seems remiss. Nonetheless, if the count is correct then clearly, the Little Apocalypse was critically important in Paul's thinking as he pondered Israel's condition and fate in Romans 9-11.

[217] Pitre, (2005, 229) agrees with this assessment, and includes Isaiah 25:1-12 in his comments on "the city of chaos" that was to be destroyed. He fails to see that if Jerusalem is the city of chaos to be destroyed in Isaiah 25:1f, that this demands that the resurrection of v. 8 - the source of Paul's resurrection hope in 1 Corinthians 15 - was to occur at the destruction of Jerusalem. This would be in agreement with Daniel 12:2-7.

Great Tribulation (v. 17).[218] This is also posited at the Day of the Lord for the vindication of the martyrs (v. 21). I am convinced that Isaiah 26 lies behind Paul's reference to the groaning of creation and the promise of the resurrection in Romans 8:18f.

4. Isaiah 27 promised the destruction of Leviathan, so that Israel, the Lord's vineyard, could sing praises for her salvation. God's people would suffer, but, her enemies would be crushed. And then we find the passage that Paul cited in Romans 11– which is also the prediction of the destruction of the city and the temple (v.9f).[219] It is possible (likely) that Paul is echoing Isaiah 27:1 in his promise of the imminent destruction of Satan in Romans 16:20.

5. Isaiah 28 threatened Israel with the overwhelming tempest of the Lord, and His fury that would overtake them like a flood (v. 2f). Yet, "in that day" the Lord would save the remnant (v. 5). In verses 11f, we once again see a citation of the Law of Blessings and Cursings, (Deuteronomy 28:49). Paul quotes directly from this text in 1 Corinthians 14, showing again his reliance of the prophecies of Israel's last days.

In 28:16, the Lord promised to lay the foundation stone for the Messianic Kingdom temple, but he warned those who would reject that work that judgment would also come (v.22). Paul cites this text in Romans 9:33.

---

[218] See Pitre's excellent discussion of the relationship between the Great Tribulation and the restoration of Israel (2005, 219+). He shows that in Scripture and in Jewish thought, there is a clear-cut and inseparable connection between these motifs. Since Jesus posited the Tribulation for his generation, and in direct connection to the judgment on Jerusalem, this means that what we have set forth in this work is correct: the time of the salvation of "all Israel" is directly related to the time of the judgment of Jerusalem.

[219] Wagner (2003, 296) misses the point in Isaiah 27:9f, by saying that Isaiah describes the destruction of the pagan idols and altars of their temples. The text is dealing with the destruction of the fortified city and the temple altar (singular) that would fall at the judgment of the people that YHVH had created, the people of no understanding, a direct citation of Deuteronomy 32:28. The pagan idolaters are the not the focus of this. They were not the distinctive people that God had created, and who had forsaken Him.

6. In chapter 29, the prophet foretold the downfall of Ariel, which is the "city of confusion" back in chapter 24 – it is Jerusalem. She would be brought low, to the dust (29:1-4). The Lord would come "with storm and tempest" and it would be because of Israel's "spirit of slumber" - – this is the text that Paul quotes in Romans 11:8. Yet, the prophet also foretold the redemption of "Zion."

Since the NT writers, and certainly Paul in Romans in his discussion of the coming salvation of Israel, draws so much on the Little Apocalypse, what is the justification for claiming that he did not have the judgment of Israel / Jerusalem in mind also, since the texts that he cites clearly did? I propose that Paul's metalyptic citations of these texts points us to the conclusion that he expected the salvation of Israel to take place at the judgment of Israel for shedding innocent blood.

Needless to say, this would be a rich and I think important study, but I will not develop it further at this time.

WHAT ABOUT:
"BLESSED IS HE WHO COMES IN THE NAME OF THE LORD"?
DID JESUS PREDICT A FUTURE CONVERSION OF ISRAEL?

At the conclusion of his Temple Discourse, Jesus uttered the following words:

> "O Jerusalem, Jerusalem, the one who kills the prophets and stones those who are sent to her! How often I wanted to gather your children together, as a hen gathers her chicks under her wings, but you were not willing! See! Your house is left to you desolate; for I say to you, you shall see Me no more till you say, 'Blessed is He who comes in the name of the Lord!' "

It is widely held that in stark contrast to the foregoing "Woes" that he pronounced on Judah and Jerusalem, he here reversed course and held out the promise of an ultimate conversion of Israel - ostensibly in agreement with Paul in Romans 11- at his final appearing.

I believe this completely misses the point.

There is a general consensus among all schools of eschatology that in Matthew 23:29-38 Jesus was predicting the fall of Jerusalem in his generation. It is even interesting to note that the Premillennialists who normally redefine the term "this generation" in Matthew 24:34 freely acknowledge that "this generation" in 23:36 means Jesus' generation and not the "Jewish race," or some future generation.

It is very clear from the literature that verse 39 is perplexing to the majority of exegetes. Plummer says there are three major interpretations of the point of time indicated by Jesus' words:

"1. The cries of the multitude on Palm Sunday (Luke 19:38; Matthew 21:9).

2.) The Second Advent (This suggestion is commonly conflated with Romans 11:25f - involving the conversion of the Jews, DKP).

3.) The conversion of the Jews throughout all time."[220]

---

[220] Alfred Plummer, *International Critical Commentary*, (Scribner and Sons, 1900)353.

It is not our intent to examine each of these postulates individually since we have covered them above. Rather, we will suggest a positive contextual construct for verse 39 that allows the verse to stand in full harmony with the context of judgment on Israel.

A Historical Note

Virtually all commentators take note of the fact that Matthew 23:39 is a citation of Psalms 118:26. However, few connect the dots of the historical significance of this fact.

There is a logical, contextual and historical application of the Song of Ascent to the events of AD 70. Psalms 118 was called a Song of Ascent or a Song of Degrees. What this meant was that the Psalm was sung to pilgrims by the inhabitants of Jerusalem as the travelers approached the city of Jerusalem to observe one of the sacred feast days of the Jewish calendar. As Rawlinson says, it was, "an antiphonal hymn, composed for joyful occasion, when there was to be a procession to the Temple, a welcoming of the procession by those inside, and the solemn offering of a sacrifice upon the altar there."[221] Manson says Psalms 118 was, "a psalm which has connections with the great pilgrim feasts of Judaism, but especially the feast of Tabernacles."[222]

Psalms 118 then, especially verse 26, was a song especially associated with the three great feast days of Israel. Let us refresh our minds about those feast days.

The Jewish Feasts

The Jews had three major "pilgrimage" feasts. In total, there were seven feasts, observed at those times of pilgrimage. That is, these were the three times a year when every Jewish male that was of age was required by Mosaic mandate to travel to Jerusalem and worship the Lord (Exodus 23:17). Those feasts are sometimes called by different names, but they are generally known as Passover,

---

[221] G. Rawlinson, *Pulpit Commentary,* Psalms Bk. V, *(Grand Rapids,* Eerdmans,, 1977)87.

[222] T. W. Manson, *The Mission and Message of Jesus*, (E.P. Dutton, 1946)420.

Pentecost, and Tabernacles.[223] Passover is otherwise known as the Feast of Unleavened Bread. (Technically, the Feast of Unleavened Bread began on the day after Passover, but was so inextricably linked with it that the terms are sometimes used interchangeably). Pentecost is the Feast of First fruits, and the Feast of Tabernacles is also called the Feast of Booths, and the Feast of In-Gathering (Exodus, 23:14; Leviticus 23).

The Feast of Passover began the Jewish Calendar and lasted for seven days (Exodus 12; Leviticus 23:4-8). The Feast of Pentecost, or First fruits, was almost two months later (fifty days - Leviticus 23:15f). The seventh month of the Jewish Calendar was especially significant, since on the first day was the Feast of Trumpets, Rosh Ha Shanah. On the 10th day was the Day of Atonement, considered by some rabbis to be the most Holy Day in the year. On the 15th day was the beginning of the Feast of Tabernacles. This Feast lasted for 7 days (Leviticus 23:33f).

The Jewish Calendar therefore, provided for a significant number of days to be dedicated to worship. In all, counting the 49 day interim between Passover and Pentecost since normally that was almost considered as part of the Festival complex, the time involved in the Feasts involved two full months. What is the point to all of this?

Remember, it was Psalms 118 that was sung to the pilgrims as they approached the city of Jerusalem to observe these feasts. Thus on three different occasions, once at the beginning of the year, once almost two months later, and again in the seventh month Psalms 118:26 would reverberate through the streets of Jerusalem: "Blessed is he who comes in the name of the Lord!" Now let us make the connection with Matthew 23:39.

Jesus' Prediction

As already noted, there is little controversy among commentators that Jesus, in Matthew 23:29-38, predicted the judgment on Jerusalem in AD 70. But these same commentators believe that verse 39 strikes a dissonant cord to that message of doom, offering instead a "silver lining" to the dark cloud of pronounced judgment.

---

[223] The seven feasts were: Passover, Unleavened Bread, Feast of Weeks, Pentecost, Rosh Ha Shanah (Trumpets), Atonement and Succot, or the Feast of Harvest.

I suggest however, that verse 39 was in fact a statement of Jesus *predicting the time of his coming in judgment against Israel*. It is very clear that the point of Jesus' statement in verse 39 is *when he would come*: "you will not see me again until you say." Most agree with this assessment to a degree, but again, it is claimed that v. 39 refers to a yet future conversion of the Jews at the end of the age, e.g. Romans 11:26f. But this ignores several facts.

First, Paul, in Romans 9:28, places the predicted salvation of Israel within an imminent time-frame, actually linking it to his personal ministry in 11:25 and 15:16f. This cannot be ignored.

Second, it also ignores the fact that Israel's salvation would come at the time of Israel's judgment as we have sufficiently demonstrated above. See Isaiah 2-4; 27, 59, 64-66; Zechariah 12-14, etc.. In other words, Israel would be saved by judgment, not from judgment. She would be saved by eschatological transformation, not national restoration.

Take particular note of the fact that verse 39 begins with the connective, "for I say to you" (*lego gar humin*). Grammatically, this ties verse 39 directly to verse 38. Thus, the time of verse 39 is the time of verse 38 - the time when Israel's house would be desolated! So, if one wishes to posit verse 39 as the time of Israel's salvation, it cannot negate that linguistic and grammatical connection to the time of Israel's judgment in AD 70.

Third, it ignores the fact that the New Testament writers indisputably taught that they were living in the last days, in the end of the age (1 Corinthians 10:10-11; Hebrews 1:1; 9:26, 1 Peter 1:5-7, 18-20). It is a dubious hermeneutic that denies this and extends the last days for a period of two thousand years - so far!

But again, the point of Jesus' prediction is the timing of his parousia. The purpose of his return in the context is judgment. When would he come in judgment? At the time when they would be singing the Song of Degrees (Psalms 118:26)! Jesus was saying he would return in the judgment he had just pronounced during one of the three Feast Days of Israel. Is this what really happened?

Anyone familiar with Josephus know this to be true. He says,

> "Now the number of those that were carried captive during this whole war was collected to be ninety-seven thousand; as was the number of those that perished during the whole siege eleven

hundred thousand, the greater part of whom were indeed of the same nation (with the citizens of Jerusalem), but not belonging to the city itself; for they were come up from all the country to the feast of unleavened bread, and were on a sudden shut up by an army."[224]

Thus, Josephus confirms that the siege of Jerusalem began at the time of one of the three major feast days, one of the distinctive times when Psalms 118:26 would be sung.

Someone might object that such a prediction by Jesus isolating his coming to one of the feast days was tantamount to predicting, "the day and the hour" of his coming. That is not the case at all. In Matthew 24, Jesus predicted his coming in that generation (v. 29-34). He even gave some signs (v. 14-15) whereby, "when you see all these things then know that he is near even at the doors." (ASV). They could know by these signs that his coming was near, "but of that day and hour knoweth no man" (v. 36).[225] Knowing something is near, that it is even to be in your generation, does not tell you the day or the hour of its occurrence.

Considering the span of time involved in the feast days of the Jews it would hardly be possible for anyone to calculate the day or the hour of Jesus' coming. After all, literally months were spanned in these feasts, both at the first of the year and in the seventh month.

If I were to tell you that I was going to come to your house next year for sure and that it would be at one of the national holidays, could you predict the specific day and hour I would arrive? Certainly not. Just so, when Jesus pronounced

---

[224] *Works of Josephus*, *Wars of the Jews*, Book 6, chapter 9, paragraph 3.

[225] It should be noted that the language of not knowing "the day and the hour" is itself taken from Israel's festal calendar. Rosh Ha Shanah, the Feast of Trumpets, which foreshadowed the Day of Judgment, was observed on the New Moon. It could not begin until the new moon was sighted. Often, inclimate weather, fog, etc. prevented the sighting of the new moon. Thus, the rabbis actually called Rosh Ha Shanah the feast of which "no man knows the day or the hour." This actually serves as a double attestation to the point we are making on Matthew 23:39.

judgment against Israel in Matthew 23:29-38 and then enigmatically stated that this would occur on one of the occasions when they would be singing the Hallel Hymn of Psalms 118, *he was not specifying the day and hour of his coming.* He was, however, indicating that it would be fulfillment of Rosh Ha Shanah, the feast that foreshadowed the Day of Judgment.

This view of Matthew 23:39 is consistent with the context. It prevents us from interjecting into the context some idea that has not been previously mentioned or hinted at, i.e. a national conversion of the Jewish nation. But, not only is this view consistent with the context, it becomes very significant for helping us understand the disciples' question in Matthew 24.

Questions about Questions

Jesus' disciples heard his prediction of coming judgment. As they were leaving the temple they began to show him the incredible stones of the temple. Many commentators believe they were pointing out its beauty to him; and this is certainly not unreasonable. But is it not just as reasonable, and contextual, to believe that they, after just overhearing him predict judgment on this edifice, were pointing out its size and invulnerability as well? But whether beauty or bulk was their focus, the point is the same and must not be ignored; the disciples were pointing to the temple in immediate response to Jesus' prediction to come in judgment against it.

Since, as we have already seen, it is widely agreed that Matthew 23 is a prediction of Jesus' coming in judgment on Israel in that generation, where is the justification for changing from that and insist that in 24:2 the disciples were asking about some "end of time" coming of Jesus? If one accepts our postulate on 23:39 this argument becomes even stronger. If the disciples understood Jesus in 23:39 to be speaking of his coming in judgment against Jerusalem then the most natural and unforced interpretation of their question in 24:2 is that they were asking for more information about what Jesus has just predicted.

Matthew 24:2 cannot contextually be viewed as "New News" to the disciples. Jesus had already pronounced coming judgment in chapter 23. Chapter 24:3 should therefore be viewed as an inquiry about that impending disaster. They wanted more information on when and the signs precursory to the event.

In spite of this it is common to read in the commentaries the claim that the disciples considered these three events, (the fall of Jerusalem, the end of the world and the final coming of Jesus, DKP), to be synchronous events, but that they were. This claim - once held by me - is, however, based on nothing but presuppositional theology and not solid exegesis. This claim assumes without proof the idea of an end of material creation at the end of time, it falsely charges the disciples with misunderstanding a subject that inspiration specifically says they understood.

I well understand that the disciples did not, far too often, comprehend Jesus' teaching. But, the only way we know they misunderstood is because the record tells us they did. See particularly the book of John on this. But, where in Matthew 23-24 are we informed of the disciples' gross misunderstanding of the subject at hand? There is no indication at all. The fact is we are told they did understand.

In Matthew 13, Jesus told three parables about the end of the age and the kingdom. In verse 51, Jesus specifically asked them, "Have you understood all these things?" Their response was, "Yes, Lord." Now did they lie, or were they too embarrassed to admit confusion? If so, where is the indication? What is so significant about this? It is because one of the parables has a direct impact on our understanding of Matthew 24.

The parable of the Tares in Matthew 13 tells of the coming of the Son of Man with the angels to gather the elect and cast out the Tares at the end of the age (v. 37f). Jesus said that time would be when, "the righteous will shine forth as the sun in the kingdom" (v. 43). This is a direct echo of Daniel 12:3.

Daniel 12 deals with the Great Tribulation (v. 1), the "time of the end" (v. 4), the Abomination of Desolation (v.9-11). Jesus directly alludes to Daniel 12 in Matthew 24:15 and 21, and the disciple's question about the end of the age is grounded in Daniel 12 as well. Now watch.

In Daniel 12 the prophet overheard one angel ask another when all these things would be fulfilled and was told that, "when the power of the holy people has been completely shattered all these things will be fulfilled" (v. 7.) The disciples were well aware of Daniel 12 and its prediction of judgment on Israel. Jesus cites Daniel 12 and applied it to his coming at the end of the age (Matthew 13). He quoted Daniel 12 no less than twice in his prediction of Jerusalem's fall in Matthew 24. Jesus asked them if they understood and they said, "Yes!" Therefore, unless the disciples lied then they understood from Daniel and Jesus' teaching in Matthew 13 that his coming would be at the end of the age judgment on Israel. Did they lose their understanding in Matthew 24? Had they become confused since Jesus spoke his words of Matthew 13? We hardly think so.

In this light the questions of the disciples in Matthew 24 are perfectly consistent with the context of Matthew 23, with the earlier teaching of Matthew 13 and with the prophetic background of Daniel 12. The disciples had heard Jesus predict Jerusalem's judgment. They were familiar with the prophecies of her fall at the end of the age, and were now inquiring for more information about when it would happen and the signs to signify its approach. Any other interpretation of the questions accusing the disciples of lying, bad memory or confusion is misguided. There is nothing in Jesus' words to indicate that those disciples were confused or in error as they connected the destruction of Jerusalem with Jesus' parousia and the end of the age.

As just noted, many commentators agree that the disciples linked Jesus' prediction of Jerusalem's demise with the end of the age and his parousia. Those commentators insist that the disciples were thinking of the end of the time-space continuum when Jesus predicted the destruction of the temple.

Calvin made this claim:

> "It must be remembered that, having believed from their infancy that the temple would stand until the end of time, and having this opinion deeply rooted in their minds, they did not suppose that, while the building of the world stood, the temple could fall to ruins. Accordingly, as soon as Christ said that the temple would be destroyed, their thoughts immediately turned to the end of the world; and, as one error leads to another – having been convinced that, as soon as the reign of Christ should commence they would be in every respect happy, they leave warfare out of the account and fly all at once to the triumph. They associate the coming of Christ and the end of the world as things inseparable from each other; and by the end of the world they mean the restoration of all things, so that nothing may be wanting to complete the happiness of the godly."[226]

The trouble with this claim is that it totally overlooks Scripture and history. Did the disciples not know that the temple had been destroyed in the sixth century BC, and yet, time, history and the cosmos continued? To suggest that the

---

[226] John Calvin, *Calvin's Commentaries, Harmony of Matthew, Mark, Luke and John 1-11*, Vol. XVII, (Grand Rapids, Baker, 2005)116.

disciples could not conceive of the destruction of the temple without thinking of the destruction of the material cosmos is simply illogical.

Wright is surely correct to note:

> "What the disciples had naturally wanted to know was, when would Jesus actually be installed as king? He responded, equally surprisingly, with a reworking of scriptural passages about great cities being destroyed, and about the vindication of the true people of Israel's god. All was focused on the central point, that the Temple's destruction would constitute his own vindication. Once grant this premise, and the nightmare of puzzled textual reconstruction is in principle over." (1996, 342).

He adds:

> "Matthew 24:3, therefore, is most naturally read, in its first century Jewish context, not as a question about (what scholars have come to call, in technical language) the 'parousia', but as a question about Jesus' 'coming' or 'arriving' in the sense of is actual enthronement as king, consequent upon the dethronement of the present powers that were occupying the holy city" (1996, 346).

While Wright makes the connection between the end of the age, the vindication of the martyrs and Jesus' parousia (But not, as he says, in the popular sense) in AD 70, he is totally silent about any connection of that time and those events with the vindication of the martyrs, the salvation of Israel and the coming of the Lord in Romans 11.

Since the disciples associated the destruction of the temple with the end of the age and Christ's coming, perhaps it is the wise course to realize that the end of the age did come with the fall of Jerusalem in AD 70. This is especially true in light of what we have seen in Matthew 13 and its relationship to Daniel 12.

Speaking of the impending catastrophe on Jerusalem, Jesus said, "These be the days of vengeance in which all things that are written must be fulfilled (Luke 21:22). The fall of Jerusalem was the *terminus ad quem* (point of ending) of fulfillment, not the *terminus a quo* (point of beginning).

There is therefore, only one coming in the context of Matthew 23-24.

After hearing Jesus' portentous words in 23:29f the disciples naturally wanted to know more, and thus the questions of Matthew 24:3. Unless one can demonstrate that: The coming of 23:39 is not the judgment coming of the previous verses, and, that the coming of verse 39 is therefore, a reference to national Jewish conversion, it therefore seems unavoidable that verse 39 is a reference to the AD 70 coming of Jesus in judgment against Israel.

This also provides the context for identifying the coming in 24:3. This means that if the coming of 24:3 is the coming of 23:39, and if the coming of 23:39 is AD 70, then there is no basis at all for postulating an "end of time" coming in Matthew 24.

A final thought here. In Luke 21:28, when Jesus promised, "when you see these things come to pass, lift up your heads, for your redemption draws nigh." As we have noted above, judgment and salvation are siamese twins and a proper understanding of the Olivet Discourse proves this. On the one hand, it would be when Israel's house would be desolated. On the other hand, it would be the time of redemption.

There is nothing in the Olivet Discourse that anticipated the national conversion of Israel. The Discourse did promise the salvation of the elect (24:30-31) - which is Romans 11:25f - and posited it for that generation, at the coming of the Lord. That coming of the Lord was in judgment of Israel.

Space will not permit a fuller discussion, but, an issue that is critical to observe is that Jehovah never allowed, or caused, Israel to be attacked and pillaged unless she had violated the covenant.[227] See Psalms 41:11.

To suggest that the Abomination would be/will be a horrible act of desecration placed on the "innocent" nation, by a traitorous Man of Sin, completely ignores the covenantal nature of any and all attacks and desecrations against Israel's land, city and temple. Simply stated, if Israel was attacked and her city and temple conquered or desecrated, it was proof positive that she was in violation of her covenant!

---

[227] See my *Daniel 12: Fulfilled or Future?* book, (2016) for a full discussion of this issue. To this date, I have not seen a single Dispensational writer address this issue.

A further point that must be repeated here, is the fact that the Millennialists claim that the Mosaic Covenant has been forever fulfilled and removed in Christ. Yet, they then appeal to Deuteronomy 30 as a proof text to support a future restoration of Israel. This is a logical contradiction. You cannot say that the Mosaic Covenant has been forever removed, and then appeal to the Mosaic Covenant to support the idea of a future restoration of Israel.

Our point in regard to the redemption promised in Luke is that it had to refer, not to the nation of Israel and a national repentance and conversion. Jesus was speaking to his followers about what would befall them at the hands of Old Covenant Israel. He then spoke of what would befall Old Covenant Israel for her persecution of His disciples. Jesus was not speaking to or about Old Covenant Israel when he said, "when you see all of these things come to pass, your redemption draws nigh." He was speaking to those who followed him in faith.[228]

Conclusion

Identifying the context and background of the Song of Ascent in Matthew 23:39 is helpful in properly interpreting the entire Olivet Discourse. Our interpretation avoids the pitfalls of introducing unprecedented subject matter into the context and is consistent with the judgment context of Matthew 23.

Just as in chapter 24, Jesus foretold the fact of his coming and the general time of its occurrence, he had already given the forecast of his coming in judgment, and a general statement as to the time for its happening. Jesus would come in judgment against Jerusalem. He would come on one of the Holy Days of the year when they would be singing "Blessed is he who comes in the name of the Lord." And this is exactly what happened.

Seen in the light of the rest of this work, Matthew 23:39 cannot be manipulated to speak of a still future coming of the Lord for the salvation of the mass body of ethnic Jews. Just like Romans 11:25f, when viewed within the purview of the ministry of John the Baptizer, Israel's salvation would take place at the time of Israel's judgment. That occurred in AD 70.

---

[228] I am not by any means suggesting any kind of "replacement theology" here. I am simply pointing out what Jesus said, and that is that national Israel, the corporate body, was to be destroyed and the righteous remnant of Israel, who had accepted Jesus as Messiah, would be those who were saved.

"JERUSALEM SHALL BE TRODDEN DOWN OF THE GENTILES, UNTIL THE TIMES OF THE GENTILES ARE FULFILLED." (Luke 21:24).

It is common in Dispensational literature to link Matthew 23:39 and Luke 21:24 with Romans 11. The end of the "times of the Gentiles" is seen as the restoration of Israel at the coming of Christ and the kingdom. Millennialists define the times of the Gentiles as the period of Gentile domination and control over Jerusalem. Some date it from the Babylonian Captivity,[229] while others believe it began in AD 70 with the Roman destruction of the city. All commentators who posit the times of the Gentiles as Gentile domination over Jerusalem, whether from BC 586 or from AD 70 onward agree with Ice's assessment: "At the parousia the times of the Gentiles cease and the focus of history once again turns to the Jews."[230] But there is an elephant in the room for those holding this position.

The linguistics of Luke 21:24 forbid the Millennialists' definition of the times of the Gentiles. Virtually 100% of those commentators seem unaware of the term "trodden down" and its impact on the definition of the times of the Gentiles.

The word translated "trodden down" is *pateo* and contrary to the Dispensational idea that it refers to the socio-economic, political "Gentile" domination and control of the city over the span of the last 2000 years and more,[231] this word means *active warfare, active conquest* and *active destruction*.

---

[229] Cf. Michael F. Blume, commenting on the vision of Daniel 2: "In essence, this awesome dream describes the fullness of the 'times of the Gentiles - that is, the 'times' and seasons when Gentile kingdoms, or Gentile-influenced kingdoms, would rule over the world, or vast sections thereof. In other words, from the time of king Nebuchadnezzar of Babylon, till the present time, today, the world has been living under or within the 'times of the Gentiles' - the times GENTILE KINGDOMS would dominate and have the supremacy over the nations of the world!" (His emphasis). (http://mikeblume.com/timesgen.htm)

[230] Thomas Ice and Timothy Demy, *Prophecy Watch*, (Eugene, Or., 1998)264.

[231] Actually, I have yet to find a Dispensational commentator that even examines *pateo*. It is totally ignored.

Ardnt and Gingrich says the word means to tread down, to trample, "of the undisciplined swarming of a victorious army through a captured city."[232] All lexicons agree on this definition. This linguistic fact alone destroys the concept of the trodding down of Jerusalem for the last 2000 years.[233] There have been *long* periods of time when there was no active military war taking place in Jerusalem. In fact, even though there certainly have been times of active military action in Jerusalem, for the most part, active military "down trodding" i.e. active trampling of the city by a victorious army, *has not characterized the last 2000 years*. To drive the point home even more, there have been periods of time – even the present time - when the Israeli forces have controlled the City! You can hardly say that the trodding down by the Gentiles is on-going when Israel and Jerusalem is not being trodden down - or even controlled - by the Gentiles.

Not only does history demonstrate that Israel has not been actively "trodden down" by the Gentiles for the last 2000 years, a quick study of how the word *pateo* is used in scripture verifies what we are saying.

While the LXX uses *pateo* in the same way as the NT, we will confine our study to the NT occurrences of the word with one quick exception.

In Lamentations 1:17, where Jeremiah looks back at the siege and destruction of Jerusalem under the Chaldeans as the *treading down* (a cognate of *pateo*) of the city. He was living in the time of socio - economic - political *domination that followed that treading down*. But that subsequent time of domination was not the time of her *pateo*.

Pateo is only used five times in the NT and as just suggested invariably refers to a violent action – it *never* refers to a simple socio / economic / political, control over a people.

---

[232] *A Greek English Lexicon of the New Testament,* (University of Chicago Press, 1979)635.

[233] The proper definition of *pateo* likewise falsifies the Amillennial view of Beale who posits the treading down of the holy city in Revelation 11 as reference to the persecution of the church throughout time, until the end of time (Beale, NIGTC, *Revelation*, 1999, 569f). This is a gross abuse of *pateo*. The church has not been actively, militarily trodden down for 2000 years.

☞In Luke 10:19 – Jesus told his disciples, "I have given you authority to *tread* on serpents and snakes." Jesus was patently not talking here of simple "domination" of snakes, but the active crushing.

☞Luke 21:24 - The context of Luke is clearly referent to the active war and siege of Jerusalem. Notice the reference to Jerusalem surrounded, and the men of Jerusalem falling by the sword. This is *active warfare*. This is the context of the trodding down. The army and the siege are part and parcel of *pateo*. The context gives no credence to the idea of a 2000 year period of political domination.

☞Revelation 11:1-4 – John was told that, "the holy city shall be trodden down for time, times and half time." Unless one can make this referent to be 2000 years, then the context refers to the active, military, war time conquering of the city. This is the city, "Where the Lord was slain" (Revelation 11:8). The parallels between Luke 21 and Revelation 11 define the, "times of the Gentiles" as the period of the Jewish War. It was "42 months." It was, to express it another way, the time appointed by God for the destruction of Old Covenant Jerusalem.

☞Revelation 14:20 – This text also describes the judgment of Babylon and she is, "trodden down in the winepress of God's wrath." Imagery could not be clearer. The treading down is the time of active destruction - not geo-political domination.

☞Revelation 19:15 - Just as in Revelation 11 and 14, in chapter 19, Jesus is described as the one that makes war on Babylon: "He treads the winepress of the wrath of God." There is not a hint of an idea of long term, geo-political, domination. It is the active, real time of war against "Babylon" – her time of destruction.

The impact of this linguistic evidence is quite devastating for the Dispensational and Premillennial paradigm. In July of 2015, I had a formal YouTube debate with Dr. Michael Brown, a renowned apologist and debater. I made the point on *pateo*, with the scriptural support. Dr. Brown did not initially respond. Near the end of the debate, when I had no opportunity to respond, he quickly stated that Jerusalem had undergone several times of military conflict during the last 2000 years, therefore my point, said he, was negated. This is as false as can be. As just demonstrated, the fact that there have been several times of active military conflict, *interspersed between long periods of peace*, does not meet the linguistic demands of *pateo*. Not to mention the fact - mentioned just above - that some of those supposed times of conflict were times when the Israeli forces controlled

Jerusalem.

P*ateo* in Luke 21:24, gives no support whatsoever to the Dispensational view that Jerusalem has been "trodden down" for the last 2000 years. It gives no hint that at some future coming of Christ Jerusalem will be restored. This means there can be no link with Romans 11, with the exception that the judgment of Jerusalem foretold in Luke is the same time as the salvation of Israel foretold in Romans 11. But, as we have demonstrated, the commonality between the two texts is that both of them were to be fulfilled in the judgment of Old Covenant Jerusalem for shedding innocent blood. But there is even more here than the meaning of *pateo*.

As I show extensively in another work,[234] the Abomination of Desolation and the Great Tribulation must be viewed as *the imposition of Covenant Wrath on Israel for violation the Law of Moses*. This fact is virtually unnoticed in the literature, but it is critical. The same can be said of the times of the Gentiles.

According to Leviticus 26 and the Law of Blessings and Cursings (Deuteronomy 28-30) the only way that YHVH allowed the Gentiles to control the land of Israel, Jerusalem and the temple, was when / if Israel had broken Torah. The invasions of the land and the capturing of the City were invariably viewed – according to the prophets - as God's judgment on the people for violating the Mosaic covenant. This is important.

Dispensationalists and Historic Premillennialists alike affirm that the Law of Moses is not in effect today. In my debate with Dr. Brown, I asked if the Law of Moses was still in effect and he answered, "No." However, one cannot affirm on the one hand that Israel remains God's people, that Jerusalem has been in subjection to the Gentiles for the last 2000 years and at the same time say the Law of Moses passed away 2000 years ago. The only way that Jerusalem and Israel could be enduring the times of the Gentiles is if the Law of Moses - every jot and every tittle of the Law of Blessings and Cursings- remains in effect and binding today.[235]

---

[234] Don K. Preston, *The Resurrection of Daniel 12: Future or Fulfilled?*, (Ardmore, Ok. JaDon Management Inc., 2016). The book is available on Amazon, my websites and other retailers.

[235] A glaring inconsistency in this regard came to light in my debate with Dr. Brown. Even though he affirmed that the Law of Moses

It is self-evident that if a law or a covenant has been annulled the provisions of that covenant are no longer applicable. This is beyond dispute. So, it was the Law of Moses that made provision for "the times of the Gentiles" i.e the appointed times of judgment against Israel for violating the covenant.[236] If therefore, the times of the Gentiles have been in existence since AD 70 this is *prima facie* proof that the Law of Moses has remained in effect - and remains in effect - to this very day.

The Dispensationalists and Premillennialists cannot have their cake and eat it too. If the Law of Moses passed away in the first century as they all claim, the times of the Gentiles ended in the first century.

If the times of the Gentiles have been in effect since AD 70 – or BC 586 - then Torah remains in effect and will remain in effect until the end of the times of the Gentiles end, at the Second Coming of Christ. And since Millennialists conflate Romans 11 with Matthew 23 and Luke 21, the problem is compounded. If our posit above concerning Matthew 23 and the parousia of Christ at the time of festal observance is correct, then of necessity, Christ must come at a time when Israel is "obeying" Torah.

There is therefore no way, Biblically or logically, to divorce the topic of the times of the Gentiles from the fundamental fact of Israel's violation of the Mosaic Covenant. Since the Millennialists insist that the Mosaic Covenant is no longer valid, (and, they likewise say the Mosaic Law will never be restored) this demands that the times of the Gentiles had to have occurred at a time *when the Mosaic Covenant was still in force*. This agrees perfectly with our comments above on Malachi 3:5 and chapter 4:4f.

---

has been done away, he then tried to prove that the judgment and resurrection must be yet future *because we are still waiting for Israel's last three feast days, Trumpets, Atonement and Succot (Harvest) to be fulfilled!* How could the Law of Moses have been done away, yet the climatic feast days - an integral part of the Law of Moses - have not been fulfilled?

[236] Deuteronomy 28-30 and Leviticus 26 speak at length of Gentile invasion and Gentiles taking Israel captivity if / when she violated Torah. Thus, the "times of the Gentiles" is inextricably tied to Israel's observance - or disobedience to - Torah.

So, an examination of the linguistics of Luke 21:24 along with the issue of Torah precludes any application of the "times of the Gentiles" to our day, or to a future event. *Pateo* absolutely does not refer to a long period of time of mere geo-political, economic domination *without active war*. Thus, the times of the Gentiles cannot refer to the last 2000 years since AD 70, a period that has witnessed long periods of no war. Furthermore, the fact that the Israeli forces have actually controlled Jerusalem for many years falsifies the Millennial interpretation of Luke 21.

Finally, while Millennialists affirm that the Law of Moses has been nullified, they then turn around and make application of prophecies from the Law of Moses to apply to the last 2000 years and to yet future events. But, it is specious to apply a dead law to current events.

Based on these facts, it is safe to say that the only connection between Romans 11, the salvation of Israel, Luke 21, and the times of the Gentiles is that the judgment on Israel for shedding innocent blood was in AD 70. The times of the Gentiles was the time designated by God for that judgment. But, it was then that Israel's soteriological history reached its destiny in Christ.

UNEXPLORED, BUT CORROBORATIVE ISSUES

There is a great deal more that could be said about Romans 11:25-27. A full exploration of these additional themes would expand this book far beyond my target, however. Just a few of the additional subjects that could be investigated and that help to corroborate the view set forth in this book are:

The Blindness of Israel - This motif leads us directly to the judgment of Israel in AD 70 - as well as that being the time of the salvation of Israel. Our brief comments above barely scratch the surface of this theme. Jesus and Paul cited the OT prophecies of Israel's obstinate blindness, and the texts they cited invariably tied that blindness to impending national judgment.

The Fulness of the Gentiles. We have briefly hinted at the significance of this issue and Paul's distinctive, exclusive role in bringing in the fullness of the Gentiles. Paul's personal ministry and stewardship was to "fulfill the word of God, the mystery" bringing the "fulness of the Gentiles" to a reality. Thus, the salvation of Israel was inseparably tied to the completion of Paul's Gentile ministry.

The Salvation of the Remnant - If the salvation of the remnant would be consummated in the salvation of "all Israel" then Paul unequivocally posited that consummation within a short time (Romans 9:28f) in full agreement with the other texts of imminence we have examined herein. Our brief examination of Revelation and the salvation of the remnant should be enough to demonstrate how it relates to Romans 11 and demands a first century fulfillment.

The Redeemer Shall Come Out of Zion. This rich motif carries with it clear cut eschatological overtones. We have hinted at its significance in our brief discussion of the Lord coming out of His place in Isaiah 26.

When I Take Away Their Sin. This would be a deeper study of Daniel 9 and the Day of Atonement typological praxis which we have discussed briefly above. But there is much more that could be investigated.[237]

---

[237] See my *Seventy Weeks Are Determined...For the Resurrection*. The book is available on my websites, Amazon, Kindle and other retailers.

This Is My Covenant With Them. This concept leads us inexorably to the climax of Israel's Old Covenant aeon, in AD 70. As we have noted, the salvation of Israel at the coming of the Lord in Romans would be in fulfillment of God's covenant with Israel. One cannot therefore, divorce Torah from the Telos, or extrapolate the salvation of Israel into the distant future, without establishing (re-establishing) Israel as the covenant people of God - along with the body of Christ. To put it another way, as noted above, is, that to say that the salvation of Israel promised in Romans 11:25f is still future is to establish the Two Covenant Doctrine, which most scholars say is false.

What we have seen in this work is sufficient to establish the validity of my premise. The role of John the Baptizer, as *The Voice, The Messenger* and *Elijah*, while virtually ignored in the literature as it relates to Romans 11, nonetheless has a determinative role in our understanding of that great text. Once a person grasps how pervasively John's message influenced the rest of the NT writers - and Romans 11 - our eschatology is profoundly impacted.

In the literature, scholar after scholar comments on how important of an "end time prophet" John was. They show how in the rabbinic literature, Elijah was tied directly to the end of the age resurrection and establishment of the kingdom. They document for us from the ancient sources that Elijah was in fact, the key end times prophet. Jesus undeniably identified John as the predicted Elijah.

But then, with the martyrdom of John, it is almost as if John and his role as *The Voice, The Messenger* and *Elijah* drops off the map in discussions of eschatology. But, why so? It is because so many - most - commentators believe that John's mission was - ultimately - a failure. After all, he was to "restore all things" and everyone knows he did not do that, right? Well, if John failed, then Jesus failed, because they shared the same role and mission.

The problem, it seems to me, is that the scholars are overlooking the incredible importance of the doctrine of the last days avenging of the martyrs. When properly considered, the martyrdom of John and Jesus was vital to the accomplishment of God's eschatological schema. Their death did not prevent fulfillment, *it was the necessary means of fulfillment*, "Ought not the Christ to suffer and to enter into his glory?"

Did not Peter say that the OT prophets had spoken of, "the sufferings of Christ, and the glory to follow" (1 Peter 1:11– cf. Romans 8:17)? For Jesus, the Cross was the pathway to the Crown, the Crown of life (Hebrews 12:1-3), the Crown of the Kingdom. And that is true of the entire doctrine of the vindication of the martyrs, including the martyrdom of John and all of the Worthies (cf. Hebrews 11).

The additional problem in consideration of John's eschatological role is the traditional, literalistic view of the Day of the Lord and resurrection. Some scholars, as we have documented, acknowledge that John did not predict the end of time or a literalistic Day of the Lord with Jesus coming out of heaven on a cumulus cloud. Nonetheless, in the broader view of eschatology that is precisely what is laid at the feet of John, Jesus and the apostles. Thus, just like Jesus and his apostles, his and their predictions of the end failed. However, by accepting the well documented nature of the Day of the Lord as set forth even in the OT prophecies of the message of *The Voice*, *The Messenger* and *Elijah*, such an ascription of failure is itself misguided. Neither John, nor Jesus or his disciples were wrong. The Day of the Lord - national judgment on Israel - came as predicted, when predicted - in AD 70.

THE IMPLICATIONS OF OUR PROPOSAL FOR FUTURIST ESCHATOLOGIES OF THE DAY

The position set forth in this work is virtually unexplored and undeveloped in the literature - unless I have completely missed it. As I have noted, I have not, at the time of this writing, found a single scholar who addresses the relationship between John the Baptizer and Romans 11. I believe that I have sufficiently demonstrated that the connections are undeniably present.

I have likewise not found a single commentator who has acknowledged or suggested that in Romans 11:25f Paul's citation of Isaiah 27 & 59 demands that he had the vindication of the martyrs in mind. Yet, that motif is more than abundantly clear in both prophecies. In fact, it is *explicit* in both of those texts. I see no justification for ignoring or denying that evidence, and yet, that is precisely what happens in the literature. If *metalepsis*[238] is valid, as most scholars now admit, how can we exclude martyr vindication from Paul's citations of Isaiah 27 and 59? No one, *virtually no one*, even addresses this issue.

Likewise, while some scholars see the dangers of a Two Covenant Doctrine in their discussions of Romans, they nonetheless, by positing the salvation of Israel in the future, fully establish that very doctrine. So, while on the one hand, those who espouse the Two Covenant Doctrine are castigated, the very scholars who condemn that view, establish it by putting the fulfillment of Romans 11 in the future.

So, if my proposal is correct, how does this, how *would* this, impact our views of eschatology, theology - and *society*? Needless to say, the impact would be revolutionary. In effect, it would turn the current world of evangelical eschatology on its head. Here is why.

Dispensationalism / Premillennialism – Romans 11:25-27 is foundational to the Millennial world, whether one speaks of Dispensationalism, or Historic

---

[238] Once again, *metalepsis* is the hermeneutical principle, widely practiced and understood in ancient Israel, that when a writer or speaker cited just a few key words, terms or phrases from an OT prophetic text, it was assumed that the reader / listener was to bring the entire OT prophetic text into their minds for consideration.

Premillennialism.[239] If, however, what we have presented here is accurate, then religious Zionism is false and has no Biblical merit.

This means that every TV evangelist that speaks of an imminent coming of the Lord to save "all Israel" is false.

It means that all ministries such as John Hagee, Hal Lindsay, Tim LaHaye, Thomas Ice, Grant Jeffrey, et. al. are completely false. It means that all of their charges of "anti-Semitism," "Replacement Theology," etc. that they level against non-Millennialists are false.

It means that we can dispense with the endless, embarrassing, harmful predictions that "the signs of the end are everywhere,"[240] or, "1948 was the Super Sign of the End."

If the view presented here is true, then all forms of Premillennialism and the attendant doctrines are wrong, and it is time to stop with the false predictions.

If my thesis and proposition is true, it means that national Israel is no longer the chosen, covenant people of God, and the "holy land" no longer belongs to them

---

[239] I have had two formal YouTube debates with noted Christian Zionist apologist Dr. Michael Brown. He describes himself as a Historic Premillennialist. Romans 11:25 is absolutely essential to his Zionist eschatology. When I argued from the position presented in this work, Dr. Brown had no answers. The first of those two debates can be viewed here: https://www.youtube.com/watch?v=H1fP1xB1gsM.

[240] As I write this, Tim LaHay has just recently released a revised and updated version of one of his books, "Are We Living in the End Times?" In this "new" book, LaHaye: "gives reasons for believing that the Rapture and the Tribulation could occur during our generation. Our's is the first generation that has the technology and opportunity to fulfill many of the prophecies of Revelation." Lamentably, few will remember that in 1973, he said that the end was coming very soon! Dispensationalists have the unfortunate and harmful practice of re-cycling their failed prophecies, depending on what the latest newspaper says. It is an embarrassment to Christianity.

by divine right.[241]

I do not have the space here to develop the incredible implications for American foreign policy if one accepts the views presented here. The impact of Dispensationalism on American politics has been - and continues to be - profound and *negative*. President after president has affirmed their belief that modern Israel remains as God's covenant people, and that America must support them unconditionally. This policy has led to horrific loss of countless lives around the world.

Postmillennialism / Dominionism - The classic Postmillennial view is that Romans 11:25f will be fulfilled at the end of the current Christian age. There are now a few representatives of the Dominionist world that quietly admit to an AD 70 fulfillment of Romans 11,[242] but, they fail to see, or discuss, the implications of that admission. They most assuredly do not see that their view establishes the Two Covenant Doctrine.[243]

---

[241] I am painfully aware that I will be charged with "anti-semitism" for making these comments. But, the charge is false. How can it be anti-semitism to say that God has been faithful to His promises to Israel? How can it be anti-semitism to point out that the OT prophets, that John, that Jesus and that the rest of the NT writers all predicted that national judgment was coming on Israel? After all, Dispensationalists themselves agree that Jesus foretold the total destruction of the Old Covenant temple and city (Matthew 23 / Luke 21:20-24). Was Jesus anti-Semitic? Are Dispensationalists anti-Semitic for taking note of this? Far too often, the label of anti-Semitic is thrown out by those who cannot give scriptural answer to the facts presented by non-Zionists.

[242] Joel McDurmon, in his *Jesus V Jerusalem* book, rejects the Westminster Confession of faith (Gentry's view) and strongly hints at a first century fulfillment. (American Vision, Powder Springs, Ga, 2012, 220). DeMar is more decisive in positing an AD 70 fulfillment: http://www.preteristsite.com/docs/demarisrael.html

[243] Joel McDurmon, in private correspondence prior to our public debate, expressed the view that the Law of Moses, and God's covenant with Israel, will remain valid until the end of the current Christian age. Of course, McDurmon tries to say that the ceremonial aspects of Torah passed, while the Mosaic Covenant remains. This is a false dichotomization of "the Law" and "the covenant" as I demonstrated in our formal public debate.

I suggest that to admit to an AD 70 fulfillment of Romans 11 falsifies any futurist eschatology.[244] It most assuredly knocks the props out from under the Classic Postmillennial Reformed view.

Postmillennialists, as a general rule, agree that John the Baptizer was Elijah. That admission demands that Romans 11 stands fulfilled - unless they wish to posit another, yet future coming of the literal Elijah, something they seem loathe to do.

If Romans 11:25f was fulfilled in AD 70 that means that all resurrection texts are fulfilled, since Paul's anticipation of the salvation of Israel is directly tied to Israel's resurrection promises (Isaiah 25:8-10). If Romans 11 is fulfilled, then, as suggested above, Revelation stands fulfilled. Thus, the Postmillennial admission that John fulfilled the role of Elijah is, in truth, destructive of the Dominionist eschatology.

Amillennialism - Once again, there are a few isolated voices in the Amillennial world who have suggested a first century fulfillment of Romans 11. However, this is not the dominant view. Scholars such as Riddlebarger, Middleton, Pate, Wright, etc. (some of whom may not be classified as traditional Amillennialists) connect Romans 11 with their expectation of a future restoration of literal creation to an Edenic utopia at the "end of time." But, if Romans 11 and Romans 8 speak of the same time of redemption and salvation, and if Romans 11 was fulfilled in AD 70 at the "Climax of the Covenant" – God's Old Covenant dealings with Israel - then any such utopian eschatology falls by the wayside.

Amillennialists, like Postmillennialists, generally agree that John was *The Voice, the Messenger* and *Elijah*. Some, like Riddlebarger posit the Baptizer as a type of a still future, literal Elijah, but that is not the norm. So, Amillennialism, like Postmillennialism, in admitting that John was Elijah, they are tacitly, but logically admitting that the end time resurrection has been fulfilled.

---

[244] To avoid this conundrum, many Postmillennialists and Amillennialists as well, say that while Romans 11 *may* have been fulfilled in AD 70, those end of the age events were a typological foreshadowing of the "real end." This claim has no Biblical support as I prove definitively in my book *AD 70: A Shadow of the "Real" End?* It is an argument born of theological desperation. That book is available on my websites, on Amazon, Kindle and other retailers.

Full development of the implications of our proposal lies well outside the scope of this work. Clearly, some of the implications are stunning, not to mention challenging. However, we should not be deterred by such challenging implications. If our desire is to know and establish Truth, then we must march boldly where that Truth is to be found. If that leads to the overturning of long cherished, firmly established traditions, then so be it.

In sum, if my proposal is correct, the following is true:

The view that Paul had the Incarnation of Jesus in view in Romans 11 is false, since Paul anticipated the salvation of Israel at the coming of the Lord foretold in Isaiah 27 and 59. Neither of those texts has anything to do with the Incarnation. What is the hermeneutic for turning Isaiah's predictions of salvation through judgment for shedding innocent blood, into a prediction of the Incarnation of Jesus?

The view posited by Wright and others, that Paul had in mind the salvation of individual Jews throughout the Christian era is false, for that view likewise ignores the prophetic source of Romans 11.

The view that Romans 11 is about a future conversion of a vast number of ethnic Jews at, or immediately before Jesus' coming at some proposed end of human history is negated, unless those proposing that view wish to extrapolate the judgment of Israel for shedding innocent blood to that event. I am unaware of any scholar that suggests this.

The only view of Romans 11:25f that honors all of the datum is the view presented herein, even it my view does raise the question of, "How was Israel saved?" if AD 70 was the appointed time. What we do know is that it involved the taking away of their sin. It involved the Remarriage of Israel. It related to the bringing the Gentiles into full equality with Israel in the one body of Christ. It involved the full establishment of the kingdom, fulfilling the message of John. There is much, much more to be said about this issue, but, space considerations forbid it here.

I suggest that it is long past time to re-examine the traditional views of eschatology and find fulfillment where Scripture firmly and undeniably posits it: At the end of the Old Covenant age of Israel that arrived with the dissolution of the temple - the very expression of that Old Covenant - and the destruction of the "holy city." That is when God's covenant dealings were consummated and the promised New Covenant creation came to full bloom. That is when "all

Israel' all of the Worthies of faith entered into their promised "eternal inheritance" at the "second appearing" of Christ for salvation.

Thus, the message and ministry of John the Baptizer, *The Voice*, *The Messenger* and *Elijah*, as the herald of the salvation of Israel, firmly, unequivocally and undeniably posits the salvation of "all Israel" in AD 70.

John was not under any misguided idea that he was predicting an end of time, earth burning (or earth renovating), Day of the Lord when he proclaimed the salvation of Israel (i.e. the kingdom). As we have shown, *he fully understood that he was predicting a time of national judgment on Israel for violating Torah*. Paul continued that message in Romans, and the rest of the NT writers echoed John's message of the impending Day of the Lord.

The acknowledgment of John's impact on Romans 11 definitively establishes the fact that the Law of Moses, with its Law of Blessings and Cursings, was to remain in effect until it was fully implemented in the judgment of Israel in AD 70. *Torah* endured until the eschatological *Telos*. You simply cannot posit the application of Mosaic Covenant sanctions of national judgment in AD 70, without thereby affirming that Torah was still in effect at that time. Since, as we have shown, John's message as The covenant Messenger, was not fulfilled between the time of his ministry and the cross, this establishes beyond dispute that the Law of Moses did not pass at the cross. Since Paul, Peter and John were all still anticipating the fulfillment of John's message, then patently, Torah would stand firm until the Telos - the Day of the Lord.

That coming was very imminent 2000 years ago. By honoring the context and framework of fulfillment, as McKnight, Wright and others have admitted, Jesus and the apostles were vindicated in their predictions. But, if they were vindicated in those expectations, *there is no other eschatological expectation in the NT.*

By accepting the views set forth here, the church has a viable and defensible answer for the skeptics who say that Jesus' predictions and those of his apostles failed.

They did not fail.

Scripture Index

Exodus

Ex. 19.6 24
Ex. 22.18-24 32
Ex. 22.21 42

Numbers

Num. 35.9-15 73
Num. 35.30 73

Deuteronomy

Dt. 27.19 31
Dt. 27.19f 42
Dt. 28-29 64
Dt. 28.15-16 31
Dt. 28.28f, 29.4 65
Dt. 30 176
Dt. 31.26 31
Dt. 31.29 110
Dt. 33.2 19
Dt. 32.28 66
Dt. 32.35 120
Dt. 32.43 74, 112

II Samuel

II Sam. 7.14 53

I Kings

I K. 8.33-34 42

Psalms

Ps. 118.26 167

Isaiah

Isa. 1.27-28 3
Isa. 2.2f 29
Isa. 6.9f 65
Isa. 10.22-23 3
Isa. 24-27 71
Isa. 26-27 157
Isa. 26.19f 38
Isa. 26.20 74
Isa. 26.21 4, 72, 79
Isa. 27 ii, 71
Isa. 27.1-5 124
Isa. 27.10-12 158
Isa. 27.11f 4
Isa. 27.9f 4-5, 65, 72
Isa. 28.16 164
Isa. 28-29 71
Isa. 29.10 66
Isa. 40 76
Isa. 40.1-2 46
Isa. 40.1-11 13, 29
Isa. 40.3 7
Isa. 40.6-8 133
Isa. 40.21 16
Isa. 40.28 16
Isa. 49.6f 47
Isa. 52.11 53
Isa. 59 ii, 4, 71, 77-83
Isa. 59.1-15 78
Isa. 59.16ff 78
Isa. 65.1-2 110
Isa. 65.6f 110
Isa. 65.13f 43
Isa. 66.15f 25

Jeremiah

Jer. 3.14f 54
Jer. 31.29f ii

Lamentations

Lam.1.17 178

Ezekiel

Ezek. 37 29
Ezek. 37.27 53

Daniel

Dan. 7.13f 92
Dan. 9.24 28, 45
Dan. 9.24-27 81-82
Dan. 9.26 47
Dan. 12.2-3 73

Hosea

Hos. 6.1-2 73

Zechariah

Zech. 6.13 29

Malachi

Mal. 3.1-2 37
Mal. 3.1-3 26
Mal. 3.1-6 114
Mal. 3.5 27, 29, 32
Mal. 3.24 7
Mal. 4.1-2 64
Mal. 4.2-3 38
Mal. 4.3-4 36

Mal. 4.5-6 45, 64

Matthew

Mt. 3.2 28, 42
Mt. 3.7 24, 59
Mt. 3.7-10 111
Mt. 3.10 61
Mt. 3.11, 12 150
Mt. 3.12 63
Mt. 4.4 64
Mt. 4.17 45
Mt. 11.9 7
Mt. 11.9f 12
Mt. 11.10 23
Mt. 11.11-15 39
Mt. 16.27-28 92-93
Mt. 17.9-13 40
Mt. 17.10f 49
Mt. 17.12 107
Mt. 23.29f 66, 114, 130
Mt. 23.37 44
Mt. 23.39 166, 168, 176
Mt. 24.3 174
Mt. 24.29f 28, 62
Mt. 24.46 122

Mark

Mk. 1.1-2 23
Mk. 1.1-3 13, 29, 47
Mk. 1.4 20

Luke

Lk. 1.17 12
Lk. 1.67-80 7
Lk. 1.72f 104
Lk. 1.79 38
Lk. 10.19 179
Lk. 18.1-8 130
Lk. 21.22 35, 174
Lk. 21.24 177-182

John

Jn. 4.20f 54

Acts

Ac. 1.6f 49
Ac. 3.19f 105
Ac. 3.23f 16
Ac. 3.27f 73
Ac. 17.30-31 24
Ac. 24.14f 102
Ac. 28.25f 65

Romans

Rom. 1.16-17 79
Rom. 1.18 95
Rom. 1.18f 160
Rom. 2.1f 17
Rom. 2.1-9 85
Rom. 2.5 137
Rom. 3.1f 17
Rom. 3.3 16
Rom. 3.3f 22
Rom. 5.1-3 88
Rom. 5.9 160
Rom. 7.25-8.1f 91
Rom. 8.16-23 90
Rom. 8.18f 69
Rom. 8.18f 123
Rom. 8.23 95
Rom. 8.33f 95
Rom. 8.34-39 112
Rom. 9.3f 111
Rom. 9.27-29 4
Rom. 9.33f 164
Rom. 10 110
Rom. 10-11 64
Rom. 10.18 16
Rom. 10.20-21 16
Rom. 10.21 78
Rom. 10.21f 110
Rom. 11 83
Rom. 11.1f 16
Rom. 11.7 22, 51
Rom. 11.13-26 72

Rom. 11.13-32 69
Rom. 11.22 62
Rom. 11.25f 26, 42, 54, 72
Rom. 11.25-27 i, 122
Rom. 11.26f 4, 22
Rom. 11.28 16
Rom. 11.28f 54
Rom. 12.10-19 119
Rom. 13.11-14f 68
Rom. 13.11f 145
Rom. 16.20 124

I Corinthians

I Cor. 4.9 69, 113
I Cor. 15 69

II Corinthians

II Cor. 4.8-16f 130
II Cor. 5-6 50
II Cor. 6.1-2 51
II Cor. 6.16 53

I Thessalonians

I Thes. 1.10 24, 86
I Thes. 2.14 160
I Thes. 2.14f 66
I Thes. 2.14-16 31, 159
I Thes. 2.16 151
I Thes. 4.13-18 69
I Thes. 4.16 17
I Thes. 5.9 160

II Thessalonians

II Thes. 1.7-12 130-131
II Thes. 2.1f 157

Philippians

Phil. 1.6, 27, 4.5 130

Colossians

Col. 1.24-27 130

Hebrews

Heb, 8.13 35
Heb. 10.37 131

James

Jas. 5.6-10 131

I Peter

I Pet. 1 24
I Pet. 1.5f 132
I Pet. 2.9 24

II Peter

II Pet. 3 25, 61

I John

I Jn. 2.8 122

Revelation

Rev. 6.9-17 25, 134
Rev. 7.14-17 143
Rev. 11.1-4 179
Rev. 14.20 179
Rev. 17.16f 87
Rev. 19.15 179

Topic Index

1948
    has nothing to do with the fulfillment of prophecy 26
    restoration of Israel in 1
    supersign of the end? 1
144,000, the remnant of Israel that is saved 143

A

A Case For Amillennialism Kim Riddlebarger 17
A New Testament Biblical Theology Greg Beale 49, 118
A New Vision for Israel Scott McKnight 6, 9
Abrahamic covenant
    John the Baptizer and 10
    not fulfilled through the law 104
    related to Torah 104
Acts and the Isaianic New Exodus David Pao 108
Acts: An Exegetical Commentary Craig Keener 109
AD 70, if Mosaic law foretold, must have been in force 36
Adam, Peter *The Message of Malachi* 32
Alford's Greek Testament, Matthew-John, Vol. 1 60
all Israel *See* Israel, all i
Allison, Dale Jr. *Jesus and the Restoration of Israel* 56
amillennialism, implications of relation between John the Baptizer and Rom. 11 189
Anchor Bible, Malachi Andrew Hill 25

anti-Semitism vs. anti Zionism 188
atheists, majority of Jews in modern state of Israel are 1

B

Baldwin, Joyce *Tyndale Old Testament Commentaries, Haggai, Zechariah, Malachi* 27
Balz, Horst and Gerhard Schneider *Exegetical Dictionary of the New Testament* 95
baptism of repentance preached by John the Baptizer 20
Beale, Greg *A New Testament Biblical Theology* 49, 118
Beale, Greg *Commentary on the New Testament Use of the Old Testament* 15, 57
Before Jerusalem Fell Kenneth Gentry 96, 135
Best, Ernest *The First and Second Epistles to the Thessalonians* 159
Biblical Hermeneutics: A Treatise on the Interpretation of the Old and New Testaments Milton S. Terry 124
birth pains in Rom. 8 98
Blaising, Craig and Darrell Bock *Progressive Dispensation-alism* 34
Blass-DeBrunner, *A Greek Grammar of the New Testament and Other Early Christian Literature* 96
"blessed is he who comes in the name of the Lord" 166-176
blindness of Israel 183

blood atonement
- demanded death of murderers 5
- Isa. 59 and Israel's salvation 78-83
- when temple destroyed 73-74

Brown, Colin *New International Dictionary of New Testament Theology* 62, 154

Brown, Colin on Mt. 24.29 62

Brown, Dr. Michael
- Christian Zionist apologist 187
- debated Preston on Rom. 11.25f 3

Bruce, F. F. on wrath about to come 159

Bruce, F. F. *The Time is Fulfilled* 45

Bruce, F. F. *Word Biblical Commentary, 1 & 2 Thessalonians* 159

Bruce, F. F. *New International Commentary on the New Testament, Acts* 106

C

Caird, George *Jesus and the Jewish Nation* 57

Calvin, John
- on end of the world 173
- on end of time 173

Calvin, John *Calvin's Commentaries, Harmony of Matthew, Mark, Luke and John 1-11* 173

Charting the End Times Thomas Ice and Tim LaHaye 1

Clarke, Adam *Clarke's Commentary* 24

Climax of the Covenant N. T. Wright 103

Cline, Meredith *Death, Leviathan, and Martyrs: Isaiah 24:2-37:1 in A Tribute to Gleason Archer*: ed. by Walter C. Kaiser, Jr. and Ronald R. Youngblood. 125

coming of the Lord
- Hester on record on coming of the Lord in Rom. 11 18
- in Rom. 11

discussed 18
- incarnation? 18
- Isa. 26.21 cf Rom. 11.25f 72
- new creation at the 72
- of Rom. 11.26f 21
- only one in context of Mt. 23-24 175
- out of Zion i
- out of Zion in Isa. 27 and 59 18
- resurrection at the 72
- salvation of Israel at the 18
- vindication of martyrs at the 72
- what kind did John the Baptizer, Jesus, and Paul expect? 150-156

Commentary on John Craig Kenner 38

Commentary on the New Testament Use of the Old Testament Greg Beale 15, 57

Contours of Pauline Theology Tom Holland 80

conversion of Israel, did Jesus predict a future? 166-176

Conversion of the Imagination Richard Hayes 4, 111

corporate guilt 74

Cranfield, C. E. B. *Romans, A Shorter Commentary* 84

creation
- restoration to Edenic utopia 99
- still awaiting redemption of 91

cross, the, all futurist eschatologists say Mosaic Law abrogated at 33

D

darkness, Hebraism for death 11

Davidic kingdom promises fulfilled in John the Baptizer 10

Davies, W. D. *The Gospel and the Land* 53

Davies, W. D. and Dale Allison Jr. *International Critical Commentary, Matthew 1-7* 59

day and the hour, the, taken from festal calendar 170
day of the Lord, the
See also Great and Terrible Day of the Lord 60
a day of fire 25
about to be fulfilled in Heb. 10.37 131
application of Mosaic covenant sanctions 34
can't be end of time earth-brning event 89
covenantal judgment 56
in judgment 19
in Mal. 3 was national judgment 32
in Malachi the time of judgment on Israel for violating Torah 42
in Rom. 11.25f 54
Isa. 26.21 4
Israel's sin taken away at 46
John as the messenger and 26
John as The Messenger foresaw a national judgment 28
McKnight on 58
Mosaic covenant wrath 32
nature of as proclaimed by John the Baptizer 56-70
nature of in John The Messenger's teaching 30
Paul and John the Baptizer anticipating the same 56
Paul vs. John the Baptizer? 71-77
Perryman on 89
Sadducees didn't believe in 111
the great and terrible day 25, 36
Thessalonians believed it had already come 89
took place as John the Baptizer predicted 99
Wright on 5, 151
day or the hour of the parousia 122
death, Hebraisms for
darkness 11
shadow of death 11

deliverer
Jesus as the and the wrath to come 157-162
John the Baptizer and the coming of in Rom. 11 156
DeMar, Gary *Last Days Madness* 94
DeMar, Gary, on vindication of martyrs 94
destruction of Jerusalem, significance of 129
dispensationalism
implications of relation between John the Baptizer and Rom. 11 186
dispensationalism
John the Baptizer forces rejection of 22
postponement theory falsified 112
two covenant doctrine 103
Divine Marriage Tom Holland 127
dominionism, implications of relation between John the Baptizer and Rom. 11 188
Drury, John *The Elijah who was to Come: Matthew's Use of Malachi* 41
Dubis, Mark *Messianic Woes in First Peter, Suffering and Eschatology in I Peter 4:12-19* 132
Dunn, James D. G. *The New International Greek Testament Commentary* 116
Dunn, James D. G. *Word Biblical Commentary, Romans 1-8* 84
Dunn, James D. G. *Word Biblical Commentary, Romans 9-16* 15, 126

E

eager expectation an indication of imminence 97
Echoes of Scripture Richard Hayes 120
Edwards, James *The Pillar New Testament Commentary* 7, 12

Elijah
- had a ministry of reconciliation 54
- has already come! 38-43
- Jesus identified John the Baptizer as 38
- John the Baptizer the eschatological iii
- Mt. 17.9-13 40
- prepared Israel for great tribulation 38

end of the world
- and the time of the end 172
- Calvin on 173
- not end of material creation 172
- Origen on 151
- Wright on 174

end of time
- Calvin on 173
- charges Paul with failed eschatology because assumes 69
- France on 154
- increasingly rejected by scholars 151
- John the Baptizer didn't anticipate 155
- McKnight on 152
- Nanos on 154
- scholars who believe it exists in Bible 151
- Wright on 154

end of world

End Times Dilemma: Future or Fulfilled? Don K. Preston 11

eschatological groaning 95

eschatological spirit, related to kingdom 109

eschatological suffering
- from *pathemata* 95
- I Cor. 4.9 113
- I Thes. 1.10 86
- in all New Testament epistles expected imminently 138
- in Rom. 11 84-139
- Moo on 119
- of the Romans 88, 90
- of the Thessalonians 87
- Paul's afflictions 117
- Rom. 2.1-9 86
- Rom. 13.11-12 121
- Rom. 12.10-19 119
- Rom. 16.20 124
- Romans 10 110
- tribulation and 87

eschatology, did John the Baptizer have a failed? 100

Evangelism in the Early Church Michael Green 116

Exegetical Dictionary of the New Testament Horst Balz and Gerhard Schneider 95

exile, forgiveness of sins another way of saying end of 20

Exodus, second 14

F

feast, Jewish 167

Ford, J. Massyngberd, posited the view that John the Baptizer wrote Revelation 148

forgiveness of sins, another way of saying return from exile 20

France, R. T.
- no end of time in Bible 154
- on John the Baptizer 8

France, R. T. *Jesus and the Old Testament* 62, 154

France, R. T. *Matthew, Tyndale New Testament Commentaries* 8

fulness of the Gentiles 183

futurist escchatologies
- all hold that Law was abrogated at the cross 33
- implications of relation between John the Baptizer and Rom. 11 186

G

Galilee, Vespasian's invasion of 19

Gentiles

fulness of 183
times of
   fulfilled 177-182
   provided for by Law of Moses 181
Gentry, Kenneth
   condemns preterism because non-creedal 142
   non-creedal views 142
   on *mello* 96
   thinks Rev. 21-22 isn't the final new creation 142
Gentry, Kenneth *Before Jerusualem Fell* 96, 135
Gentry, Kenneth *He Shall Have Dominion* 1, 45
Gentry, Kenneth *Navigating the Book of Revelation* 142
Gibbons, Edward *Rise and Fall of the Roman Empire* 136
Gibbons, Edward, Neronian persecution caused by Jews 136
glory about to be revealed, DeMar on 102
Great and Terrible Day of the Lord, the
   discussed 36
   Hagner on 60
   Nolland on 60
great tribulation, John the Baptizer prepared Israel for the 38
Green, Michael *Evangelism in the Early Church* 116
groaning, eschatological 95

H

Hagner, Donald *Word Biblical Commentary on Matthew* 8, 60
Harnack, Adolph *Mission and Expansion of Christianity* 135
Harnack, Adolph, Roman persecution of the church not in view 135
Hayes, Richard *Conversion of the Imagination* 4, 111

Hayes, Richard *Echoes of Scripture* 120
Hayes, Richard *Reading Backwards* 15
He Shall Have Dominion Kenneth Gentry 1, 45
Hendrickson, William *New Testament Commentary, Romans* 17, 84
Heralds of the Good News J. Ross Wagner 4
Hester, Dr. David
   Dan. 9 irrelevant to return of Christ 81
   insists law nailed to cross 33
   on Dan. 9.24-27 81
   on hope of Israel 11
   on imminence in Rom. 8 97
   on record on coming of the Lord in Rom. 11 18
   which coming in Rom. 11 17
Hill, Andrew *Anchor Bible, Malachi* 25
Holland, Tom
   on the Satan in Romans 126
   significance of partial quotations 80
Holland, Tom *Contours of Pauline Theology* 80
Holland, Tom *Romans the Divine Marriage* 85, 127
hope of Israel
   Dr. David Hester on 11
   in Heb, 11 11
   Joel McDurmon on 11
   unity of in Abraham, David, and Israel 11
hope, unity of in Abraham, David, and Israel 11
How Is This Possible? Don K. Preston 89

I

Ice, Thomas and Kenneth Gentry *The Great Tribulation Past or Future?* 35

Ice, Thomas and Tim LaHaye *Charting the End Times* 1
Ice, Thomas and Timothy Demy *Prophecy Watch* 177
Ice, Thomas, on continuation of Torah 35
imminence
    eager anticipation indicates 97
    eager expectation an indication of 97
    Hester on 97
    in Rom. 8.18f 96
    Milton Terry on statements of in Bible 123
    Paul certainly expected the final events in his lifetime 69
implications of relation between John the Baptizer and Rom. 11 186
International Critical Commentary Alfred Plummer 166
International Critical Commentary, First Corinthians Robertson and Plummer 113
International Critical Commentary, Matthw 1-7 W. D. Davies and Dale Allison Jr. 59
Into All The World, Then Comes the End Don K. Preston 109
Isa. 24-27 *See* Little Apocalypse
Isaiah's New Exodus in Mark Rikki Watts 81
Israel
    all, what did Paul mean? i
    blindness of 183
    deliverance in resurrection 10
    did Jesus predict a future conversion of? 166-176
    majority in modern state are atheists, agnostics and unbelievers 1
    restoration in 1948 1
    restoration of
        and John the Baptizer 22
        reconciliation through the 49
    salvation of all
        See also salvation of Israel
        tied to vindication of martyrs ii
Israel 1948: Countdown to No Where Don K. Preston 1
Israel, all, Isa. 59 helps define in Rom. 11 147
Israel's Last Prophet David Turner 8
Israel's salvation
    at end of Christian age? 104
    at end of Mosaic age 104
    Isa. 59 and blood atonement 78-83

J

Jerusalem
    Josephus on seige of 169
    trodden down of the Gentiles 177-182
Jerusalem in the New Testament N. T. Wright 152
Jesus, did he predict a future conversion of Israel? 166-176
Jesus and Judgment Marius Reiser 63, 154
Jesus and the Jewish Nation George Caird 57
Jesus and the Old Testament R. T. France 62, 154
Jesus and the Restoration of Israel Dale Allison Jr. 56
Jesus and the Victory of God N. T. Wright 5, 9, 39
Jesus V Jerusalem Joel McDurmon 91
Jesus, The Tribulation and the End of Exile Brant Pitre 38, 59
Jewish feasts 167
Jewish persecution prior to Roman persecution 138
Jews, did Paul envision a massive conversion of in Rom. 11.25-27? i
John the Baptist, Prophet of Purity for a New Age Catherine M. Murphy 8

John the Baptizer
- a prophet of God
  - Edwards on 12
  - Wright on 12
- an eschatological prophet 10
- and God's covenant with Abraham 10
- and resurrection 10
- and the coming of the deliverer in Rom. 11 156
- anticipated judgment of Rev. 20 25
- as Elijah, a martyr of God 101
- as the messenger
  - and the nature of the day of the Lord 26
  - discussed 23-37
- as the voice 13
- connection to Rom. 11 16
- Davidic kingdom promises
  - fulfilled in connection with 10
- didn't anticipate an end of time 155
- Elijah has already come! 38-43
- end time prophet 7-12
- eschatological role in Isa. 40.1-11 13-22
- forces rejection of dispensationalist claims 22
- full of the Spirit from his mother's womb 12
- Hagner on 8
- implications of relation between Rom. 11 and 186
- J. Massyngbert Ford posited the view that he wrote Revelation 148
- Jesus identified as Elijah 38
- message of wrath to come and Jesus the deliverer 157-162
- ministry foretold in Isa. 40 iii
- mission as The Voice 17
- mission challenges all prevailing views of Romans 11 9
- more than a prophet 7
- most overlooked eschatogical figure 10
- Mt. 11.9f 12
- nature of Israel's restoration 22
- nature of the day of the Lord
  - proclaimed by 56-70
- preached baptism of repentance 20
- prepared Israel for great tribulation 38
- R. T. France on 8
- scholars ignore in discussions of salvation of Israel in Romans 11 9
- scholars think mistaken on eschatology 150
- summary of eschatological importance 67-68
- the day of the Lord took place as he predicted 99
- the eschatological Elijah iii
- the messenger and Elijah 67
- the voice in the wilderness 67
- Turner on 8
- vs. Paul on the day of the Lord? 71-77
- was he successful? 100
- was the fulfillment of prophecy 7
- what kind of *parousia* did he expect? 150-156
- would be instrumental in salvation of Israel in Rom. 11.25 9
- Wright on 8

John the Baptizer and Prophet Robert Webb 10, 61

Josephus
- believed Song of Moses was fulfilled in first century 121
- describes Vespasian's invasion of Galilee 19
- on seige of Jerusalem 169

Josephus, Flavius *Works of Josephus, Wars of the Jews* 170

judgment
- salvation of Israel by means of 72

and salvation, siamese twins *See also* salvation and judgment discussed 3-7

K

Keener, Craig *Acts: An Exegetical Commentary* 109
Keener, Craig *Commentary on John* 38
kingdom related to eschatological spirit 109

L

land promise
   Old Testament messianic 53
   Paul never mentions 52
Last Days Madness Gary DeMar 94
law of Moses provided for times of the Gentiles 181
Like Father, Like Son, On Clouds of Glory Don K. Preston 28
Little Apocalypse
   discussed 71
   Isa. 24 163
   Isa. 25.6-9 163
   Isa. 26.1-3, 19f 163
   Isa. 27 164
   Isa. 28 164
   Isa. 28.16 164
   Isa. 29 165
   outline of 163
   Paul and the 163-165
   Pitre on 163
   Wagner on 163
Longenecker, Richard *The New International Greek Testament Commentary, Romans* 85

M

Malachi
   impact on New Testament eschatology 23
   New Testament writers cite as source of eschatology 150

Manson, T. W. *The Mission and Message of Jesus* 167
martyr vindication *See* vindication of martyrs
Matthew, Tyndale New Testament Commentaries R. T. France 8
Mayor, Joseph *The Epistle of St. Jude and the Second Epistle of St. Peter* 154
McDurmon, Joel
   on hope of Israel 11
   still awaiting redemption of creation 91
McDurmon, Joel *Jesus V Jerusalem* 91
McKnight, Scott
   Mt. 16.27-28 93
   on end of time 152
   on the day of the Lord 58
   on vindication of martyrs 93
McKnight, Scott *A New Vision for Israel* 6, 9
mello
   A. T. Robertson on 97
   Blass-DeBrunner *A Greek Grammar of the New Testament and Other Early Christian Literature* 96
   discussed 96
   Gentry on 96
messenger, John the Baptizer as the 23-37
messianic land promise 53
messianic temple vs. second temple 29
Messianic Woes in First Peter, Suffering and Eschatology in I Peter 4:12-19 Mark Dubis 132
metalepsis
   See also partial quotations
   discussed 81
   Richard Hayes on 4
Minear, Paul *New Testament Apocalyptic* 61

ministry of reconciliation
    Elijah had one 54
    John as Elijah and the 44-55
Misreading Scripture With Western Eyes Randolph Richards and Brandon J. O'Brian 90
Mission and Expansion of Christianity Adolph Harnack 135
Moo, Douglas *New International Commentary on the New Testament, The Epistle to the Romans* 56
Moo, Douglas, on eschatological suffering 119
Mosaic law
    futility of man under 91
    futurist eschatologies say abrogated at cross 33
    if AD 70 foretold, must have been in force 36
Moyter, J. Alec *The Prophecy of Isaiah* 4, 19
Mt. 21 and the Parable of the Wicked Vineyard workers 130
Mt. 22 and the Parable of the Great Wedding Banquet 130
Munck, Johannes *Paul and the Salvation of Mankind* 115
Murphy, Catherine M. *John the Baptist, Prophet of Purity for a New Age* 8

N

Nanos, David
    charges Paul with a failed eschatology 69, 123
    no end of time in Bible 153
    on Rom. 8.18f 123
Nanos, David *The Mystery in Romans* 69
Navigating the Book of Revelation Kenneth Gentry 142
Neronian persecution caused by Jews 136

new creation
    at the coming of the Lord 72
    Gentry thinks Rev. 21-22 isn't the final one 142
New International Commentary on the New Testament, Acts F. F. Bruce 106
New International Commentary on the New Testament, The Epistle to the Romans Douglas Moo 56
New International Dictionary of New Testament Theology Colin Brown 62, 154
New International Greek Testament, Commentary on 1 & 2 Thessalonians 3
New Testament Apocalyptic Paul Minear 61
New Testament Commentary, Romans William Hendrickson 17, 84
no understanding in Israel, quoted from Dt. 32.38 66
Nolland, John *New International Greet Testament* 60
Nolland, John, on The Great and Terrible Day of the Lord 60

O

Olivet Discourse
    no anticipation of national conversion of Israel 175
    questions about questions 171
Origen on end of the world 151

P

Pao, David *Acts and the Isaianic New Exodus* 108
parousia, what kind did John the Baptizer, Jesus, and Paul expect? 150-156
partial quotations
    See also metalepsis
    Andrew Perriman on significance of 80
    Rikki Watts on significance of 81

significance of 80-81
Tom Holland on significance of 80
Pate, C. M. *The End of the Age Has Come* 84
pathemata, eschatological suffering 95
Paul
  and the little apocalypse 163-165
  certainly expected the final events in his lifetime 69
  never mentioned land promise 52
  vs. John the Baptizer on the day of the Lord? 71-77
Paul and the Faithfulness of God N. T. Wright 6, 12, 20
Paul and the Salvation of Mankind Johannes Munck 115
Paul's afflictions were eschatological suffering 117
Perriman, Andrew
  day of the Lord can't be end of time earth-burning event 89
  on imminence in Rom. 8.18f 96
  on Rom. 8.18f 123
  on Rom. 11.13-26 73
  significance of partial quotations 80
Perriman, Andrew *The Coming of the Son of Man* 80
Perriman, Andrew *The Future of the People of God* 73, 96
Pitre, Brant
  on the Little Apocalypse 163
  on John being Elijah 42
Pitre, Brant *Jesus, The Tribulation and the End of Exile* 38, 59
Plummer, Alfred *International Critical Commentary* 166
postmillennialism, implications of relation between John the Baptizer and Rom. 11 188
postponement theory
  falsified 112
  John the Baptizer and 22

premillennialism, implications of relation between John the Baptizer and Rom. 11 186
Preston, Don K.
  debate with Dr. Michael Brown 3
  debating Rom. 11.25f i-ii
Preston, Don K. *End Times Dilemma: Future or Fulfilled?* 11
Preston, Don K. *How Is This Possible?* 89
Preston, Don K. *Into All The World, Then Comes the End* 109
Preston, Don K. *Israel 1948: Countdown to No Where* 1
Preston, Don K. *Like Father Like Son, On Clouds of Glory* 28
Preston, Don K. *Seal Up Vision and Prophecy* 82
Preston, Don K. *Seventy Weeks Are Determined...For the Resurrection* 46
Preston, Don K. *The Resurrection of Daniel 12:2: Fulfilled or Future?* 33, 175
Progressive Dispensationalism Craig Blaising and Darrell Bock 34
Prophecy Watch Thomas Ice and Timothy Demy 177
prophet
  John the Baptizer an eschatological prophet 10
  John the Baptizer and end time 7-12
  John the Baptizer more than a 7
Pulpit Commentary, Psalms G. Rawlinson 167

Q

quotations, partial *See* partial quotations

R

Rawlinson, G. *Pulpit Commentary, Psalms* 167

Reading Backwards Richard Hayes 15
reconciliation
  ministry of
    See also ministry of reconcciliation
    discussed 44-55
    nothing but forgiveness 44
    on corporate level 44
    Paul's longest discourse on 50
    through restoration of Israel 49
Redeemer out of Zion 183
redemption of creation, is the restoration of all things still awaiting? 91, 108
redemption of the body 102
Reiser, Marius *Jesus and Judgment* 63, 154
remnant
  Romans about the salvation of the 140
  salvation of the 183
replacement theology 176
restoration of all things
  in AD 70 101
  is the redemption of creation 108
restoration of creation, Edenic utopia? 99
restoration of Israel
  at time of crushing of Satan 124
  foretold in Dt. 30? 176
  Isa. 27.1-5 124
resurrection
  at the coming of the Lord 72
  the deliverance of Israel 10
Resurrection of the Son of God N. T. Wright 59
return of the Lord, never a physical presence 105
Revelation
  J. Massyngbert Ford posited the view that he wrote it 148
  Roman persecution of the church not in view 135

Richards, Randolph and Brandon J. O'Brian *Misreading Scripture With Western Eyes* 90
Riddlebarger, Kim *A Case For Amillennialism* 17
Rise and Fall of the Roman Empire Edward Gibbons 136
Robertson and Plummer *International Critical Commentary, First Corinthians* 113
Robertson, A. T. *Word Pictures in the New Testament* 97
Robertson, A. T., on *mello* 97
Roman persecution of the church
  not in view in Revelation
    Gentry on 135
    Harnack on 135
    Vanderwaal on 135
    Wright on 136
  occurred after Jewish persecution 138
Romans
  about salvation of the remnant 140
  martyr vindication fulfills Dt. 32 138
  Paul expects vindication of martyrs imminently 138
  summary of suffering and martyrdom in 137
Romans 9-16, Vol. 33b James Dunn 15
Romans the Divine Marriage Tom Holland 85
Romans, A Shorter Commentary C. E. B. Cranfield 84

S

Sadducees didn't believe in the day of the Lord 111
salvation and judgment
  conjoined in Isa. 1.27-28 3
  in Isa. 59 4
  siamese twins 3-7
  synchronous events 6
  Wright on 4

salvation of all Israel
  concerns the salvation of the remnant 140
  discussed 140-149
  in Revelation 7, 14 140
  Rom. 11 about the salvation of the remnant 140
salvation of Israel
  by means of judgment 72
  fulfilled
    Isa. 27.13 76
    Isa. 59 77
    Isa. 40 76
  in Romans and Revelation is the same 145
  introduced i
  John the Baptizer and Paul connected 2
  occurred in AD 70 76
  the 144,000 is the remnant that is saved 143
salvation of the remnant 183
Satan
  crushed at restoration of Israel 124
  crushed in Rom. 16.20 124
  destruction of in Rev. 20 124
  Tom Holland on 126
Seal Up Vision and Prophecy Don K. Preston 82
second coming of Christ, Dr. David Hester on Dan. 9 81
second Exodus 14
second temple didn't have Spirit 12
siege of Jerusalem, Josephus on 169
Seventy Weeks Are Determined ...For the Resurrection Don K. Preston 46
shadow of death, Hebraism for death 11
Song of Moses
  echoed in Isa. 27 74
  five citations in Romans 120
  Josephus believe it was being fulfilled in first century 121
  Wright on 120

Spirit, second temple didn't have 12
suffering of this present time was eschatological suffering 84
suffering, eschatological *See* eschatological suffering
supersign of the end, is 1948? 1

T

Taylor, Richard and E. Ray Clendenen *The American Commentary, Haggai-Malachi* 31
temple
  destroyed when martyrs avenged 74
  messianic vs. second 29
  second did not have the Spirit 12
Terry, Milton S. *Biblical Hermeneutics: A Treatise on the Interpretation of the Old and New Testaments* 124
Terry, Milton, on imminence statements in Bible 123
Tertullian on Mal. 4.2-3, Isa. 26.19f 38
The American Commentary, Haggai-Malachi Richard Taylor and E. Ray Clendenen 31
The Church's Bible, Isaiah Robert Lewis Wilken 38
The Coming of the Son of Man Andrew Perriman 80
The Elijah Who Was to Come: Matthew's Use of Malachi John Drury 41
The End of the Age Has Come C. M. Pate 84
The Epistle of St. Jude and the Second Epistle of St. Peter Joseph Mayor 154
The First and Second Epistles to the Thessalonians Ernest Best 159
The Future of the People of God Andrew Perriman 96
The Gospel and the Land W. D. Davies 53

The Great Tribulation Past or Future? Thomas Ice and Kenneth Gentry 35
The Message of Malachi Peter Adam 32
The Mission and Message of Jesus T. W. Manson 167
The Mystery in Romans David Nanos 69
The New International Commentary on the Old Testament Peter A. Verhoef 155
The New International Greek Testament Commentary James D. G. Dunn 116
The New International Greek Testament Commentary, Romans Richard Longenecker 85
The Pillar New Testament Commentary James Edwards 7, 12
The Prophecy of Isaiah Alec Motyer 4, 19
The Resurrection of Daniel 12:2: Fulfilled or Future? Don K. Preston 33, 175
The Time is Fulfilled F. F. Bruce 45
Thessalonians, the
   believed the day of the Lord had already come 89
   eschatological suffering of the 87
times of Gentiles
   introduced 177-182
   law of Moses provided for 181
Torah, Abrahamic covenant's relation to 104
transfiguration 40
tribulation
   eschatological suffering and 87
   eschatological suffering in Rom. 5.1-3 88
   Romans enduring in Rom. 12.10-19 119
   usage in New Testament 90
Turner, David *Israel's Last Prophet* 8

Two Covenant doctrine
   dispensationalism and the 103
   Wright on 103
Tyndale Old Testament Commentaries, Haggai, Zechariah, Malachi Joyce Baldwin 27

V

Vanderwaal, Cornelius *Hal Lindsey and Biblical Prophecy* 135
Vanderwaal, Cornelius, Roman persecution of the church not in view in Revelation 135
Verhoef, Pieter A. *The New International Commentary on the Old Testament* 155
Vespasian's invasion of Galilee 19
vindication of martyrs
   at the coming of the Lord 72
   Col. 1.24-27 130
   DeMar on 94
   Heb. 10.32f 131
   I Pet. 1.5f 132
   II Cor. 4.8-16f 129
   II Thes. 1.7-12 130
   in Rom. 11 84-139
   in Romans fulfills Dt. 32. 138
   Jas. 5.6-10 131
   Jesus' three parables about 94
   Lk. 18.1-8 129
   McKnight on 93
   Mt. 21 and the Parable of the Wicked Vineyard workers 128
   Mt. 22 and the Parable of the Great Wedding Banquet 129
   Mt. 23.29f 129
   Paul an end time martyr 117
   Paul in Romans expected imminently 138
   Phil. 1.6, 27, 4.5 130
   Rev. 6.9-17 134
   Rom. 2.1-9 86
   Roman persecution of the church not in view 135
   salvation of all Israel tied to ii

summary of in Romans 137
when temple destroyed 74
wrath about to come, Rom. 2.5 138
Wright on 92
voice, the
coming of the Lord in judgment 19
John the Baptizer as 13
John's mission as 17
of Isaiah 17

W

Wagner, J. Ross
on the Little Apocalypse 163
Paul draws from Dt. 28-29 in Rom. 10-11 64
Wagner, J. Ross *Heralds of the Good News* 4
Wanamaker, Charles *New International Greek Testament, Commentary, Commentary on 1 & 2 Thessalonians* 3
Watts, Rikki *Isaiah's New Exodus in Mark* 81
Watts, Rikki, on significance of partial quotations 81
Webb, Robert *John the Baptizer and Prophet* 10, 61
Wilken, Robert Lewis *The Church's Bible, Isaiah* 38
"witness" indicates covenantal judgment 31
Word Biblical Commentary on Matthew Donald Hagner 8
Word Biblical Commentary, 1 & 2 Thessalonians F. F. Bruce 159
Word Biblical Commentary, Romans 1-8 James D. G. Dunn 84
Word Biblical Commentary, Romans 9-16 James D. G. Dunn 126
Word Pictures in the New Testament A. T. Robertson 97
Works of Josephus, Wars of the Jews Flavius Josephus 170

wrath about to come
and Jesus the deliverer 157-162
Bruce on 159
discussed 150
I Thes. 2.14-16 159
Isa. 26-27 157
Isa. 40 158
Isa. 59 158
Mal. 3 158
Mal. 4 158
Rom. 1.18f 160
on end of the world 174
Wright, N. T.
on Dan. 7.13f 92
on I Thes. 2.16 151
on Mt. 16.27-28 92
on Mt. 24.3 174
on Song of Moses 120
on the day of the Lord 151
on two covenant doctrine 103
on the day of the Lord 5
on vindication of martyrs 92
Roman persecution of the church not in view in Revelation 136
Wright, N. T. *Climax of the Covenant* 103
Wright, N. T. *Jerusalem in the New Testament* 152
Wright, N. T. *Jesus and the Victory of God* 5, 9, 39
Wright, N. T. *Paul and the Faithfulness of God* 6, 12, 20
Wright, N. T. *Resurrection of the Son of God* 59
Wright, N. T. *The Letter to the Romans, New Interpreters Bible* 1

Z

Zion
coming of the Lord out of i
redeemer out of 183
Zionism
and national judgment of Israel 155

are anti-Zionists anti-Semitic? 188
Dr. Michael Brown an apologist 187
modern built on faulty foundation 26
Rom. 11.25 essential to 187

Made in the USA
Middletown, DE
17 June 2019